3000 800064 68250

St. Louis Community College

Meramec Library
St. Louis Community College
11333 Big Bend Blvd.
Kirkwood, MO 63122-5799
314-984-7797

WITHDRAWN

D0069008

America's Natural Places

Regional Volumes in *America's Natural Places*

East and Northeast, Donelle Nicole Dreese

Pacific and West, Methea Kathleen Sapp

Rocky Mountains and Great Plains, Kelly Enright

South and Southeast, Stacy Kowtko

The Midwest, Jason Ney and Terri Nichols

AMERICA'S NATURAL PLACES

ROCKY MOUNTAINS AND GREAT PLAINS

Kelly Enright

Stacy Kowtko, General Editor

GREENWOOD PRESS
An Imprint of ABC-CLIO, LLC

Santa Barbara, California • Denver, Colorado • Oxford, England

Copyright 2010 by Kelly Enright

All rights reserved. No part of this publication may be reproduced,
stored in a retrieval system, or transmitted, in any form or by any means,
electronic, mechanical, photocopying, recording, or otherwise, except for
the inclusion of brief quotations in a review, without prior permission in
writing from the publisher.

Library of Congress Cataloging-in-Publication Data

Enright, Kelly.
    America's natural places. Rocky Mountains and Great Plains / Kelly Enright.
        p. cm. — (Regional volumes in America's natural places)
    Includes bibliographical references and index.
    ISBN 978-0-313-35088-7 (set hardcover : alk. paper) — ISBN 978-0-313-35089-4 (set ebook) —
ISBN 978-0-313-35314-7 (alk. paper) — ISBN 978-0-313-35315-4 (ebook)
1. Protected areas—Rocky Mountains Region.   2. Protected areas—Great Plains.   3. Endangered
ecosystems—Rocky Mountains Region.   4. Endangered ecosystems—Great Plains.   I. Title.
    S932.R63E57   2010
    333.780978—dc22   2009032384

14   13   12   11   10   1   2   3   4   5

This book is also available on the World Wide Web as an eBook.
Visit www.abc-clio.com for details.

ABC-CLIO, LLC
130 Cremona Drive, P.O. Box 1911
Santa Barbara, California 93116-1911

This book is printed on acid-free paper ∞
Manufactured in the United States of America

CONTENTS

Series Foreword

The United States possesses within its borders some of the most diverse and beautiful natural wonders and resources of any country on earth. Many of these valuable natural places exist under a constant threat of damage from environmental pollution, climatic change, and encroaching civilization, just to name a few of the more destructive forces. Some natural areas enjoy the care and protection of neighboring human societies, but some have fallen to the wayside of concern. This series of reference volumes represents a collection of distinct areas of preservation concern in the following five geographical divisions of the United States: the East and Northeast, the Pacific and West, the Rocky Mountains and Great Plains, the South and Southeast, and the Midwest. The goal is to present representative challenges faced across the country, providing information on historical and ongoing preservation efforts through the process of identifying specific sites that representatively define the United States as an environmental entity. Individual entries were chosen based on the following criteria: biodiversity, ecology, rare or endangered species habitats, or unique environmental character. Many of the entries are nature preserves, state or national parks, wildlife habitats, or scenic vistas. Each selection focuses on a particular area and describes the site's importance, resident flora and fauna, and threats to the area's survival, along with historical and current information on preservation efforts. For sites that are physically accessible, there is information on location, access methods, and visiting tips. Although each volume is organized by state, many natural places cross state borders, and so the larger focus is on environmental ecosystem representation rather than state definition. The goals are to inform readers about the wide variety of natural places across the country as well as portray these natural places as more than just an exercise in academic study. The reality of natural preservation in the United States has an immediate impact on everyone.

Each volume contains a short introduction to the geographical region, including specific information on the states' natural environments and regionally specific concerns of restoration and preservation. Content entries represent one or more of the following criteria: ecological uniqueness; biodiversity; rare or endangered species habitat; exceptional natural beauty; or aging, fragile, or disappearing natural environs. By reading the various entries in each volume, readers will gain understanding concerning environmental issues of consequence as demonstrated by the representative entry choices. The audiences especially suited to benefit from this series are high school and undergraduate students as well as hobbyists and nature enthusiasts. Readers with an interest in local, regional, and environmental health will find easily accessible, useable information throughout the series. The following paragraphs offer short excerpts from the introductions of the regional volumes in *America's Natural Places*.

The East and Northeast United States is a corridor, a doorway to America that has facilitated movement and migration into the continent. The subject of corridors is revisited frequently in the East and Northeast volume as it covers natural areas beginning as far west as Kentucky, as far south as Virginia, and voyages up the coast to Maine. Smaller corridors are described here as well, because many of the places featured in this book have their own respective passageways, some more wild than others. This volume is also about larger corridors—those that connect the past to the present and the present to the future. These natural areas are storytellers chronicling the narratives of cultural and ecological histories that not only have much to tell about the region's past, but also are microcosmic indicators of the earth's current global health. They are corridors into our future as they tell us where our planet is going—toward the loss of countless native species, archeological treasures, and ecosystems that are vital for a sustainable planet. These natural areas are themselves guided paths, passageways into a healthier future as they teach us what is happening within their fragile ecological significance before their lessons are lost forever.

The American Pacific and West is a place of legendary proportions; its natural resources have beckoned to entrepreneurs, prospectors, immigrants, adventurers, naturalists, writers, and photographers, thereby deeply embedding the region into U.S. history, culture, commerce, and art. J. S. Holliday wrote. "I think that the West is the most powerful reality in the history of this country. It's always had a power, a presence, an attraction that differentiated it from the rest of the United States. Whether the West was a place to be conquered, or the West as it is today, a place to be protected and nurtured. It is the regenerative force of America." Over the course of its history, the ecosystems of the Pacific and West have been subject to a variety of forces, both restorative and destructive. Individual entries in the Pacific and West volume seek to not only detail the effects of these forces but to describe the flora, fauna, and topography that make each entry unique. As a cumulative effect, the volume offers an inclusive depiction of the region as a whole while echoing the famous call to "Go West."

"The western landscape is of the wildest variety," Wallace Stegner wrote of his homeland. "There is nothing in the East," he continued, "like the granite horns of Grand Teton or Teewinot, nothing like the volcanic neck of Devil's Tower, nothing like the travertine terraces of Mammoth Hot Springs." Consisting of deserts, grasslands, alpine mountains, plateaus, canyons, cliffs, and geyser basins, the Rocky Mountains and Great Plains is a region of great biodiversity and natural beauty. From the 100th meridian over the peaks of the Rocky Mountains, this landscape has been the source of frontier legends, central to the nation's geography as well as its identity. Home to the world's first national park and some of the most extractive industries in the nation, this landscape displays the best and worst of human interactions with the natural world. Fossils in Colorado are evidence of ancient inland seas. Tall-grass prairies reveal pre-Anglo American ecology. This volume teaches students to read natural landscapes as products of interacting dynamics between culture and nature. People of many backgrounds, ethnicities, and cultures have contributed to the current state of the environment, giving readers a strong, provocative look at the dynamics of this ever-changing landscape.

"The American South is a geographical entity, a historical fact, a place in the imagination, and the homeland for an array of Americans who consider themselves southerners. The region is often shrouded in romance and myth, but its realities are as intriguing, as intricate as its legends." So states Bill Ferris. This volume explores the variable, dynamic South and Southeast through the details of its ecoregions and distinct areas of preservation. Individual entries provide the elements necessary for examining and understanding the threats, challenges, and promises inherent to this region. State partitions serve as geographical divisions for regional treatment, but the overall goal of this work is to present representative examples of the varying ecosystems across the area rather than focusing on the environmental character of individual states. When combined, the sections present a total picture of the South and Southeast through careful selections that portray not only the coastal wetlands and piedmont areas characteristic of the region but also the plateaus, mountains, highlands, plains, and woodlands that define the inland South and Southeast. The goal is to produce a comprehensive picture of the South and Southeast natural environs as they combine to present a unique character and quality that shapes Southern reality today.

The Midwest stands historically as the crossroads of America, the gateway to the West. The region is incredibly diverse, long shaped by geological forces such as the advance and retreat of glaciers. It is a transitional region, where the eastern temperate forests meet the Great Plains of the West and where the southern extent of the northern forests transitions from the mixed-wood plains to the Ozark forests and southeastern plains of the South. Human presence and interaction, however, have greatly reduced and currently threaten this diversity. The Midwest's rich soils and forests, along with its abundant lakes and streams, make this region's natural resources some of the county's most desirable for farming, logging, and development. As a result, little of the once-vast prairies, forests, and wetlands remains. Nonetheless, many efforts, both public and private, are underway to restore and protect the diversity of the Midwest. By taking a holistic approach, individual entries in this volume exemplify the varied ecosystems of the region with the volume as a whole covering all the major Midwest ecoregions. As readers explore the various entries, a comprehensive understanding of the natural systems of the Midwest will emerge, grounded in the region's natural and cultural history and shaped by its current and future challenges.

ACKNOWLEDGMENTS

To complete such an encyclopedic volume, I sought the expertise of many. My thanks goes to those whose lives are spent working in, and for, these protected natural places, and who assisted in checking my facts were up-to-date and my descriptions accurate. The help and generosity of those at our national forests, national parks, national wildlife refuges, and the Nature Conservancy was invaluable. I am grateful for series editor Stacy Kowtko's patience which never tired, from proposal to publication, and for the careful and organized work of all editors at ABC-Clio, who also found wonderful photographs to capture the beauty of these natural places.

Writing this manuscript forced a move from New Jersey to Colorado. Yet, I continued to find guidance from my mentors at Rutgers University, and from my family. I found inspiration in my drive through the prairies of Kansas and in the views of the Rocky Mountains from the windows of my many Colorado homes. Exploring the natural places of the Rocky Mountains and Great Plains allowed me to breathe life into this manuscript. I thank all those who came along on these adventures, and who helped me see these places through their eyes, as well as my own.

PREFACE

"The western landscape is of the wildest variety," Wallace Stegner wrote of his homeland. "There is nothing in the East," he continued, "like the granite horns of Grand Teton or Teewinot, nothing like the volcanic neck of Devil's Tower, nothing like the travertine terraces of Mammoth Hot Springs." Consisting of deserts, grasslands, alpine mountains, plateaus, canyons, cliffs, and geyser basins, the Rocky Mountains and Great Plains is a region of great biodiversity and natural beauty. From the 100th meridian over the peaks of the Rocky Mountains, this landscape has been the source of frontier legends, central to the nation's geography as well as its identity. Home to the world's first national park and some of the most extractive industries in the nation, this landscape displays the best and worst of human interactions with the natural world. Rich are the sites in which the ecological history of the region can been seen. Fossils are evidence of ancient inland seas. Tall-grass prairies reveal pre-Euro-American ecology. Redirected rivers indicate human intervention in nature's course, while melting mountaintop glaciers expose more ethereal human effects on the environment.

Rocky Mountains and Great Plains describes the flora, fauna, geology, and geography of this varied region by highlighting specific locations of ecological interest, from the depths of Wind Cave to the highest peak of Mount Elbert. This volume of *America's Natural Places* asks readers to read natural landscapes as products of interacting dynamics between culture and nature. It asks you to question the idea of wilderness, trace the history of land preservation, show the gradual change of vegetation, address natural disasters, and follow species shifts from local extinctions to reintroductions.

I selected sites in consultation with the Nature Conservancy, Wildlife Conservation Society, and the National Park Service. Some places are representative of larger local ecologies. Others, I chose for their unique characteristics. Where many choices were available for similar landscapes, I located the one site that best represented the complexity of human-landscape encounters.

Each entry addresses the ecology and history of the site. Readers will understand that nature is not separate from human activity. Human-environment interactions are as much a part of history as the stories told about human interactions—from conflicts over land rights, manipulation of rivers for human use, to management for preservation of a wilderness ideal. Additionally, this volume includes sites and perspectives of a variety of inhabitants of the region. Ancient peoples, French traders, Spanish conquistadors, American pioneers, Native, African, and Mexican Americans have all inhabited, used, and changed the landscape of the Rocky Mountains and Great Plains. People of many backgrounds, ethnicities, and cultures have contributed to the current state of the environment. From trade routes of the Anasazi to the ski trails of Aspen, *Rocky Mountains and Great Plains* offers readers a strong and provocative look at the dynamics of this ever-changing landscape.

America's Natural Places

Rocky Mountains and Great Plains

ROCKY MOUNTAINS AND GREAT PLAINS

CANADA

N

Helena ★
MONTANA

NORTH DAKOTA
★
Bismarck

Boise ★
IDAHO

SOUTH DAKOTA
★ Pierre

WYOMING

NEBRASKA

Salt Lake City ★   Cheyenne ★

Omaha •

Boulder •
★ Denver

Lincoln ★

UTAH

COLORADO

Topeka ★ • Kansas City
KANSAS

Oklahoma City ★
OKLAHOMA

MEXICO

Pacific
Ocean

0   500 mi

0   500 km

Gulf of
Mexico

INTRODUCTION

Looking northwest and southwest from the rolling landscape of Denver, the Rocky Mountains appear as a monochromatic mass save for, perhaps, a snowcapped peak. Traveling into the foothills, the road cuts through dramatic outcroppings of red, orange, yellow, and ochre sandstone. Keep driving and the highway leads past mining towns and over the Continental Divide, up some 11,990 feet through Loveland Pass, then down to the mountain valley containing the artificial Lake Dillon, a reservoir bringing water all the way back down to Denver. A few former mining towns now serve the ski industry. Continuing west, the interstate ascends 10,662 feet through the White River National Forest to the top of Vail Pass, then winds back down into Eagle Valley, where ranches fill the dry valley.

The subject of this volume consists of two major American landscapes that could not be more dissimilar. The Rocky Mountains and Great Plains region contains eight physiographic provinces: the Great Plains; the northern, middle, and southern Rocky Mountains; the Wyoming Basin; the Columbia and Colorado plateaus; and the Basin and Range. From rolling plains to mountain peaks to high desert valleys, the Rocky Mountains and Great Plains comprise a landscape of contrasts. The Rocky Mountains alone have more than a dozen ecosystem types, plus smaller regional or specific particularities. Diversity ranges along latitude as well as longitude. The southern Rockies are drier and taller than the northern Rockies. Northern prairies consist of mixed grasses, while southern prairies are primarily short grass. Despite their seeming monotony, prairies are one of most diverse and complex ecosystems in the world, second only to the rainforest. Prairie was once North America's largest continuous natural habitat, covering 170 million acres in the United States. Today, only four percent of this acreage remains native grassland.

One does not need to leave paved roads to see natural places here. Interstates run right through national forests, and national parks contain dramatic scenic roadways. But wandering beyond pavement, the Rocky Mountains and Great Plains contain about 16.5 million acres of designated wilderness. National wildlife refuges, state parks and forests, and private preserves flesh out the area's protected natural places. Half of Idaho is public land. Wyoming and Colorado are 42 and 37 percent protected lands, respectively.

In the center of the North American continent is a vast grassland. Stretching 2,000 miles north to south from Canada to Texas, the Great Plains passes through the states of New Mexico, Oklahoma, Kansas, Colorado, Wyoming, Nebraska, South Dakota, and North Dakota. Prairie is identified by grass, few trees, flat or sloping landscape, and a low altitude. From the foothills of the Rocky Mountains, the plains slope eastward over 500 miles, dropping from 6,000 feet in elevation to 1,500 feet. More rain falls in the east, making grasses grow up to 10 feet in the tall-grass prairie. As the landscape rises westward, grasses decrease in height, forming mixed and short-grass prairie.

The Great Plains used to be an inland sea, which accounts for its flatness. Sedimentary rock in layers makes up most of the ground. In places, igneous rocks have sprouted up, creating higher elevations. The shallow underground Ogallala (or High Plains) Aquifer, one of the world's largest, covering 174,000 square miles, provided and provides water for irrigation and consumption. Average yearly rainfall is only 24 inches, with most areas receiving only 16 inches.

A tall-grass prairie ecosystem once covered 190 million acres from southern Texas to southern Manitoba, Canada. Only one percent of this habitat remains. Grasses and wildflowers grew in abundance. Wetlands dotted the landscape. More than 300 species of plants once thrived here. Bison were a major part of the Great Plains ecosystem; Native Americans had long hunted them, but, with western settlement, bison became all but extinct.

By the 1930s, overuse and poor management of land and soil made the Great Plains the site of one of the worst natural disasters in the nation's history. The Dust Bowl blew topsoil from the ground, not only destroying crops but creating large clouds of dust that obscured the view. These storms were called dusters or black blizzards and occurred for several years during the 1930s. Lands formerly ranched were planted in part because of the demand for wheat during World War I. In Kansas, Texas, Oklahoma, and New Mexico, livestock was returned to this depleted soil, further destroying the ground cover. Farmers abandoned their land, and the federal government stepped in with restoration projects and new agricultural techniques.

Today, sorghum, flax, and cotton are grown here, though the main crop is wheat, grown mostly north of Nebraska. Ranches raise cattle and sheep. Energy development is ongoing with oil, natural gas, and coal deposits as well as gold.

The Rocky Mountains run more than 3,000 miles across the western portion of North America, from central New Mexico through the states of Utah, Colorado, Wyoming, Montana, Idaho, part of northeastern Washington, Canada, and finally reach their end in northwestern Alaska. They divide the dry basins and plateaus further west from the rolling grasslands of the Great Plains. They were formed between 180 and 50 million years ago, uplifted in a series of pulses lasting millions of years. Glacial activity caused erosion and created mountains and valleys. Additional uplift and volcanic activity also sculpted the landscape. The mountains' overlying sedimentary rock has, in places, given way to older rock, exposed and clearly visible on some mountainsides. The ancient spine of the Rockies is comprised of metamorphic and igneous rock.

The most dramatic geographical feature is the hydrological divide known as the Continental, or Great, Divide, which runs along the spine of the Rocky Mountains, marking the spot where watersheds drain east to the Atlantic Ocean (some via the Gulf of Mexico) and west to the Pacific Ocean (and further north, to the Arctic Ocean). The Continental Divide runs the entire length of the Americas, from Alaska's Seward Peninsula to the tip of Patagonia. In the Rocky Mountains lie the headwaters of the continent's major rivers, including the Porcupine-Yukon, the Columbia, the Fraser, the Missouri-Mississippi system, the Colorado, and the Rio Grande. Trickling down mountainsides or roaring through canyons, eastbound waters of the Rio Grande, and the Arkansas, Platte, Yellowstone, Missouri, and Saskatchewan rivers empty into the Atlantic Ocean. Running down the west side of the range are the Pacific-bound Colorado, Columbia, Snake, Fraser, and Yukon rivers. Glacier National Park contains the only place in the world where two ocean divides converge. At Triple Divide Peak, the Continental and the Northern Divides meet, marking the spot where water flows into three oceans—Atlantic, Pacific, and Arctic—and is the feature behind Glacier's nickname, Crown of the Continent.

Over 30 mountain ranges are part of the Rocky Mountains. The highest peaks are in its southern portion. The Sawatch range in Colorado contains both Mount Elbert (14,431 feet) and Mount Massive (14,418 feet). Colorado is the highest overall state in the region, with an average elevation of 6,800 feet and 59 "fourteeners" (peaks measuring over 14,000 feet). Wyoming is a close second, with an average elevation of 6,700 feet. North of the Wyoming Basin, in Utah and Wyoming, rise the Wind River range and the Teton range. These middle ranges run to Yellowstone National Park in northern Wyoming, where, north of the park, lie the Bitterroot and Lost River ranges. In Montana's Beartooth range, Pacific marine weather affects ecology, bringing higher precipitation. Ponderosa pine dominates the forests, except in Idaho, where limber pine survive better in its drier climate. The northern ranges contain more whitebark pine. By contrast, the Lost River and Lemhi ranges are so dry that vegetation shows little variety, with grassland, sagebrush, or mountain mahogany dominating all elevations, even tundra.

In the mid-19th century, gold rushes, ranching, and lumbering encouraged settlement in the Rocky Mountains. Most overland migrants passed through the Rockies at a place known as South Pass, in southwest Wyoming, at the end of the Wind River range. South Pass runs from the Great Plains to the Wyoming Basin. The Oregon and Mormon trails also passed through here. Today, the mountains are still valued for their lead, zinc, copper, silver, and gold deposits. Oil shale is another valuable commodity for the energy industry, but it is expensive to extract and largely untapped. The Rocky Mountain environment is threatened by invasive species, fire suppression, development, oil and gas exploration, and overgrazing. Overcrowding in the quickly developing Rocky Mountains has made forests susceptible to mountain pine beetle infestation. Thousands of acres of ponderosa and lodgepole pine have been destroyed.

Vegetation zones are created by different conditions of altitude. The Rocky Mountains' zones are classified as foothills, montane, subalpine, and alpine. Generally, as altitude increases, temperature drops, winds pick up, and precipitation increases. This affects soil conditions and climate, which in turn creates variation among plant and animal life. The higher the elevation, the smaller and less diverse the plant and animal species. In the Rocky Mountains, the foothills consist of sagebrush and pine-dominated woodlands containing ponderosa, limber, juniper, piñon, Gambel oaks, and an assortment of shrubs. The montane zone begins as a landscape of Douglas fir. Farther up into the mountains, lodgepole pines and aspen dominate. Subalpine vegetation consists of spruce fir, white and Englemann spruce, and white pine. At the peaks of the highest mountain, the alpine zone is decorated with krummholz (wind-shaped trees), grasses, sedges, sagebrush, and tiny moss and lichens. North-south location affects the elevation range of vegetation zones.

Ponderosa pines create the tallest forests of the foothills and lower mountain elevations. They survive best in mid-elevations, moderate climates, and in areas that receive between 16 and 25 inches of precipitation. In the ponderosa forest, snow does not remain long on the ground, and generally less than a foot falls at a time. Ponderosa communities include sparse shrubs and herbaceous plants on the forest floor. This varies throughout the range from Gambel's oak in previously cut areas to populations of wax currant, boulder raspberry, waxflower, kinnikinnick, common juniper, bitterbrush, mountain mahogany, and big sagebrush. Some sloping ponderosa communities contain grasses (mountain muhly, and timber oatgrass). Ponderosa forests have a hidden helper—mushrooms. Although they rarely appear above the surface, a species of mushroom winds itself around ponderosa roots. In the heavy rainfalls of midsummer, these mushrooms help the ponderosa by absorbing excess moisture. This symbiotic relationship is known as mycorrhiza (fungus-root). Ponderosa forests also revive themselves through natural cycles of fire. Dry ground cover can be sparked by lightning. The resulting burn clears the floor of debris and thins seedling stands, allowing more sunlight to reach the forest floor and providing less competition for growth with mature trees. Fire also increases soil fertility. Wildlife here consists of the flammulated owl, Abert's squirrel, golden-mantled ground squirrel, least chipmunk, coyote, cottontail, mule deer, elk, ermine, yellow-bellied marmot, mountain lion, northern pocket gopher, porcupine, dwarf shrew, montane vole, long-tailed weasel, bushy-tailed and Mexican wood rat, deer mice, myotis, Williamson's sapsuckers, Steller's jay, pygmy nuthatch, western tanager, evening grosbeak, pine siskin, and mountain and western bluebird.

The montane zone begins as Douglas fir–spruce forests with floor vegetation of a shrub called mountain lover, a lichen called old man's beard, and wildflowers, including fairy slipper orchid, twinflower, and heartleaf arnica. Great horned owls, hairy woodpeckers, mountain and black-capped chickadees, dark-eyed juncos, and Cassin's finches fly and rest in the canopy. Coyote, mule deer, elk, snowshoe hare, mountain lion, myotis, shrews, squirrels, vole, weasel, and wood rat comprise the majority of wildlife. As the montane zone reaches to higher elevations, lodgepole pine and aspen forests take over the fir-spruce forest. Rocky Mountain lodgepole pine and common juniper are the primary arboreal species. Shrubs include kinnikinnick and wild rose. Wildflowers such as one-sided wintergreen, mountain pussytoes, and fireweed add color to the forest floor. A few parasitic plants enforce the relationships among species; among them are pinedrops, dwarf mistletoe, and spotted coralroot orchid. Chickaree (red or pine squirrel) help spread conifer seeds, which are their primary food. Mammals here are the southern red-back vole, hoary bat, black bear, bobcat, least chipmunk, cottontail, coyote, mule deer, elk, ermine, snowshoe hare, American marten, moose, mice, porcupine, masked shrew, and long-tailed weasel. Avian species include sharp-skinned hawk, downy woodpecker, white- and red-breasted nuthatch, and brown creeper. Aspen forests mix in among all the ecological zones, except alpine tundra, and are common in the montane zone. Quaking aspen rarely reproduce through seed; they more often sprout asexually from the root system as clones. Aspen groves provide a sunlit forest floor for shrubs such as red-osier dogwood, ninebark, shrubby cinquefoil, and sticky laurel. Wildflowers thrive here as well, including mariposa lily, common harebell, Fendler's meadowrue, Colorado blue columbine, heartleaf arnica, showy daisy, and black coneflower. The occurrence of aspen within pine-dominated regions increases forest diversity. Wildlife species include silver-haired bat, western jumping mouse, black bear, northern goshawk, red-naped sapsucker, tree swallow, house wren, yellow-rumped warbler, chipmunk, cottontail, coyote, mule deer, elk, ermine, snowshoe hare, moose, mice, porcupine, shrew, squirrels, voles, and weasels.

The subalpine zone is dominated by Engelmann spruce and subalpine fir. Some aspen, corkbark, Rocky Mountain bristlecone pine, limber pine, Rocky Mountain lodgepole pine, Colorado blue spruce, and white fir mix in the forests. Parasites are common, including witches' broom, snow molds, and spruce galls. Shrubs include the fruitful blueberry, huckleberry, buffaloberry, and red elderberry. Wildflowers are smaller here than in the montane region and include wood nymph, curled lousewort, Parry's primrose, Jacob's ladder, globeflower, heart-leaved twayblade, and brownie lady's slipper. Wildlife consists of snowshoe hare, marten, long-tailed weasel, blue grouse, northern saw-whet owl, three-toed woodpecker, gray jay, red-breasted nuthatch, ruby-crowned kinglet, hermit thrush, pine grosbeak, white-crowned sparrow, black bear, bobcat, chipmunk, cottontail, mule deer, elk, ermine, red fox, lynx, deer mice, northern pocket gopher, porcupine, montane shrew, squirrel, and vole.

In the highest mountain elevations, the alpine tundra, wind speeds of 100 miles per hour are frequently recorded. Gusts of 200 miles per hour are not uncommon, though the average is 25 to 30 miles per hour. Such wind influences alpine ecology. Temperatures are lower, and transpiration rate is higher. Alpine plants are uniquely adapted to wind abrasion, snow, and ice. Engelmann spruce, subalpine fir, limber and lodgepole pines are all capable of twisting to the wind, forming stunted and deformed trees known as krummholz. Soil is rocky, and the landscape is marked by peaks, cliffs, steep slopes, and boulder fields. In this extreme environment survives a small, delicate community known as fellfields. Amid rocks and gravel in coarse soil grow cushion, or matlike, plants such as alpine phlox, moss campion, big-rooted spring beauty, dwarf clover, and mountain dryad.

Some wildflowers and grasses find a footing in this landscape as well, including black-headed daisy, old-man-of-the-mountain, rose crown, Parry's clover, bog sedges, Drummond's rush, and Rocky Mountain sedge. Shrubs consist of shrubby cinquefoil, bog birch, and willows. Hearty wildlife includes yellow-bellied marmots, pikas, ermine, bighorn sheep, white-tailed ptarmigan, horned lark, water pipit, and rosy finch.

The history of conservation in the Rockies is the history of the nation's conservation. The Rocky Mountains are the site of the first designated national park (Yellowstone, 1872) and the first recovered endangered species (the American bison). The landscape's unique geography and unusual thermal features earned Yellowstone National Park protection from development and misuse. The region's largest national parks were established in the early decades of the 20th century—Glacier in 1910 and Rocky Mountain in 1915. In 1932, at the Canadian border in Montana, the world's first international peace park—Waterton-Glacier—was established.

At the end of the 20th century and into the 21st, conservation began to concentrate on the health of larger ecosystems and wildlife corridors. Previously, protection of nature and wildlife tried to impose boundaries on preserved areas. But the interconnectedness of watersheds and the mobility of wildlife have proven that the future protection of Yellowstone National Park, for example, lies both within and outside its borders. Conservation methods in the Rocky Mountains include regulations for broad ecoregions, generally through networks of public, nonprofit, and scientific organizations. The Wildlands Project has designated three large ecosystems for which to advocate: Yellowstone to Yukon, Heart of the West, and Southern Rockies. Ecosystem protection is supported by the Greater Yellowstone Coalition and the Southern Rockies Wildlands Network. The National Park Service maintains a network of 32 natural areas and studies the ecosystems of each to predict, and hopefully prevent, future threats.

The nonprofit the Nature Conservancy has been especially active in the plains region, where conservation easements have been successful in protecting land, wildlife, and resources on private lands. After farms were destroyed in the Dust Bowl, the federal government took over much of the land on the Great Plains. It restored the fertility of some land for reseeding with commercial crops, but returned other parcels to native vegetation. At the same time, these grasslands and their water—both artificial and natural wetlands, marshes, rivers, and lakes—were recognized as critical to wildlife, particularly migrating birds and waterfowl. The National Wildlife Preservation System began designating parcels of land for protection here in the first decades of the 20th century.

Public lands regulated by federal or state agencies are the largest contributor to the protection of natural places in these regions. National forests are managed as multiple-use areas. The U.S. Forest Service regulates extractive industries such as timber and mining, provides healthy grazing land for livestock (cattle, sheep), monitors and maintains healthy wildlife populations, and protects designated wilderness areas. Many national forests have been combined to make administration easier. In the plains, national grasslands, part of the national forest system open to diverse use such as hunting, grazing, mining, and recreation. There are 20 national grasslands, all but three of which are in the Great Plains. Together, they total about four million acres.

Wildlife preservation in the Rocky Mountains and Great Plains has included saving species from extinction, reintroducing species to former ecosystems, and protecting migration corridors. The animals of this region are the iconic species of North American nature. Conservation efforts target the region's threatened and endangered species, as designated by the U.S. Fish and Wildlife Service including grizzly bear, Canada lynx, Preble's meadow jumping mouse, Mexican spotted owl, greenback cutthroat trout, and piping plover. Endangered species are the Uncompahgre fritillary butterfly, whooping crane, black-footed ferret, gray wolf, Eskimo curlew, least interior tern, pallid sturgeon, American burying beetle, and black-capped vireo.

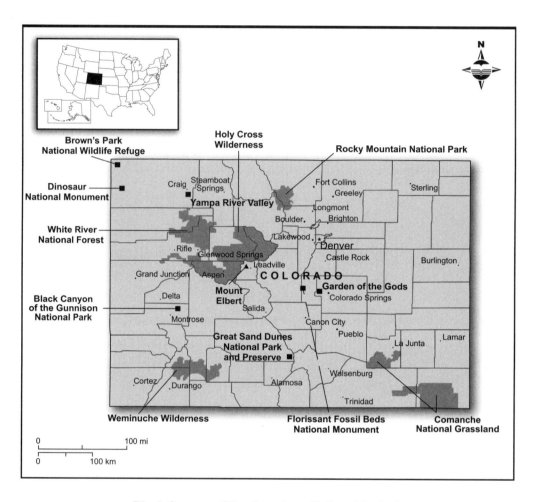

Black Canyon of the Gunnison National Park, 2

Brown's Park National Wildlife Refuge, 3

Comanche National Grassland, 4

Dinosaur National Monument, 5

Florissant Fossil Beds National Monument, 7

Garden of the Gods, 8

Great Sand Dunes National Park and Preserve, 9

Holy Cross Wilderness, 11

Mount Elbert, 12

Rocky Mountain National Park, 13

Weminuche Wilderness, 15

White River National Forest, 16

Yampa River Valley, 17

COLORADO

From the golden eastern plains to the mountains' outcroppings of pink Pike's Peak granite, Colorado's natural places live up to the state's name, derived from the Spanish word for colorful. The gray walls of the Black Canyon of the Gunnison, the bright orange of the Garden of the Gods, the vibrant green of pine forests, and the flash of fall's yellow aspen all attest to the state's famous hues. The Rocky Mountains reach their highest point in the state, which contains the most "fourteeners" (mountains over 14,000 feet), of any in the United States. The expansive White River National Forest was the site of the U.S. Forest Service's earliest preserved wilderness, created in 1920 when Forest Service employee Arthur Carhart suggested a road slated for Trappers Lake be stopped. Colorado residents have since sought to preserve the legacy of the state's wildness, preventing the imprint of highways and water systems in mountain ecosystems.

The mountains are straddled by agricultural regions. Colorado's eastern plains grow wheat, corn, and soy beans, while the cool nights of its western slope foster sweet cherries and peaches. Ranches lie throughout the state's mountains and valleys. Gold and silver were 19th-century stimuli for development and settlement. Many of Colorado's scenic mountain towns and resorts are former mining villages. Oil shale, coal, and uranium are dug and blasted from the mountains today.

The state is interested in restoring historic wildlife populations. But the task in not an easy one. Even existing wildlife, specifically predators, are controversial. In 1990, five dead black bears were discovered near a lamb carcass found to be poisoned. There are few legitimate cases in which bears have taken livestock, but the fear of future losses pits ranchers against environmentalists who encourage rising numbers of coyote, mountain lions, and wolves. In 2009, two extirpated species returned to Colorado—a wolf and a wolverine. Both were radio-collared in Yellowstone National Park. Residents have reported wolf sightings for nearly 10 years. Though the state has no plan to reintroduce the species, state law gives free range to any migrant wildlife.

BLACK CANYON OF THE GUNNISON NATIONAL PARK

Dramatic. Foreboding. Inaccessible. This is Black Canyon of the Gunnison National Park. Humans have never occupied its gorge. Ferdinand Vandeveer Hayden, who explored the canyon on his 1873–1874 geological expedition, described the gorge as impassable. In 1900, local residents floated the river for one month exploring for irrigation potential. One year later, two explorers spent nine days navigating the river on a rubber mattress.

The Black Canyon of the Gunnison is a 48-mile-long chasm in southwestern Colorado. It is the deepest narrow canyon in the United States, nearly twice as deep (some 2,400 feet) as it is wide—1,300 feet rim to rim at its narrowest point, near the North Rim Nature Trail. For some two million years, the Gunnison River's consistent path slowly cut through the hard, uplifted rock of the Gunnison Uplift enhanced by Spring surges of upstream snowmelt. Although rock falls and landslides added to the process, it was the river itself that formed this canyon's depth. It did so by speed. In its 14 miles through the park, the Gunnison River loses an average of 96 feet a mile. In its natural flow, the river sped through at up to 12,000 cubic feet per second and with the power of 2.75 million horsepower. In one two-mile stretch, it drops 480 feet.

The canyon is painted with streaks of lighter-colored rock. The walls are a pre-Cambrian gneiss that lay deep in the ground during the earth's formation, subjecting it

Black Canyon of the Gunnison National Park. (Doc Searls)

to extreme pressure and heat. When the gneiss cracked molten rock worked its way into these openings. The pink stripes are granite, and the gray rock is pegmatite.

The depth and sheerness of the canyon prohibit most animal life. Birds, however, are undeterred. Great horned owls, mountain bluebirds, Steller's jays, peregrine falcons, white-throated swifts, canyon wrens, and American dippers live all or part of the year here. Canyon wrens live off the steep walls of the canyon, plucking insects from alcoves and ledges. Plants along the gorge bottom reflect typical western riparian diversity with river birch, willow, serviceberry, and cottonwood. Weasel, badger, cougar, and black bear find food and shelter in this landscape. The river contains the state's largest trout population. At the rim, oak brush, piñon-juniper forest, and ponderosa pine are the primary vegetation. Sagebrush grassland spreads away from the rim, providing a nutritious browse for mule deer in winter and other mammals seeking its high fat content (nearly 12 times higher than alfalfa). It is truly a native form of nutrition; imported cattle cannot digest the plant. Sagebrush is the foundation for these types of grasslands, but it suffers competition from opportunist invaders like cheatgrass, a nonnative species.

Black Canyon of the Gunnison National Park is 30,244 acres, of which 15,599 are designated wilderness areas. The park is adjacent to the Gunnison Gorge National Conservation Area and the Curecanti National Recreation Area. Locals lobbied to make the canyon a park in the 1930s, and it was made a monument in 1933. The land below the rim gained additional protection as part of the National Wilderness Preservation System in 1976. It was not designated a national park until 1999, preserving 14 miles of the canyon's most dramatic scenery. Locals had lobbied for this designation for nearly 15 years. The bill included the Gunnison Gorge National Conservation Area, an early Bureau of Land Management wilderness area, and gave 4,400 acres to the national park. The Gunnison Diversion Tunnel is a six-mile irrigation structure that was built between 1905 and 1909. The river is now managed by a series of dams.

Further Reading

Hansen, Wallace, Carolyn Dodson, and T. J. Priehs, eds. *Black Canyon of the Gunnison: In Depth.* Tucson, AZ: Western National Parks Association, 1993.

BROWN'S PARK NATIONAL WILDLIFE REFUGE

In 1963, Brown's Park National Wildlife Refuge was preserved as a sanctuary for migrating birds, to conserve endangered and threatened species, and offer wildlife-dependent recreational opportunities. Its river and wetlands are a retreat from the semiarid environment surrounding it. Waterfowl, migrating birds, 68 species of mammals, and 15 species of reptiles and amphibians use these resources.

Brown's Park National Wildlife Refuge lies along the Green River in northwestern Colorado between the Cold Springs and Diamond mountain ranges. The refuge contains a variety of habitats—riparian, wetland, grassland, and upland. In the riparian environment of the Green River and Vermillion and Beaver Creeks, cottonwoods, buffaloberry, and willows thrive. This habitat is important for migrating songbirds and makes a more permanent home for Woodhouse's toad and Bullock's oriole. Moose and river otter find protection and nourishment for their young in this environment.

The refuge's seven wetland areas of 1,245 acres offer imperative support for migratory waterfowl in the spring and fall. Pied-billed grebes and ducks nest in the summer, and American bitterns, Woodhouse's toad, and white-faced ibis all use this habitat. Park staff pumps water into these areas from the river and two creeks. These are the only wetlands large enough to support this life for miles around the semidesert uplands. Nineteen hundred acres of grassland support diverse grasses like inland salt grass, western wheatgrass, and Great Basin wild rye. This vegetation supports montane vole and damselflies; waterfowl and songbird nesters; and wintering elk and mule deer. Refuge staff sets controlled fires to restore the matted vegetation from overuse. Eight thousand acres of upland habitat include semidesert shrubland and piñon and Utah juniper forests. A variety of grasses supports the sage grouse, Ord's kangaroo rat, and sagebrush vole. Forest residents include unique species like gray flycatcher, piñon jay, bats, and lizards.

This life-giving environment has been affected, however, by the damming of the Green River at Flaming Gorge in 1962. The river no longer naturally floods in spring, which deepens the channel and forces trees and willows to strain their roots for water. Cottonwoods are not taking to seed, and invasive species, which do not support native wildlife, have moved in, including perennial pepperweed and tamarisk. This multiple-use area offers hunting, fishing, observation, and photography. One popular route is the eight-mile River's Edge Wildlife Drive, which traverses a variety of the refuge's habitats. Management includes burns, hunts, and seedings, as well as biological and chemical control of invasive species.

Further Reading
Dolin, Eric Jay. *Smithsonian Book of National Wildlife Refuges*. Washington, DC: Smithsonian Institution Press, 2003.

COMANCHE NATIONAL GRASSLAND

Comanche National Grassland is 440,000 acres of prairie grassland and juniper canyon land in southeastern Colorado. Its name disguises its most striking feature—one of the only dinosaur trackways in the world. The region was covered 150 million years ago with a massive lake in the middle of a tropical forest. The soft mud and slow sedimentation preserved Jurassic footprints of apatosaurus and allosaurus. In all, the grassland contains over 1,300 fossilized dinosaur tracks.

On the surface, Comanche National Grassland represents the natural state of the Great Plains, before plow and tractor turned the soil. This is as close as one can get to a view of the landscape seen by the first Euro-American explorers and homesteaders. It is primarily short-grass prairie with sandy soil, the dominant environment of the western reaches of the Great Plains. The grassland is divided into two sections. The northern area near the town of La Junta is known as the Timpas Unit and contains the Purgatory River. The southern area, south of Springfield toward the Oklahoma border is called the Carrizo Unit. Flora here includes Andean prairie clover, Colorado Springs evening primrose, Colorado frasera, Raven Ridge false goldenweed, sandhill goosefoot, wheel milkweed, prickly pear, and cholla cactus. Rarities like the lesser prairie chicken, golden eagle, and swift fox make their homes in Comanche National Grassland. Mammals include pronghorn, coyote, badgers, and prairie dogs. Turtles, collard lizards, wild turkeys, and roadrunners share the earth, while the skies contain over 200 species, including hawks, burrowing owls, dove, and quail.

Human history here is ancient. Native Americans carved images on canyon walls 1,500 years ago. Modern oral history retains a belief in the canyon's spiritual power. Between 1821 and 1880, the Santa Fe Trail ran ruggedly through this region. Limestone markers show its path, as do the still-visible ruts of wagon wheels. Near the Timpas Picnic Area, a three-mile hike leads to Sierra Vista Overlook for a view of the Spanish Peaks—the first mountains sighted by those along the trail after the long trek through the plains. Nearby is Bent's Old Fort National Historic Site, a stop along the overland trail.

Though most who visited this landscape were headed further west, some stayed in this region, settling as farmers or ranchers during the 1870s and 1880s. Remains of these homesteads, built of stone in this tree-deficient environment, can be seen on the landscape of the Comanche National Grassland today. The Dust Bowl drove out nearly all settlers during the 1920s and 1930s, causing the federal government to take over the land. Picketwire Canyon, however, was occupied until 1971, when the Department of Defense purchased the land for their Pion Canyon Maneuvering Site. The U.S. Army may take over more land in this area. The grassland began prescribed burning in 2009.

For Further Reading

Moul, Francis. *The National Grasslands: A Guide to America's Undiscovered Treasures.* Lincoln: University of Nebraska Press, 2006.
Phillips, Dave. "The Lost World/Comanche National Grassland." *Colorado Springs Gazette,* May 16, 2003 http://findarticles.com/p/articles/mi_qn4191/is_20030516/ai_n10018721.

Dinosaur National Monument

Dinosaur National Monument has the unique trait of being the only protected historic dinosaur quarry in the national park system. The monument contains a collection of fossils that tells of the land's past ecological diversity and the Yampa River—the only remaining free-flowing tributary of the Colorado River. It lies at the confluence of the Green and the Yampa rivers, on the border between Utah and Colorado.

Dinosaur National Monument's fossils are within the Morrison Formation, a Jurassic river bed composed of sandstone and conglomerate. This 150-million-year-old rock contains fossils from a variety of habitats dating to that time. It represents 23 extinct ecosystems including arid desert. Belemnites (squid relatives) attest to ancient oceans; freshwater lakes contained clams, snails, algae, frogs, turtles, crocodiles, and small mammals. Humid araucaria (ferns, ginkgo, and moss) forests are represented by plants over 150 feet tall. Over 250 species of plants are found in this fossil record, some represented by fossilized pollen and spores. Some plant species were completely dependent on soil composition. Big wild buckwheat, for example, is found fossilized only in Mowry Shale. Four groups of dinosaurs are found here: plant-eating sauropods, stegasaurs, ornithopods, and flesh-eating theropods.

The fossil beds were discovered in 1909 by Earl Douglas, on an expedition for the Carnegie Museum. Six years later, 80 acres were designated a national monument to protect the fossils from looters. The 23 exposed layers of rock found here are the National Park Service's most complete record of a single place's changing environment through time. In 1938, the monument was extended to include surrounding lands in Utah and Colorado, giving Dinosaur National Monument its current size of over 200,000 acres. It now contains the river canyons of the Green and the Yampa rivers. The landscape is semiarid and contains cold desert shrubs, mountain piñon-juniper forests, and aquatic and riparian areas. Mammals include elk, mule deer, coyote, porcupine, prairie dogs, badger, pronghorn, bighorn sheep, river otters, and Yuma myotis bat. Birds include chickadees, hermit thrush, warblers, lazuli buntings, and grouse. The Yampa River contains three species of endangered fish.

Dinosaur National Monument was the site of an important conservation success. In the 1950s, the U.S. Bureau of Reclamation wanted to dam the Green River at a place known as Echo Park, inside monument borders, as part of the 10-dam Colorado River Storage Project that would provide hydroelectric power and develop reservoirs. Sierra Club director David Brower and the Wilderness Society's Howard Zahniser led a massive nationwide campaign, claiming that, if land in the national park system could be dammed, there was no way to protect the public parks and wildernesses. It would have set a precedent for development that would endanger not just the Green and the Yampa rivers in Dinosaur National Monument but all natural places. The Colorado River Storage Project continued, but with the caveat that dams and reservoirs could not be constructed within national parks or monuments. This 1956 victory for conservationists ushered in an era of success in protecting free-flowing rivers and the wild character of places, leading to the Wilderness Act (1964) and the Wild and Scenic Rivers Act (1968).

Further Reading

Cosco, Jon M. *Echo Park: Struggle for Preservation*. Boulder, CO: Johnson Books, 1995.

Harvey, Mark W. T. *A Symbol of Wilderness: Echo Park and the American Conservation Movement*. Seattle: University of Washington Press, 2000.

FLORISSANT FOSSIL BEDS NATIONAL MONUMENT

During the Eocene epoch, 34 to 35 million years ago, the landscape of Florissant, Colorado, was dominated by a rumbling volcano. The vast prairie that now forms the center of Florissant Fossil Beds National Monument was a 12-mile-long, 1-mile-wide lake surrounded by forests of redwoods, cedars, pines, maples, hickories, oaks, ferns, and shrubs. Mudslides from a nearby volcano buried redwood trees, petrifying their trunks. Multiple eruption episodes released ash and pumice into the atmosphere, which settled on the floor of the ancient lake, burying and preserving myriad forms of life that had died and fallen to the bottom. The fossil beds at Florissant contain delicate life forms rarely preserved in fossil records, which favor bones and hard material over soft matter. The impressions formed in the hardening of the ash and pumice represent insects, plants, seeds, and even pollen. Butterflies have been preserved with such intricacy that scientists can observe details as minute as the pattern on their wings. The fossiliferous shale contains 140 species of plants and more than 1,400 species of insects. Most of the insect life found resembles today's world species, though most of the species found here, like the tsetse fly, no longer live in Colorado. Florissant's fossil beds tell scientists of the former climate, which was more humid than today.

The fossils lie underneath the ground, while the landscape above is primarily ponderosa pine forests and mountain meadows filled with summer wildflowers. Elk, black bear, coyote, badger, porcupine, mountain lion, and Abert's squirrel all live in the valley, as well as raptors—golden eagles and red-tailed hawks—who often nest within the park. Florissant Fossil Beds National Monument also contains the 1878 Hornbeck Homestead—the remains of buildings from a pioneer farming family.

Fossils from Florissant Fossil Beds National Monument can be found in top museum collections in the United States and United Kingdom. Samuel Scudder was the first to perform major investigations of the fossil shale in the late 19th century, when most of his paleontological colleagues were looking for dinosaur bones. The unique nature of these fossil beds garnered support for its preservation in 1969. Today a short hike along the Ponderosa or Petrified Forest Loops reveals petrified redwood stumps, fossil shale exposures, along with the current ecosystem.

Further Reading

Frank, James, and Dan Klinglesmith. *Portrait of Pikes Peak Country*. Alberta, Canada: Altitude Publishing, 2000.

Meyer, Herbert W. W. *Fossils of Florissant*. Washington, DC: Smithsonian Institution Press, 2003.

GARDEN OF THE GODS

In the late 1950s, two surveyors exploring locations surrounding the future site of Colorado City ran across lands with awe-inspiring sandstone formations. One surveyor suggested that the area would serve beautifully as a beer garden once population numbers began to grow. His surveying partner, Rufus Cable, reportedly stated instead, "Beer garden! Why it is a place fit for the gods to assemble. We will call it the Garden of the Gods instead." Over the next decade, railroad expansion brought new settlement pushes into the West. By the 1870s, people in the eastern United States had access to all corners of the country. In 1871, General William Jackson Palmer established Colorado Springs while expanding the reach of the Denver and Rio Grande Railroad lines. In the process of settling into the area, Palmer bought 240 acres in the Garden of the Gods to build a home. He eventually added to his acreage but did not develop them. The idea was to leave intact the amazing wonders of the Garden of the Gods. Although the general died before he had the opportunity to arrange for permanent protection of his lands, two years later in 1909, Palmer's children acted on what would have been their father's wishes and placed almost 500 acres under the ownership and protection of Colorado Springs. Its protection charter finalized the process declaring that the Garden of the Gods would "remain free to the public . . . where no building or structure shall be erected except those necessary to properly care for, protect, and maintain the area as a public park."

The geology of the park is unusual, to say the least. The site's ancient beds of sandstone and limestone were originally horizontally deposited, but time and mountain-building geological forces tilted them vertically. Erosion has exposed the deposits, providing not only spectacular formations but also uncovering evidence of the area's ancient past. It is possible to see what landscapes once covered the land. Eroded, ancient mountain ranges, sand dune fields, alluvial fans, and coastal beaches have all left their mark in the megalithic remains that characterize this natural wonder. Overall, there are 300 million years of natural history represented in the exposed layers. Ridges and valleys dominated the surface, all running in a north-south direction. In every ridge and every valley, it is possible to examine a different geological time period. For example, ancestral Rocky Mountains that grew from the land 300 million years ago are the foundation of the Fountain Formation, which dominates much of the west side of the park. Through years of erosion, streams carried gravel, mud, and sand away from the mountains, leaving layers of sediment to collect at the base of the mountains. Fine layers and coarse layers alternate today and are easily observable at the garden's Sentinel Rock and Balanced Rock.

Tall, colored sandstone cliffs, created of ancient desert sand, offer a glimpse of a different piece of the area's history. The red in the cliffs comes from iron-rich layers that help hold the sands together. Over 250 million years ago, what would become Lyons Formation, a major section of the cliffs today, began the long process of creation, solidification, and eventually transformation into the area's contemporary natural wonders. Each section, every turn, every rock is a different page in the expansive environmental story of Garden of the Gods.

Another piece of ancient history is found at the park today. Paleontologists have found a wealth of fossil evidence to study the history of dinosaur habitation in the area. One of the most significant finds is the first evidence anywhere on the planet for a new dinosaur species. In 1878, James H. Kerr discovered what he believed to be fossils of ancient sea monsters in the east ridges of the Garden. Yale paleontologist O. C. Marsh found the discovery interesting and came to investigate in 1886. Marsh uncovered what he believed to be the skull of a camptosaurus and shipped it to the Peabody Museum in Connecticut. For over 100 years, that was the end of Kerr's fossil discovery and the skull's story. In 1994, while a visitor's center was under construction, the idea for a dinosaur exhibit was explored, so the skull was shipped back to Colorado. Planners made casts and arrangements to include these fossils in the dinosaur showcase. For more than 10 years, the dinosaur now known as Campi was a central part of the center's Jurassic exhibit. Ken Carpenter, the scientist who made the replica, had his doubts about the identification, though. Through detailed study and analysis, Carpenter and his associate, Kathleen Brill, concluded that the skull was not of a camptosaurus, but instead a remnant of a new Cretaceous species, the *Theiophytalia kerri*. They named it for the location in which it was found, the Garden of the Gods, *Theios* means "belonging to the gods" and *phytalia* means "garden." This discovery encourages preservation of Garden of the Gods for its scientific, as well as its scenic, treasures.

Further Reading

Matthews, Vincent. *Messages in Stone: Colorado's Colorful Geology.* Boulder: Colorado Department of Natural Resources, 2003.

GREAT SAND DUNES NATIONAL PARK AND PRESERVE

The Great Sand Dunes are an oddity in western America. Formed by centuries of sediment washed from the mountains to the valley, this national park represents a unique geologic process. The first Euro-American to set eyes on these dunes, explorer Zebulon Pike, wrote: "their appearance was exactly that of the sea in a storm." Great Sand Dunes National Park and Preserve is nestled at 8,200 feet elevation in the wide San Luis Valley at the foot of two mountain ranges—the San Juan to the west and the Sangre de Cristo to the east. Streams and rivers used to empty into lakes, but the waterways have changed and now deposit only sand on the valley floor. The dunes are then shaped by winds that blow southwesterly in the valley, funneling through mountain passes from the northeast. The tallest dune here is the highest in North America, at 750 feet. Surface temperature of the sand can reach 140° F, and lightning strikes here often.

The environment of the Great Sand Dunes National Park and Preserve is an unexpected one for the Rocky Mountains. Air temperatures reach 100° F. Vegetation is hardy and adapted to the dearth of water and shifting sands. Grasses like blowout and Indian ricegrass thrive, along with late summer blooms of prairie sunflowers. Animals are scarce. The kangaroo rat and giant sand treader are two inhabitants. Despite its short stock of wildlife, the dunes are host to six species of insects that are found only here. A few oddities can be found in the park. Epidote is a green rock formed as the Sangre de Cristo Mountains uplifted. Fulgurites are rough glass tubes formed by lightning melting sand at temperatures of 50,000° F as it strikes the dunes. Research in the area includes monitoring its six unique insects, stream flow, and vegetation. An extensive study of the region's bison and elk herds is ongoing, managed in part by the Nature Conservancy. This study seeks to better understand behavior, patterns of movement related to birthing and dying, as well as the effect of weather on behavior.

The surrounding mountains and valley contrast with the dunes environment. Hikers can explore dune, forest, and alpine trails. Climbing the dunes is popular—as is sliding down them. Four-wheel-drive roads climb the mountains to Medano Pass (where Pike caught his first glimpse) for views down to the sand dunes. The Nature

Great Sand Dunes National Monument. (National Park Service)

Conservancy maintains the adjacent Medano-Zapata Ranch. Its 103,000 acres contain sand dunes as well as wet meadows, desert shrubland, and piñon-juniper forest. These ecosystems support elk, bison, some 200 bird species, and the Great Sand Dunes tiger beetle.

Further Reading

Trimble, Stephen. *Great Sand Dunes: The Shape of the Wind*. Tucson, AZ: Western National Parks Association, 2001.

Tweit, Susan J., and Glen Oakley. *The San Luis Valley: Sand Dunes and Sandhill Cranes*. Tucson: University of Arizona Press, 2005.

HOLY CROSS WILDERNESS

Named for its highest peak, 14,005-foot Mount of the Holy Cross, the Holy Cross Wilderness contains over 25 mountains over 13,000 feet. The mountain's name is derived from a nearly permanent snow cover nestled in two crossing gullies at the top of the peak. This formation was made famous by 19th-century photographer William H. Jackson (though some believe he manipulated his images to make the cross appear larger than it really was). Holy Cross Wilderness lies in the Sawatch range, a stretch of mountains made of 1.7-billion-year-old schist and gneiss. Seven Sisters Lakes dramatically descend near Fall Creek Pass. Wide valleys provide habitat for deer, elk, black bear, bobcats, and lynx. Elevation ranges from 8,000 to 14,000 feet.

The wilderness area contains 122,797 acres just west of the Continental Divide. Hikers and cross-country skiers enjoy 164 miles of trail, including part of the Colorado Trail and the 28-mile Cross Creek Trail. Mount of the Holy Cross is a popular summit destination reached by a six-mile one-way trek. Isolated fishing for native cutthroat trout is found at Turquoise Lakes. The northwest corner of the wilderness is home to the Polar Star Inn, one of a series of huts built by the 10th Mountain Division. A ghost town lies near the eastern border along the Fall Creek Trail just south of Seven Sisters Lakes.

The Holy Cross Wilderness is one of the wettest places in Colorado, checkered with lakes, wetlands, streams, and waterfalls. While this adds to the scenic beauty of the landscape, the water is valued for more than its aesthetics. As with many western battles, water has been the source of conflict here for decades. During the 1960s, the Front Range cities of Colorado Springs and Aurora claimed the headwaters of the Eagle River for future water supplies. They constructed the Homestake Reservoir before wilderness designation in 1980. That assessment tried to appease the cities and environmentalists by preserving the landscape but allowing for future water use. Proposed plans to divert more northern streams (Cross and Fall Creeks) to the reservoir are still contested.

Further Reading

Fielder, John, and Mark Pearson. *Complete Guide to Colorado's Wilderness Areas.* Boulder, CO: Westcliffe, 1994.

MOUNT ELBERT

Mount Elbert is the highest mountain peak in the North American Rocky Mountain range, and it is the second highest peak in the continuous United States. It reaches 14,440 feet, only 65 feet shorter than Mount Whitney in California. The peak is named for Samuel Hitt Elbert, the territorial governor of the Colorado territory and a leader in the region's conservation and irrigation. The first recorded ascent was in 1874, completed by H.W. Struckle of the Hayden Survey. In the many years since its first ascent, climbers have attained the summit through several methods, including horse, mule, jeep, all-terrain vehicle, and helicopter. While Mount Elbert was already established as the second highest peak in the continental United States, the official height was raised in 1993 from 14,433 feet to 14,440. That doesn't mean its status went uncontested. Some people who wished the state's second highest peak, 14,421-foot Mount Massive, to be the continental U.S.'s second tallest peak, attempted to raise its height by piling rocks at its apex. Mount Elbert supporters, however, removed the rocks. This continued for some time until Mount Massive boosters tired of the contest and quit building the cairns. Thus, Mount Elbert remains on record as the tallest peak in the Rocky Mountains.

Despite its now uncontested place in the list of mountain apexes, Mount Elbert is not as popular a recreation destination as some of Colorado's other "fourteeners." Unlike Front Range mountains, Elbert is far from the state's metropolises. It lies just south of the Mount Massive Wilderness inside the Pike and San Isabel National Forests. Trailheads for Mount Elbert begin near Leadville, about 100 miles from Denver. The summer climbing season for Mount Elbert is June through September. There are five main access routes. The most commonly used route, the South Mount Elbert Trail, begins at the Colorado Trail and runs east to the peak. Another popular path for average hikers is the North Mount Elbert Trail, also known as Halfmoon Creek Route. Black Cloud Trail is the most difficult path, requiring at least 10 hours to complete. All five trails, however, gain an elevation of 4,000 feet, so altitude and weather are ever-present dangers. Mount Elbert, like Colorado's other fourteeners, gathers clouds throughout the day and frequently sees dangerous afternoon thunderstorms. In winter, these storms are not common, but there are, of course, other dangers. Avalanches, snowstorms, and extra distance due to closed roads should be considered. As in warmer months, the South Mount Elbert Trail is the most frequented. The winter trek is more demanding, as the access road is closed, making the climb an 11-mile round-trip. Many who undertake this climb in the winter camp at the upper trailhead. Snow cover may make the trail difficult to find but signage, maps specific to winter ascents, and previous climbers offer tips for staying safely on the trail.

Advance planning and research can ensure a safe and enjoyable hike up Mount Elbert no matter what the season. This highest of natural places provides year-round experiences that thrill beginning hikers and completely satisfy the experienced, making it one of few adventure spots that can appeal to everyone, young or old, novice or expert.

Although hiking is a relatively low-impact activity, erosion on the North Elbert Trail became so severe the U.S. Forest Service closed a three-mile section of trail in 1992. It constructed a temporary route, but restoration of the original trail may take 50 to 100 years. Mount Elbert's trails traverse fragile alpine environments. The U.S. Forest Service maintains trails to prevent hikers from stepping on alpine plants, such as yellow alpine avens, old-man-of-the-mountain, and blue-purple sky pilot, that may die with one imprint of a hiker's boot. In 1994, a group of climbers who observed the damage to trails like those on Mount Elbert formed the Colorado Fourteeners Initiative. They estimate over 500,000 people climb the state's mountains each year, a figure that has increased dramatically over the past three decades. The Fourteeners Initiative educates hikers, volunteers to maintain and construct trails, and partners with land agencies to protect these high, and fragile, natural places.

Further Reading
Baron, Jill. *Rocky Mountain Futures: An Ecological Perspective*. Washington, DC: Island Press, 2002.

ROCKY MOUNTAIN NATIONAL PARK

Rocky Mountain National Park's Trail Ridge Road easily accesses the tundra environment normally reached only by foot. At its highest point of 12,183 feet, this road through Rocky Mountain National Park provides a view above the tree line and an interpretive trail, the Tundra Communities Trail (near the Alpine Visitor Center). The park contains 72 peaks over 12,000 feet, including Long's Peak, which tops out at 14,259 feet—the northernmost "fourteener" in the Rocky Mountains.

This is one of the few places in the world with car access to an alpine environment. The tundra begins here at 11,400 feet. Growth is stunted yet diverse. Specialized plants have adapted to the harsh, cold winds and ultraviolet light by growing low to the ground. Despite their low profile on the surface, plants cling to thin soil with roots of up to six feet long, such as the yellow blooms of alpine avens. Harsh winters keep most animals seasonal, but ptarmigan and pikas remain all year. Marmots hibernate for the eight months of winter. Migrants include American pipits, elk, and coyote and reintroduced bighorn sheep.

A trio of glacial episodes between 738,000 and 13,750 years ago formed the mountains here. The granite is 1.3 billion years old. The 265,769-acre park preserves not only the tundra but the subalpine and montane environments as well. From 9,000 feet to the tip of the tundra, the subalpine environment hosts Engelmann spruce, fir, juniper, limber pines, and a variety of colorful wildflowers. At the line of tundra, spruce, fir, and limber pines twist from the harsh winds into krummholz (crooked wood), some of which are nearly horizontal and hundreds of years old. Martens, long-tailed weasels, chickarees, snowshoe hare, hermit thrush, and boreal owls make their homes here.

The montane environment is the liveliest, with pine forests and meadows; the smell of ponderosa pine fills the air as the sun heats the fragrant bark. These pines leave plenty of space for sunlight to penetrate through to the forest floor, which is filled with grasses, shrubs, flowering plants, and bushes (chokecherry, wax current, and serviceberry). Mountain bluebirds and Abert's squirrels enjoy the abundance. On north-facing slopes, Douglas fir, lodgepole pine, and Engelmann spruce mix with ponderosa and create a less diverse forest floor. Meadows are comfortable homes for deer, elk, coyote, black bear, red-tailed hawks, and goshawks. These glacier-created meadows provide streams and wetlands for a variety of life, with succulent grasses, wildflowers, and aspen groves at the edges.

Rocky Mountain National Park has been inhabited little, but Utes used its seasonal abundance 6,000 years ago. Cheyenne and Arapahoe passed through, and Euro-Americans began hunting beaver here in the 1800s, until prices for fur fell in the 1840s. An 1858 gold rush created nearby cities, but these mountains were relatively poor. Gold-rusher Joel Estes found a better fortune hunting for meat for camps and farmers. In the 20th century, the mountains became valued for their scenery, and tourism entered through the east in Estes Park and the west in Grand Lake. The land was first set aside as a forest preserve and was made a national park in 1915, thanks to the efforts of conservationists, most famously, Enos Mills. For the past 30 years, most of the land in the park has been managed as a designated wilderness area.

Rocky Mountain National Park. (Linda Yvonne)

Further Reading

Buchhotz, C. W. *Rocky Mountain National Park: A History*. Boulder: University Press of Colorado, 1987.

Gellhorn, Joyce. *Song of the Alpine: The Rocky Mountain Tundra through the Seasons*. Boulder, CO: Johnson Books, 2002.

WEMINUCHE WILDERNESS

Nestled between the Rio Grande and San Juan National Forests, the Weminuche Wilderness is Colorado's most isolated stretch of mountains. Encompassing nearly half a million acres, it is the largest wilderness area in the state and the site chosen for fragile populations of lynx and wolves. Reintroduction of grizzly bears has also been proposed. Average elevation is 10,000 feet dominated by alpine meadows and spruce forests.

Three "fourteeners" (peaks over 14,000 feet) mark this wilderness: Mount Elous (14,083 feet), Sunlight Peak (14,059 feet), and Windom Peak (14,082 feet). In fact, the lowest elevation in the wilderness is a lofty 8,000 feet. Headwaters here lead through streams and rivers to the Rio Grande and the San Juan River, feeding the arid southwestern United States Vallecito Creek, Los Pinos River, Piedra River, and the San Juan headwaters drain to the San Juan, which becomes the Colorado River. On the east side of the Continental Divide, the Ute and Weminuche Creeks lead to the Rio Grande. These are two of the most important rivers in the ecology and culture of the Southwest.

The landscape here is a diverse mixture of glacial valleys, alpine lakes, harsh ridges, and dramatic summits. In the western region, the granitic Needle Mountains tower over the Animas River. The southern portion of the wilderness features limestone mesas, and the eastern region showcases the cliffs and peaks of formerly active volcanoes.

In 1999, the Colorado Division of Wildlife reintroduced 50 lynx to the Weminuche Wilderness. They are now a thriving, self-sustaining group, producing wild-born kittens. Elk also thrive in this remote location. At the start of the 20th century, their numbers were as low as 100 individuals. Sixty years later, they numbered 10,000. This abundance has led the Colorado Division of Wildlife to propose wolf reintroduction to naturally control the elk population.

The Weminuche Wilderness was created in 1975 when Congress set aside some 400,000 acres as roadless. The move was controversial to locals who hoped to build a road over Weminuche Pass to connect the scattered Hinsdale County, which requires a four-mile drive from one end to the other. Local loggers fought hard to maintain access to Goose Creek, and this area was released from the restraints of wilderness protection. Cutthroat trout suffered, and, five years later, Congress added Goose Creek to the Wilderness. In 1993, the West Needle Mountains and adjoining Animas River were annexed.

Visitors can ride the Durango-Silverton Narrow Gauge Railroad through the scenic canyon cut by the Animas River or experience isolated wilderness. Hikers traverse the extent of the Weminuche on a portion of the 80-mile Continental Divide National Scenic Trail or on 21 miles of the statewide Colorado Trail. This is the most visited wilderness area in the state, however, and trails show signs of use and abuse. There are two less popular roadless areas nearby, Carson Peak and San Miguel.

Further Reading

Boucher, B. J. *Walking in Wildness: A Guide to the Weminuche Wilderness.* Durango, CO: Durango Herald Small Press, 1999.

Fielder, John, and Mark Pearson. *Complete Guide to Colorado's Wilderness Areas.* Boulder, CO: Westcliffe, 1994.

WHITE RIVER NATIONAL FOREST

Stretching over two million acres through the heart of Colorado, outdoor enthusiasts consider the White River National Forest one of the top forests in the country for its beauty and serenity. Eight wilderness areas—Flat Tops, Eagles Nest, Ptarmigan Peak, Holy Cross, Hunter-Fryingpan, Maroon Bells-Snowmass, Collegiate Peaks, and Raggeds—lie within national forest boundaries, the largest concentration in the state. Many portions of forest and wilderness lie within easy reach of urban populations, making this a highly-used recreational forest. Consequently, management is challenged with balancing recreation and wilderness needs. All motorized equipment, from bicycles to all-terrain vehicles are forbidden in wilderness areas where, says the forest, nature exists "on its own terms." Rangers monitor camp locations and dog-leash usage, as well. Meanwhile, the non-wilderness areas of the White River National Forest, allow snowmobiling, hunting, mountain biking, and even the massive ski resorts Vail and Aspen. There are twelve ski areas in the national forest, attracting over 8 million visitors a year from all over the world.

In addition to balancing recreation and wilderness areas, White River National Forest staff is charged with maintaining a healthy ecosystem. The national forest contains the headwaters of the Upper Colorado River Watershed, producing 75 percent—some 200,000 acre feet—of the Colorado River's flow in the state. Along its course, the river is channeled for irrigation and water supply. Other headwaters within forest boundaries include the Blue, Eagle, and Roaring Fork Rivers (all tributaries to the Colorado River), the Yampa River, and the headwaters of its namesake river, the White. Overall, the White River National Forest contains some 4,000 miles of perennial streams, 14,000 acres of lakes, 120,000 acres of riparian and wetland areas, and five reservoirs. Swimming in these waters are Bluehead sucker, Roundtail chub, and the recovery Colorado River cutthroat trout. Black bear, elk, bighorn sheep, deer, purple martin, and Townsend big-eared bats inhabit the forest. Threatened and endangered species include the Canada lynx and Penland's alpine fen mustard (a perennial left over from the Ice Age). Perhaps the biggest threat to White River National Forest's ecosystem is one of its smallest inhabitants—the mountain pine beetle and spruce bark beetles. Throughout eastern portions, pine trees stand in swaths of brownish-red where they used to be green. These dead trees are often cut by forest staff to limit beetle range and prevent wildfires. The timber is used for fuel in surrounding counties. Forest staff monitor wildfires, noxious weeds, and water and air quality. Near Sunlight Ski Resort, the national forest monitors water and air quality for the nationwide program of the Environmental Protection Agency, the National Acid Deposition Program.

Further Reading

Fielder, John and Mark Pearson. *Complete Guide to Colorado's Wilderness Areas*. Boulder, CO: Westcliffe, 1994.
Outdoor Books & Maps. *White River National Forest Recreation Guide*. Denver, CO: Outdoor Books & Maps, 1996.

YAMPA RIVER VALLEY

The Yampa River is one of the only remaining waterways in the Colorado River Basin that resembles its natural flow. As such, it can support a streamside riparian ecosystem rare in the West. The Yampa still experiences seasonal flooding, which gently erodes and deposits sediment on the riverbank in what is called a river dance. The winding course of the river creates new forests and wetlands. Cottonwood forest, willows, and cattail marshes decorate the valley. The riparian habitat of the Yampa River Valley consists of rare box elder, narrowleaf cottonwood, and red-osier dogwood. Nearby sage and oak hills are home to Colorado's only population of Columbian sharp-tailed grouse. These hills also shelter the state's second largest elk herd during winter, and bald eagles breed and nest along the banks of the Yampa. Sandhill cranes migrate through in spring and fall. Beaver, elk, mink, mule deer, Swainson's thrush, river otter, and gray catbird use the river's habitat.

The Yampa River Valley was identified by the Nature Conservancy as a biologically rich landscape. In the Yampa Valley, the Nature Conservancy has preserved more than 9,000 acres of land since 1985 through conservation easements. The 235-acre broad floodplain of the Nature Conservancy's Yampa River Preserve is open for limited public recreation. In all, the Nature Conservancy has protected over 10,500 acres in the valley.

Further Reading

Stegner, Page. *Adios Amigos: Tales of Sustenance and Purification in the American West*. Berkeley, CA: Counterpoint Press, 2008.

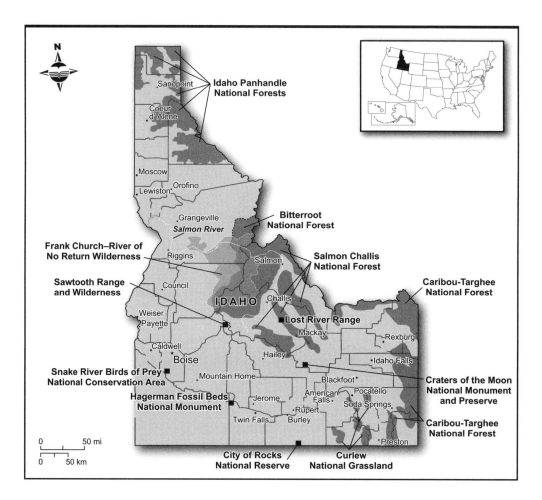

Bitterroot National Forest, 20

Caribou-Targhee National Forest, 21

City of Rocks National Reserve, 22

Craters of the Moon National Monument and Preserve, 23

Curlew National Grassland, 24

Hagerman Fossil Beds National Monument, 25

Frank Church–River of No Return Wilderness, 27

Idaho Panhandle National Forests, 28

Lost River Range, 30

Salmon-Challis National Forest, 31

Salmon National Scenic River, 32

Sawtooth Range and Wilderness, 33

Snake River Birds of Prey National Conservation Area, 34

IDAHO

Idaho, like many of the states of the Rockies and the Great Plains holds a wealth of natural beauty and diversity. Subalpine forests, granite mountains, fertile farmland, and arid deserts are all within state borders. Hell's Canyon, the deepest canyon in North America, cuts through the landscape. Shoshone Falls is just a bit higher than the more famous Niagara Falls. The Rocky Mountains reach all the way from the panhandle in the extreme north to the Wyoming border in the southeast. In Idaho's 80 mountain ranges, 50 peaks reach higher than 10,000 feet above sea level. In addition to the Rocky Mountains, Idaho contains two other distinct geographical regions—the Columbia Plateau and the Basin and Range Province. The Columbia Plateau follows the Snake River east from Washington to the base of the state's southern panhandle. Southeastern Idaho contains part of the Basin and Range Province, where plateaus and valleys create stark geographic contrasts.

Idaho is rich in natural resources. The Columbia Plateau contains some of the most fertile lands in the state, with potatoes and sugar beets thriving in the ancient lava flow soils of the Snake River plain. Idaho contains various minerals and is the top extractor of silver in the country. The gold, lead, zinc, and copper produced may not match the silver output, but the quality and quantity of these resources is high and plentiful. The environmental impact of this long mining history has turned the state's attention to restoration and conservation. The action of mining requires significant disturbance of land, air, and water systems. Though historically mining companies paid little attention to their effects on the environment, today the industry attempts to find an equitable balance between extraction and conservation.

Idaho's natural diversity offers a wealth of natural exploration, observation, and learning opportunities. Natural places present challenges to preservation. Fire, for example, is an integral player in the rejuvenation process of many ecosystems across the state. Natural burns are necessary to maintain a proper balance of native species and invasive varieties. Even some indigenous plants can take over and become aggressive environmental dominators if fire is not allowed to burn. Fire suppression over the last 50 years has dramatically changed many of the natural environments throughout the state, resulting in disproportionate species, disease infestation, and insect influxes. Whitebark pine stands have been reduced by more than 50 percent—and in some areas as much as 90 percent—due to the repression of natural burns and insect infestations. If the climate continues to change, becoming progressively warmer and drier, more of this vital habitat will disappear, leaving animals such as the grizzly bear with less and less valuable habitat. Human incursions such as mining are not the only threat to natural health and stability in Idaho. Efforts strive on many fronts to curb environmental degradation and establish a baseline of ecosystem stability that can direct future restoration and conservation efforts to preserve Idaho's natural treasures.

BITTERROOT NATIONAL FOREST

The Bitterroot National Forest encompasses 1.6 million acres in east-central Idaho and southwest Montana and contains parts of the Selway-Bitterroot, Frank Church–River of No Return, and Anaconda Pintier wildernesses. In all, some 743,000 acres are designated wilderness. From the 3,200-feet elevation of the Bitterroot River Valley, the Bitterroot National Forest rises to 10,157 feet on top of Trapper Peak. Lowest elevations are on the Selway and the Salmon rivers, bottoming at 2,200 feet.

In the valley, precipitation is low, giving way to an arid landscape of grass and shrubland and ponderosa pine and cottonwood forests. Both wildlife and livestock use grasslands. Higher elevations contain Douglas fir, lodgepole pine, and western larch, leading up to Engelmann spruce, subalpine fir and larch, and whitebark pine. Forests are managed to yield timber, including saw timber, post, poles, and firewood.

The Bitterroot National Forest provides habitat for mule and white-tailed deer, elk, bighorn sheep, mountain goat, black bear, mountain lion, and moose. When Lewis and Clark traveled through the region in 1805, they wrote of a healthy population of grizzly bears, which are now a threatened species in the contiguous United States. In 1953, not a single grizzly was seen in the Bitterroot region. There are plans to reintroduce grizzlies to 5,600 square miles known as the Bitterroot Recovery Zone. Because the Bitterroot National Forest is part of a 10,000-square-mile Bitterroot ecosystem, it has been identified as ideal grizzly habitat. This reintroduction was approved in 2000 but never funded.

Human history in the area dates to over 8,000 years ago. This land was the ancestral home of the Bitterroot Salish and frequently used by the Nez Perce. The forest contains a portion of the Nez Perce National Historic Trail (Nee-Me-Poo) that traces the flight of the tribe from their Idaho homeland into north-central Montana. Gold was found in the Bitterroot Valley in the 1860s, bringing white prospectors and settlers. Lumbermen followed in the 1880s. In 1897, the Bitterroot Forest Reserve was created to protect the forests from further unorganized harvesting. In 1907, it was one of the original areas put under the management of the U.S. Forest Service.

There are 1,600 miles of hiking trails, along with fishing, hunting, rafting, kayaking, boating, and horseback riding. Downhill and cross-country skiing and snowboarding, as well as snowmobiling are permitted in the forest.

Further Reading

Baird, L., and Dennis Baird. *In Nez Perce Country: Accounts of the Bitterroots and the Clearwater after Lewis and Clark.* Moscow: University of Idaho Press, 2003.

Oko, Dan. "The Debate That Roared: A Plan To Reintroduce the Grizzly in Idaho Causes Considerable Growling." *Outside,* March 1998 http://outside.away.com/magazine/0398/9803dispwildlife.html.

CARIBOU-TARGHEE NATIONAL FOREST

The Caribou-Targhee National Forest is in southeastern Idaho, between the borders of Montana, Utah, and Idaho. The three-million-acre forest is part of the Greater Yellowstone Ecosystem and contains two wilderness areas: Jedediah Smith Wilderness (123,451 acres) and Winegar Hole Wilderness (10,721 acres). The latter preserves essential grizzly bear habitat adjacent to Yellowstone National Park. Two areas, Italian Peaks and Lionhead, are recommended for wilderness designation. Mountain ranges here include the Lemhi Mountains, Medicine Lodge/Beaverhead Mountains, Centennial Mountains, and the Red Conglomerate Range, as well as the western slope of the Teton Range.

The Henrys Fork, the Snake, and the Bear rivers flow through Caribou-Targhee National Forest, which contains two undisturbed waterfalls. The Upper and Lower Mesa Falls are among the few natural falls in the Columbia River system.

Grizzly and black bear, coyote, elk, deer, wolverine, moose, mountain goats, pika, and spotted frogs are among the forest's 85 mammal species and 17 amphibian and reptile species. Three hundred species of birds have been sighted in the forest, including wintering trumpeter swans and nesting sandhill cranes. Ferruginous hawk, osprey, and golden and bald eagles are regular avian species. Caribou-Targhee contains three endangered or threatened species: grizzly bear, Rocky Mountain wolf, and peregrine falcon. The U.S. Forest Service manages habitat for these rare species; the wildlife itself is managed by the Idaho and Wyoming Department of Fish and Game.

Of all the land in the Greater Yellowstone Ecosystem, Caribou-Targhee National Forest has been the most heavily logged. Each year, 10 million board feet of timber are harvested. Clear-cut areas remain, as do logging roads. Environmental effects include continued sediment flow into streams and recreational use of roads. Phosphate mining has leaked selenium into soils, streams, and plants.

Caribou-Targhee National Forest was recently made into one unit. Land here was initially preserved to manage the watershed, as Pocatello Forest Reserve in 1903. The forest manages 140 grazing allotments; recreational boating at Palisades Reservoir; and two ski areas, Grand Targhee and Kelly Canyon.

Further Reading
Craighead, Frank C., Jr. *For Everything There Is a Season: The Sequence of Natural Events in the Grand Teton-Yellowstone Area.* New York: Falcon, 2001.

CITY OF ROCKS NATIONAL RESERVE

Along the rolling sagebrush grassland rises a striking formation of granite known as the City of Rocks. Pinnacles and monoliths protrude more than 600 feet high. These features are two and a half billion years old. Named formations include the Twin Sisters, which are 100 years apart in age. This rock formation was a major landmark for those traveling the overland trail to California, from 1843 onward. More than 50,000 goldfield-bound people passed through here in 1852. Wagon ruts are still visible, as are initials and names written in axle grease on Register and Camp Rocks. There are six miles of historic trails maintained by the reserve.

City of Rocks National Reserve sits on the northern edge of the Great Basin, in southern Idaho's Albion Mountains. Although the reserve is only 14,320 acres, it contains diverse habitats characteristic of the Great Basin desert region: piñon-juniper-mahogany forests, aspen-riparian, sagebrush flats, and high-elevation spruce-fir-pine forests. Here, Idaho's tallest piñons tower 55 feet tall. The forests are also Idaho's largest piñon groupings. In all, about 450 plant species thrive here, including at least 100 different wildflowers and 45 common woody plants.

This is a high desert ecosystem, providing habitat for bobcat, coyote, elk, mule deer, desert bighorn sheep, mountain cottontail, black- and white-tailed jackrabbit, yellow-bellied marmot, piñon mouse, ringtail, pygmy rabbit, golden-mantled ground squirrel, and chipmunks (cliff and least). Three individual mountain lions live here, but they are quite elusive. Endangered pygmy rabbits find refuge, feeding on grasses and sagebrush leaves. They are the only rabbits that create burrowing systems on their own rather than using those made by other animals. They have lost much habitat to agricultural land. Idaho is involved in a captive-breeding program to help restore pygmy rabbit numbers through reintroduction to the wild. Historic records identify pronghorn and bison here, but they no longer inhabit the area.

Avian life includes the black-capped and mountain chickadees, lazuli bunting, western tanager, green-tailed towhee, Virginia's warbler, mountain bluebird, piñon jay, common nighthawk, cliff swallow, Clark's nutcracker, turkey vulture, sage grouse, and rock and canyon wrens. Birds of prey consist of red-tailed, Swainson's, Cooper's, sharp-shinned, and ferruginous hawks; American kestrel; northern harrier; prairie falcon; great horned owl; and golden eagle. A total of 138 species of birds have been identified at the reserve.

In 1988, land held by the Bureau of Land Management, the state of Idaho, the U.S. Forest Service, and private landowners was combined to create the City of Rocks

National Reserve. The Idaho Department of Parks and Recreation and the National Park Service manage it cooperatively. More than 500 known climbing routes ascend the rocks within the reserve.

Further Reading

Argo-Morris, Lesley. "Ecological History of the City of Rocks." http://www.nps.gov/ciro/ naturescience/naturalfeaturesandecosystems.htm.

Droz, Dwight R. *City of Rocks*. Poulsbo, WA: Scandia Patch Press, 2006.

CRATERS OF THE MOON NATIONAL MONUMENT AND PRESERVE

The volcanic rift zone of Craters of the Moon National Monument and Preserve spreads across the Snake River Plain for over 50 miles. This composite field contains 60 lava flows and 25 cones and is the largest young basaltic lava field in the lower 48 states. It is part of the Great Rift volcanic zone, a system of fractures in the earth's crust that contains basalt lava deposits up to 10,000 feet deep.

Two-thousand years ago, volcanic eruptions carved this landscape, although some activity dates to only 15,000 years ago. Cinder cones, spatter cones, lava tubes, and lava flows are all present here. Within the monument are three young lava fields, each originating from the Great Rift. The southernmost lava fields, the Wapi Lava and the Kings Bowl, were formed by single eruptive periods. Kings Bowl contains a 280-foot-long by 100-foot-wide by 100-foot-deep steam explosion pit and represents the most recent volcanic activity at the site, 2,130 years ago. The Craters of the Moon Lava Field was created during at least eight eruptive episodes.

Lava tube caves are one unusual formation. Indian Tunnel is about 800 feet long. Others include the 700-foot basaltic cinder cone, Big Cinder Butte, and the hued Blue and Green Dragon lava flows. Crystal Ice Cave, no longer accessible, combines natural and manmade passageways and displays dikes, breccia zones, and soil horizons. Another unique feature of the modern landscape are kipukas—remnants of vegetation that lava had flown around, creating islands. There are hundreds of these islands in the Craters of the Moon and Wapi Lava Fields.

When the area was designated a national monument in 1924, President Calvin Coolidge claimed it was "a weird and scenic landscape peculiar to itself." In 1970, 43,243 acres were designated Craters of the Moon National Wilderness Area, which is managed in accordance with the Wilderness Act. This area maintains stricter regulations, including the prohibition of vehicles, logging, and mining. Camping is permitted. In 2002, Congress designated 640 square miles as Craters of the Moon National Preserve, most of which was previously identified as four distinct wilderness study areas by the Bureau of Land Management.

Further Reading

Wright, R. Gerald, and Stephen C. Bunting. *The Landscapes of Craters of the Moon National Monument: An Evaluation of Environmental Changes*. Moscow: University of Idaho Press, 1994.

CURLEW NATIONAL GRASSLAND

Curlew is the only national grassland in the Great Basin Ecosystem. Its 47,000 acres are in a semiarid valley near the Utah border which was inhabited by Bannock and Shoshone until Mormon pioneers settled the region. By the end of the 19th century, the entire Curlew Valley was checkered with homesteads. Remnants of old homesteads remain on the landscape, along with remains of a campsite on the National Register of Historic Places from the Hudspeth's Cutoff of the overland trail used by California gold rushers in 1849.

Drought and erosion brought an end to these farms and ranches, and the federal government took over management of the land in the 1930s. They reseeded the land with crested wheatgrass, Ladak alfalfa, and bulbous bluegrass. Today, only 12,000 acres of native range remain, containing indigenous species of grasses, sagebrush, bitterbrush, serviceberry, and forbs. The U.S. Forest Service manages Curlew National Grassland for wildlife, water, and recreation. Sagebrush is allowed to develop naturally. Prescribed burns and reseeding projects continue. Curlew National Grassland is challenged with invasive plant species including leafy spurge, knapweed, and dyer's woad.

Sage and sharp-tailed grouse breed on Curlew's leks in March and April. Grouse were rare in the region until the 1970s, when grassland staff planted windbreaks of trees and shrubs to block wind and prevent erosion. These breaks also created shelter for these birds to nest and mate. Grouse are well known for their elaborate courtship dances. Sharp-tailed grouse are so abundant that several have been caught to start reintroduction programs elsewhere. Pheasants and partridges also returned to the reviving landscape. The artificial Sweeten Pond led to visits by migrating Canada geese, 400 ducks, and hundreds of shorebirds. The pond is now managed for waterfowl and shorebird habitat. Curlew National Grassland also provides food and shelter for curlew, ruffed grouse, blue grouse, gray (Hungarian) partridge, golden and bald eagles, and several hawks, including marsh hawks. Mammal species include deer, elk, bobcats, mountain lions, and coyotes.

Fishing, hunting, camping, wildlife observation, and photography are the primary recreational activities at Curlew National Grassland.

Further Reading

Moul, Francis. *The National Grasslands: A Guide to America's Undiscovered Treasures*. Lincoln: University of Nebraska Press, 2006.

HAGERMAN FOSSIL BEDS NATIONAL MONUMENT

The fossils located at Hagerman Fossil Beds National Monument represent the world's richest concentration of late Pliocene fossil deposits. Three to four million years ago, just before the Ice Age, modern life began to form. Hagerman Fossil Beds National Monument contains about 200 species, including the Hagerman horse (*Equus simplicidens*). Thirty complete horse fossils have been found, as well as fossil evidence of over 200 other individual horses. Scientists believe this species is a link between the modern and the prehistoric; it is the first horse they have classified under the modern genus, *equus*. The Hagerman Horse Quarry is a national natural landmark and one of the six most important horse fossil sites in the world.

The first excavation began in 1929, led by J. W. Gidley and funded by the Smithsonian Institution. Other fossils of note include the pond turtle (*Clemmys owyheensis*); pocket gopher (*Thomomys gidleyi*); and a weasel relative, the grison (*Trigonictis idahoensis*). These fossil beds contain a wealth of information for paleontologists. Not only are they one of the largest deposits of late Pliocene fossils, they possess a high quality and diversity of specimens. The fossils here were formed in the sand, silt, and clay of the river system that flowed into the ancient Lake Idaho. The stratigraphy is undisturbed, representing three to four million years of life on earth in wetland, riparian, and savanna environments. Camel and mastodon were former residents of this landscape, as were rails, ducks, Hibbard's swan, songbirds, cormorants, pronghorn, moles, shrews, mollusks, and various fish species.

Today, the region is home to ring-necked pheasants, gray partridge, California quail, horned larks, vesper sparrows, northern orioles, marsh wrens, rufous-sided towhees, and warblers. Migrating waterfowl stop along the Snake River and natural springs, which remain warm throughout the winter and provide unfrozen winter water sources. As many as 55,000 ducks and 4,000 Canada geese are known to stop during the winter, as well as tundra and trumpeter swans, northern pintails, American wigeon, cinnamon and green-winged teals, lesser scaup, and ring-necked ducks. Other migrators are black-crowned night herons, great blue herons, Virginia rails, American avocets, and spotted sandpipers. Raptors include ospreys; rough-legged hawks; and two threatened species, bald eagles and peregrine falcons. Waterfowl such as mallards, gadwalls, redheads, ruddy ducks, and Canada geese, as well as short-eared and western screech owls use nesting area here.

The Snake River provides habitat to rainbow trout, smallmouth bass, chub, suckers, nonnative carp, and a small population of sturgeon. Much of the Snake River is designated critical habitat for Snake River sockeye salmon, an endangered species, and the threatened Chinook salmon, neither of which still inhabit the national monument because of the construction of dams. The river is also designated an evolutionary significant unit for West Coast steelhead. It is a tributary of the Columbia River and part of the Columbia River Basin, which is important habitat for bull trout. Five species of endangered or threatened freshwater snails reside in Hagerman's waterways—Snake

Hagerman Horse Fossil Beds. (Kris Calhoun)

River physa, lanx, bliss rapids, Utah valvata, and Idaho springsnail. These mollusks have declined as the river's flow has been obstructed, warming the water. Nonnative snails also threaten the habitat of native species.

Mule deer, red foxes, coyotes, badgers, cottontail rabbits, black-tailed jackrabbits, pygmy rabbits, ground squirrels, wood rats, kangaroo rats, spotted and striped skunks, weasels, bobcats, and yellow-bellied marmots live in Hagerman's uplands, while watery areas are home to river otters, beavers, muskrats, and minks. Striped whip snakes, western rattlesnakes, and gopher snakes are common, as are several lizards—the short-horned, western whiptail, and sagebrush.

The current landscape of Hagerman Fossil Beds National Monument is primarily sagebrush steppe. Sagebrush shrubs dominate with areas of grass and forbs. Before designation as a monument, this land was used for livestock grazing, which affected soil quality and allowed for the invasion of nonnative species. Grazing, water control, and other development have disturbed the landscape. Russian olive, Russian thistle, quack-grass, cheatgrass (most common), blue mustard, tansy mustard, tumble mustard, and medusa head crowd out native wheatgrass, bluegrass, Indian ricegrass, and Great Basin wild rye. Native riparian species such as cottonwood, bulrush, cattails, and willows compete with newcomers like Russian olive, purple loosestrife, and salt cedar. In need of special protection for Idaho's plant diversity are giant helleborine, cowpie buckwheat, and Owyhee mourning milk vetch. The most important botanical aspect of the monument, however, are microbiotic plants that form a soil crust incompatible with grazing lands.

Hagerman Fossil Beds National Monument contains wheel ruts from pioneer wagons that crossed the region during the 19th century and are part of the Oregon National Historic Trail.

Further Reading

Hagerman Fossil Council, Inc. *Equus Evolves: The Story of the Hagerman Horse*. Boise, ID: Black Canyon Communications, 2005.

FRANK CHURCH–RIVER OF NO RETURN WILDERNESS

The 2,366,757-acre Frank Church–River of No Return Wilderness, partly contained within the Salmon-Challis National Forest, is the largest contiguous wilderness area in the lower 48 states. Together with the neighboring Gospel Hump Wilderness and U.S. Forest Service lands, 3.3 million acres are roadless.

Mountain ranges include the Salmon River, Clearwater, and Bighorn. Mountain lakes dot the Bighorn Crags above 8,000 feet. Elevation ranges from 3,000 feet in the canyons, to peaks 7,000 to 10,000 feet high. The landscape here was sculpted more than 100 million years ago by a massive granite conglomerate known as the Idaho Batholith. The Salmon River Mountains are the dominant range in the wilderness area and are unusual in their seemingly random arrangement. While most western mountains rise in lines with a dominating trend or crest, these peaks expand in all directions.

Cutting through the Frank Church–River of No Return Wilderness is the Salmon River, the second largest tributary of the Snake River, also known as the River of No Return for its extremely fast current. The headwaters of the Salmon River lie in the Sawtooth National Recreation Area. The main flow of the Salmon River and the Middle Fork are designated national wild and scenic rivers. One hundred miles of the Middle Fork flow through the Frank Church–River of No Return Wilderness. The rivers here flow fast and rough, making rafting and kayaking popular activities. The Salmon River Canyon is deeper than the Grand Canyon.

In addition to the dramatic landscape, diverse habitats mark the Salmon River Canyon. Forests, bluffs, rock formations, and crags draw attention away from canyon walls to the vistas beyond. Coniferous forests run throughout the wilderness, marked by Douglas fir and lodgepole pine as well as shrubs such as sagebrush, ninebark, and bearberry. Ponderosa pines grow at low elevations, and Engelmann spruce and subalpine fir grow on the peaks.

A total of 258 wildlife species reside here—72 mammals, 173 birds, 23 fish, 7 reptiles, and 6 amphibians. Mammals include mule and white-tailed deer, elk, bighorn sheep, mountain goat, black bear, moose, otter, marmots, golden-mantled squirrels, mountain lion, gray wolves, black bear, lynx, coyote, and red fox. The wilderness is critical habitat for wolverines. Scientists believe the forests provide good habitat for grizzly bears, but no established groups exist at this time. Waterways are populated with steelhead, cutthroat, rainbow, and Dolly Varden trout; Rocky Mountain whitefish; white sturgeon; and Chinook salmon during their spring and summer runs. Programs to manage anadromous fish are in place. Introduced species include brook and California golden trout as well as Artic grayling. Avian species consist of blue grouse, Canadian geese, black-capped chickadees, and others.

Fur trappers and missionaries visited this area early in the nation's history. Before them, Shoshone and Nez Perce Indians lived here. Miners and homesteaders made their way later in the 19th century. Part of this region has been managed by the U.S. Forest Service since 1931, when roughly one million acres were designated the Idaho Primitive Area. The wilderness is named partly for the speedy current of the Salmon River, which prevents upstream travel and gave it the nickname, the River of No Return, and for Idaho Senator Frank Church (1924–1984) who supported the Wilderness Act of 1964 and introduced the 1968 Wild and Scenic Rivers Act. The Middle Fork of the Salmon River was included in this initial bill, ensuring preservation of free-flowing waterways and surrounding habitats. In 1980, Church passed the Central Idaho Wilderness Act that created this wilderness area and added 125 miles of the Salmon River to the National Wild and Scenic River System.

Because of preexisting permissions, the Frank Church-River of No Return Wilderness allows the use of jet boats and airstrips. About the time of this land's wilderness designation, scientists estimated only 15 individual wolves lived in all of central Idaho. They were reintroduced in 1995 along the Main Salmon River at Corn Creek. Researchers believe there are now 10 packs in the region.

Further Reading

Carrey, John, and Cort Conley. *River of No Return*. Cambridge, ID: Backeddy Books, 2003.
Scheese, Don, and Wayne Franklin. *Mountains of Memory: A Fire Lookout's Life in the River of No Return Wilderness*. Iowa City: University of Iowa Press, 2001.

IDAHO PANHANDLE NATIONAL FORESTS

At the narrow northern end of Idaho, the Idaho Panhandle National Forests straddle the state, extending into Washington and Montana. Three national forests—the Coeur d'Alene, St. Joe, and Kaniksu—were administratively consolidated in 1973 to form this 2.5-million-acre area. Mountains, lakes, rivers, and cedar groves provide habitat for wildlife and recreation for people. Fishing is popular, as are winter activities like skiing and snowmobiling.

The national forests sit on the eastern portion of the Columbia Plateau, straddling two mountain ranges—the Cascade Mountains to the west and the Bitterroot Mountains to the east. Three hundred wildlife species share habitat in this diverse environment. The forest is managed to focus on 15 of these species, 3 of which are protected under the Endangered Species Act—woodland caribou, Canada lynx, and grizzly bear. Although recently removed from the Endangered Species List, gray wolves are also a priority. Other sensitive species are the boreal toad, Coeur d'Alene salamander, common loon, harlequin duck, peregrine falcon, flammulated owl, black-backed woodpecker, Townsend's big-eared bat, northern bog lemming, fisher, and wolverine. Birds range from large raptors like bald eagles to the diminutive calliope hummingbird.

Idaho Panhandle National Forests have a history of mining and logging, which played key roles in the region's settlement. Most timbering activities today are managed to achieve fuel reduction goals to help protect communities form the threat of unwanted wildfire; to restore wildlife and fish habitat; and to provide timber to local mills including biomass for energy production. In 1910, the Idaho Panhandle National Forests experienced a devastating wildfire. This led to fire fighting policies that are still in effect today. About the same time, white pine blister rust arrived from Europe in seedlings that spread through the mountains and devastated the western white pine, and threatens whitebark pine. The U.S. Forest Service's Coeur d'Alene Nursery has been a leader in developing rust-resistant stock so that these native species may be reforested. As a result of fires and disease, these national forests suffer dense, unhealthy conditions spread over much of the range.

The fate of the species is tied to the ecological health of the region, which would be less productive without it and more susceptible to fire, insects, and pathogens. Western white pine was one of the richest carbon producers in the Interior Northwest. Without this species, this area is now one of the poorest carbon compartments in the northern Rocky Mountains. While western white pine is considered to be at lower risk of

Idaho Panhandle National Forest. (CraigZone)

extinction based on the International Union for Conservation of Nature and Natural Resources Red List classification, scientists insist that action must be taken to ensure its future existence. Some western white pines have varied genetically to resist the pathogen. The U.S. Forest Service identifies these trees to reseed.

Further Reading

Harvey, Alan E., James W. Byler, Geral I. McDonald, Leon F. Neuenschwander, and Jonalea R. Tonn. *Death of an Ecosystem: Perspectives on Western White Pine Ecosystems of North America at the End of the Twentieth Century.* General Technical Report RMRS-GTR-208. Fort Collins, CO: U.S. Forest Service, Rocky Mountain Research Station, 2008.

Miller, Char, ed. *American Forests: Nature, Culture, and Politics.* Lawrence: University Press of Kansas, 1997.

LOST RIVER RANGE

Located in central Idaho, the Lost River Range runs for approximately 75 miles from the Salmon River to the Snake River Valley. At the Salmon River, the range rises to an approximate elevation of 5,000 feet. There are peaks in the range, though, that top 12,000 feet. In fact, seven of the state's nine peaks that reach over 12,000 feet are in the Lost River Range. Over the last 11 million years, tectonic forces have shaped the land into the range seen today. Two significant glacial periods left their mark, as well. Volcanic forces have made the most impact and have had the most immediate influence on the mountains' shapes. The process of formation began with the stretching of the crust, causing large faults or cracks to form. What would become the mountains then pushed up from underneath as a result of the pressure beneath the crust. While much of this activity took place over millions of years, there are still geological forces that affect the range. In 1983, the Mount Borah Earthquake hit the region with a magnitude of 7.3. As a result, Borah Peak gained seven feet. The fracture was 26 miles long and 7 miles deep. It caused the Lost River Valley to slide away from Mount Borah. This fracture can be accessed by car, giving a unique opportunity to observe the massive forces that shape the landscape.

Many climbers visiting the Lost River Range seek out Idaho's highest peak, Mount Borah. The most popular route, just over three and a half miles, ascends 5,262 vertical feet, following the southwest ridge of the mountain. Most of this route is considered a strenuous hike, but the last section before the summit crest is a ridge with steep slopes on both sides, called Chickenout Ridge. Snow and ice increase the danger. The visual intimidation factor of the narrow ridge passing sends some less-experienced, less-confident climbers home just short of Mount Borah's summit. The north face of the mountain offers one of Idaho's only year-round snow climbing experiences and is ranked a much tougher climb than the southwest ridge. Regardless of the route chosen, as the highest mountain in Idaho, Mount Borah offers a challenging and unique way to experience the state's natural places.

Further Reading

Lopez, Tom. *Idaho: A Climbing Guide: Climbs, Scrambles, and Hikes*. Seattle, WA: Mountaineers Books, 2000.

Robertson, R. G. *Idaho Echoes in Time: Traveling Idaho's History and Geology: Stories, Directions, Maps, and More*. Boise, ID: Tamarack Books, 1998.

SALMON-CHALLIS NATIONAL FOREST

The 4.3-million-acre Salmon-Challis National Forest contains Idaho's highest elevation (Borah Peak), the Wild and Scenic Salmon River, and the Middle Fork of the Salmon River. It also contains a portion of the Frank Church–River of No Return Wilderness. The highest point on the massive Mount Borah is 12,662 feet above sea level. Here, in the 75-mile-long Lost River Range, lie 9 of Idaho's 11 peaks over 12,000 feet: Borah Peak, Leatherman Peak, Mount Church, Mount Breitenbach, Lost River Mountain, Mount Idaho, Donaldson Peak, and two unnamed peaks.

The Lost River Range is a dramatically formed vista of towering cliffs, spires, peaks, and rock folds. The landscape's mountains and hot springs stand as evidence of a long history of extreme tectonic activity. This area of central Idaho is vulnerable to earthquakes, averaging one major tremor every 20 years. In 1983, a quake hit the base of Borah Peak, topping 7.0 on the Richter scale; it was Idaho's largest recorded quake. Twenty-one miles of scarring and faults can now be seen on the southwest slope of the Lost River Range, including the base of Mount Borah.

This national forest unit is made of two formerly separate forests, the 2.5-million-acre Challis National Forest and the 1.8-million-acre Salmon National Forest. The latter's landscape is the remotest and most undeveloped forest in Idaho, lying 150 miles from the nearest urban centers of Idaho Falls and Missoula, Montana. Much of the former Salmon National Forest is alpine environment with spawning stream habitats for steelhead and anadromous salmon.

Mule deer, antelope, moose, bear, elk, bighorn sheep, mountain goats, pronghorn, and cougar share habitat here. Forest Service staff maintain 1,200 miles of trails, including portions of the Continental Divide National Scenic Trail, Lewis and Clark National Historic Trail, Nez Perce National Historic Trail, Divide–Twin Creek National Recreation Trail, and Bear Valley National Recreation Trail. Undermanagement of grazing contracts is damaging available grazing land, while overgrazing by livestock erodes streams and meadows.

Recreation in Salmon-Challis National Forest includes hunting, fishing, and whitewater rafting. There is also an 18-run ski area, the Lost Trail Ski Area. In October 2008, an plan to allow mining for cobalt, copper, and gold on Salmon-Challis National Forest land was reversed pending further information on the operation's plan and its effect on the environment. In 2005, a plan for an all-terrain vehicle trail was canceled, but off-road trails are controversial in the Lost River District, where over 30 miles are currently in use. Countering these issues is the Borah Peak Roadless Area, which covers 150,000 acres.

The U.S. Forest Service has recommended 120,000 acres of the Salmon-Challis National Forest for wilderness designation.

Further Reading
Stahl, Greg. "20 Years since Borah Earthquake." *Idaho Mountain Express*, October 22–28, 2003. http://www.mtexpress.com/2003/03-10-22/03-10-22borah.htm.

SALMON NATIONAL SCENIC RIVER

The Salmon River cuts its way through Idaho for a total length of over 400 miles. It drains 14,000 square miles and drops more than 7,000 feet. The Salmon headwaters flow from Sawtooth National Recreation Area in central Idaho to its convergence with the Snake River in the southern part of the state. The first European presence on the river was the effort made by Lewis and Clark to travel its length after they crossed the Continental Divide in August 1805. Clark named it Lewis's River, after Lewis, because he was the "first white man ever on this for the Columbia," according to Clark's journal. The name only stuck for a few years though, and, by 1810, maps were calling it the Salmon River instead. In the 1860s, the river gained new significance when gold was found along its banks. It was this gold rush that heralded the beginning of conflicts between European American arrivals and the Nez Perce over the tribe's ancestral lands. Eventually, the miners and settlers won, but the Nez Perce still hold lands in Idaho today, some of which the Salmon River runs through on the way to its mouth at the Snake River. Today, the Salmon River is a popular recreation destination. It offers some of the most beautiful scenery and exciting floats in Idaho. The Middle Fork and a section of the main river flow are designated national wild and scenic rivers. From ancient native residents to today's adventure seekers, the river has always had something to offer.

Another outstanding recreation opportunity on the Salmon River is fishing. Sections of the Middle Fork are known as some of the best catch-and-release fly-fishing waters in the country. Historically, the river hosted 40 percent of all of the steelhead salmon and 45 percent of all of the Chinook salmon in the entire Columbia River Basin. Because of human development and intervention in other basin rivers, the Salmon River now contains more than 70 percent of the entire salmon and steelhead habitat in the area. There are still large numbers of these species in the river, but, due to the presence of federal reservoirs and dams, those numbers are declining. Several of Idaho's native fish species have been listed, or are serious candidates for, protection as endangered species. Recreational fishing plays a role in population reduction, but the larger impact tends to come from habitat fragmentation or destruction. The Idaho Department of Fish and Game can help restore some of the numbers, but it only has authority to restrict harvesting and control stocking. Often these efforts are not enough to fully restore endangered populations because they do nothing to affect changes to habitat. By carefully restricting harvesting activity and intelligently planning stocking patterns, however, population numbers can be stabilized and maintained. It ultimately depends on the individual spe-cies as well as the total environmental impact whether the Idaho Department of Fish and Game activity is enough to significantly benefit endangered populations.

Almost all of the ocean-going salmon and steelhead that are natural, native spe-cies of Idaho are listed as threatened or endangered under the 1973 federal Endangered Species Act. The listing of these natural species aims to protect them from fishing, ha-rassment, and harvesting in an effort to preserve their shrinking populations. So many factors affect migrating fish populations, though, that it is difficult to completely control everything that can affect the individual count. Conditions in the freshwater environ-ments and the ocean waters affect the numbers of salmon and steelhead that return each year. The presence of dams and reservoirs is a primary factor in causing the decline of these species, because they change migration conditions. Smolts, the young salmon and steelhead fish trying to reach the ocean, are often prevented from completing their jour-ney by these constructions. Other issues are important, as well. In addition to harvesting and habitat degradation, negative interactions with hatchery fish, avian smolt predators, and adult predators that prey on adult salmon all affect the final counts. What can be controlled is an effort to effectively protect nonhatchery fish communities. While full recovery may not be possible with the conservation and restoration methods currently in place, it is possible to curb the population decline in the hopes of preserving these species for many years to come.

Further Reading

Lichatowich, James A. *Salmon without Rivers: A History of the Pacific Salmon Crisis*. Wash-ington, DC: Island Press, 2001.

Neil, J. M. *To the White Clouds: Idaho's Conservation Saga, 1900–1970*. Pullman: Wash-ington State University Press, 2005.

SAWTOOTH RANGE AND WILDERNESS

The Sawtooth Range of the Rocky Mountains runs through the Sawtooth Wilderness and the Sawtooth National Recreation Area in central Idaho. The recreation area encompasses almost 800,000 acres and offers hiking, fishing, hunting, mountain biking, kayaking, camping, and rock climbing. The Sawtooth Range is probably the best known in the entire state. Many compare the mountains to the Grand Tetons, partially because of their jagged appearance and partially because of the large lakes at their base. The area has enjoyed federal protection for its mountains, lakes, and surrounding environment for over a century. The geological history of the mountain range involves a process of glacial uplift and carving. The Sawtooths are one of the best exposed examples of thrust faulting in the larger fold-and-thrust belt that spans the western United States. Because of the significant impact of these glacial activities, the Sawtooth Range has often been the focus of scientific studies to better understand the history of glacial movement and its effects on the shape of the landscape.

The Sawtooth Mountains not only provide evidence of ancient natural history, but reveal evidence of human history. Almost 10,000 years ago, prehistoric hunters visited the region, making camp and hunting around what is today called Redfish Lake. Native American people continued to use the region's waters for fishing and the basalt quarries for tool materials. By the early 1800s, Western powers fought for control of the Pacific Northwest, and the Sawtooth region was part of this struggle. The first trapper-explorers found their way into what is today the Sawtooth National Recreation Area in 1824. By 1840, they had depleted the beaver population and began to leave. In 1849, the territorial argument between the United States and Britain ended, and, for a while, there was no reason for anyone to move into the area.

All of that changed in 1860, though, with the discovery of gold. Within 20 years miners extracted a half million dollars in this precious metal. The mining industry brought new residents from overseas. Mine construction was accomplished largely due to the utilization of Chinese immigrant labor. Conflicts periodically arose between the local tribes and the mining residents, creating a difficult environment for everyone involved. This was complicated by the discovery of silver in 1878, which brought in new speculators, adding to the area's diversity and instability. None of these economic booms made it through the end of the 1800s, however, and now the evidence of these towns has been largely reclaimed by natural forces. Though some homesteaders came to the area, sheepherding took center stage as the region's main economic endeavor. The establishment of the Sawtooth National Forest in 1905, however, called for reducing herd size and range. Today, because of the long history of careful management and environmental conservation, the range, wilderness, and national recreation area offer relatively unspoiled environments for the enjoyment of wildlife and human visitors alike.

Further Reading

Prato, Tony, and Dan Fagre. *Sustaining Rocky Mountain Landscapes: Science, Policy, and Management for the Crown of the Continent Ecosystem*. Washington, DC: Resources for the Future Press, 2007.

SNAKE RIVER BIRDS OF PREY NATIONAL CONSERVATION AREA

One of the top bird-watching spots in North America, the Snake River Birds of Prey National Conservation Area provides nesting sites for eagles, hawks, vultures, owls, and prairie falcons (America's only indigenous falcon). Nearly 800 pairs nest here, making this the continent's densest concentration of nesting raptors, who find protection in the canyon's dramatic 600-foot rise. There are 24 raptor species that use the area—16 nesting and 8 migrating. Nesting raptors include American kestrels; golden eagles; northern harriers; turkey vultures; ospreys; prairie falcons; ferruginous, red-tailed, and Swainson's hawks; and barn, burrowing, great horned, long-eared, northern saw-whet, short-eared, and western screech owls. Migrating raptors are bald eagles, gyrfalcons, merlins, northern goshawks, peregrine falcons, and Cooper's rough-legged and sharp-shinned hawks.

Just 35 miles from Boise, the Snake River Birds of Prey National Conservation Area protects 81 miles of the Snake River and a total of 484,873 acres of land. It is operated in cooperation with an additional 120,000 acres of private, state, military, and surface water lands. Sagebrush mesas are home to ground squirrels and jackrabbits, which are food for predatory raptors. The environment here supports an abundance of burrowing mammals, ensuring food for predatory raptors. Paiute ground squirrel populations are the densest concentrations of squirrels ever recorded. The same is true of the national conservation area's badger population, which averages 11 per square mile. Pocket gophers, kangaroo rats, and deer mice are common. Overall, 259 wildlife species—including 45 mammals, 165 birds, 8 amphibians, 16 reptiles, and 25 fish species—use this landscape for food and shelter.

The Bonneville Flood created the dramatic geology of the Snake River canyons. At the end of the last Ice Age, receding glaciers flooded the ancient lake on this part of the continent known as Lake Bonneville. The flood poured through the soft soil of the Snake River, trapping boulders and creating box canyons. Some of these boulders are carved with petroglyphs dating to human occupation 12,000 years ago. The Snake River Birds of Prey National Conservation Area contains historic sites from 19th-century gold mining and overland travel. It contains well-preserved portions of the Oregon National Historic Trail and three sites on the National Register of Historic Places, including the Black Butte–Guffey Butte Archaeological District and the Swan Falls Dam—the first hydroelectric dam on the Snake River, dating to 1901.

The Snake River Birds of Prey National Conservation Area was created in 1993, when research indicated a need to protect raptors and their prey. It is managed by the Bureau of Land Management, which allows for diverse uses, including ranching, power generation, and Army National Guard training. Recreation includes fishing, camping, boating, hiking, hunting, all-terrain vehicle riding, and wildlife watching. Mammal populations have been disturbed due to fires and military training. In turn, a recent study of prairie falcon nesting sites found a 50 percent decline in numbers, from 230 historical to 110 current pairs.

Further Reading

Baker, John. *The Peregrine*. Moscow: University of Idaho Press, 1996.

Gensbol, Benny, and Walther Thiede. *Collins Birds of Prey*. New York: HarperCollins, 2008.

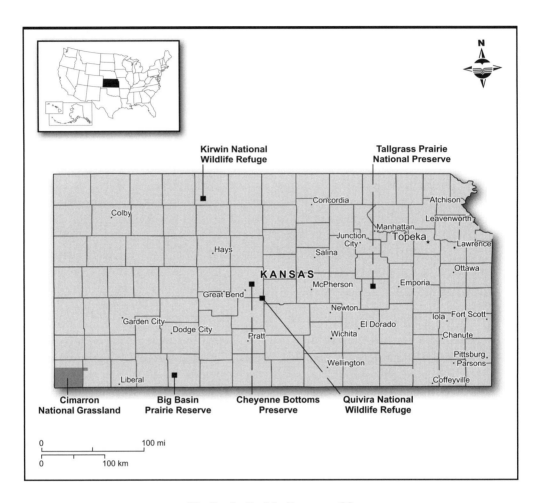

Kirwin National Wildlife Refuge

Tallgrass Prairie National Preserve

Concordia
Atchison
Leavenworth
Colby
Manhattan
Junction City
Topeka
Lawrence
Hays
Salina
KANSAS
Ottawa
McPherson
Emporia
Great Bend
Newton
Iola
Fort Scott
Garden City
El Dorado
Dodge City
Wichita
Chanute
Pratt
Pittsburg
Parsons
Wellington
Liberal
Coffeyville

Cimarron National Grassland

Big Basin Prairie Reserve

Cheyenne Bottoms Preserve

Quivira National Wildlife Refuge

0   100 mi

0   100 km

KANSAS

Kansas is a land of rolling prairie dotted with rich wetlands. What looks like a monotonous landscape is filled with botanical diversity. Tall, short-grass, and sand-sage prairies contain a diversity second only to the Brazilian rainforest. There are over 1,700 species of native flowering plants and ferns, and 250 species of grasses. Only four percent of native prairie remains in the U.S. Ninety-five percent is in Kansas. The state also contains over 60,000 acres of wetlands. These are important habitat for migrating shorebirds, sandhill and whooping cranes, and a number of raptors. The Arkansas River nourishes forested floodplains and fertile soil as it braids its way east-southeast through the state.

Westward expansion brought European settlement to Kansas in the early 1800s. Settlement, ranching, and railroad construction changed the face of the land. The fertile prairie soils of Kansas encouraged settlement in the nineteenth century. Farmers pulled up prairie grasses and replaced them with wheat, corn, and soy beans. Prairie grasses are adapted to suit their environment, to survive periodic drought and natural fires. Their roots reach deep into the soil, holding it in place. In the 1930s, drought, heat, wind, and loose soil created a series of dust storms, known collectively as the Dust Bowl. It took years for the land to recover, but the ordeals of the Dust Bowl encouraged more sustainable farming practices.

Natural places in Kansas provide scenery and habitat. Native prairie remains in the Flint Hills, which were not extensively farmed due to their rocky soil. Scientists struggle to restore disrupted prairies, increase diversity, and control invasive species. At least 400 nonnative plants grow amid the natives, including the opportunistic purple loosestrife, which crowds out native grasses. Kansas's wetlands ensure the survival of birds that cross the continent. The nature of Kansas is vital to these avian species and is an icon of a wilder America.

BIG BASIN PRAIRIE RESERVE

The Big Basin Prairie Reserve native grassland covers 1,818 acres in the Red Hills of Kansas. Keiger Creek flows intermittently through the landscape, which contains two nondraining basins. The hills, uplands, and canyons of Big Basin Prairie Preserve add contrast to the prairie, making this landscape unique.

The features here—Big Basin, Little Basin, and St. Jacob's Well—were created by solution-subsidence. This is a process by which surface water seeps underground and dissolves mineral deposits of salt, gypsum, and limestone. When these minerals dissolve, upper layers of soil, rock, and minerals sink, making small depressions in the ground. Big Basin is considered a sinkhole or sink. The one-mile diameter of Big Basin sinks 100 feet with nearly vertical walls. It catches water in small ephemeral ponds. Only two-thirds of the Big Basin lies within Big Basin Prairie Reserve. The remainder is privately owned, and a federal highway runs just west of the preserve boundary.

Little Basin lies entirely within the preserve and is just 280 yards in diameter with a depth of 35 feet. Here lies the permanent St. Jacob's Well—a pond 84 feet in diameter and 58 feet deep. It has been the source of tall tales. Some thought the well was bottomless; others reported blind fish living in its waters. St. Jacob's Well and Big Basin were important water sources for cattle drives from Texas.

The Nature Conservancy bought the land and sold it to the Kansas Department of Wildlife and Parks in 1974 with the agreement that it remain a nature preserve. It was designated a national natural landmark in 1978. The preserve provides habitat for a herd of about 50 bison.

Further Reading

Moul, Francis. *The National Grasslands: A Guide to America's Undiscovered Treasures.* Lincoln: University of Nebraska Press, 2006.

Picton, Harold. *Buffalo Natural History & Conservation.* St. Paul, MN: Voyageur Press, 2005.

CHEYENNE BOTTOMS PRESERVE

Cheyenne Bottoms is a resting and refueling ground for nearly half of the migrating shorebirds of North America and more than 250,000 waterfowl. The wide, shallow marshes have an average depth of one foot, creating the perfect environment to facilitate migration for many avian species. Birds fly thousands of miles during migration movement, fueled only by a few tablespoons of body fat. When those stores run low, it becomes necessary for the birds to stop, rest, refuel, and then continue. Cheyenne Bottoms hosts more bird species than any other site in the state. The mudflats offer feeding grounds to a wide variety of wading birds. Ducks and geese are present throughout the year, but during migration, their numbers climb significantly.

Between the mid-1950s and the late 1970s, about 40 percent of the wetlands in Kansas disappeared. Natural marshes, mudflats, and adjoining grasslands are all necessary to support native and transitory avian populations. Many areas of the state that used to be functioning wetlands are now beyond repair. The area that contains Cheyenne Bottoms also hosts the Quivira National Wildlife Refuge, another wetland of national and international importance. The Nature Conservancy of Kansas and the Kansas Department of Wildlife and Parks chose to work in Cheyenne Bottoms because of its proximity to another significant wetland and its capacity for healthy, sustainable restoration, as well as the key role it plays in the lives of so many bird species.

The most valuable characteristic of both Cheyenne Bottoms and its neighboring preserve, the Quivira National Wildlife Refuge, is that these wetlands are not comprised of just one type of ecosystem. Like a jigsaw puzzle, they are a collage of habitats ranging in size from large to small, in depth from shallow to deep, and in vegetation from weedy to open. As the largest interior marsh in the country, these wetlands are a vital part of the continent's habitat system. Without it, many species would decline and eventually disappear. On three sides of the bottoms are low bluffs that trap the waters coming out of the Blood and the Deception creeks. To maintain the site's ecological health, the Kansas Department of Wildlife and Parks uses pumps, water diversions, and pikes to control water levels and flow. These protective measures were born of efforts in the 1990s to convert the lands for agricultural use. Today, although the area is known primarily for its native and migrant bird populations, a variety of other animal species call this 60-square-mile patch home. Raccoons, beaver, deer, mink, turtles, and snakes all live among the rushes, finding food and shelter in this protected site. Endangered species depend on the bottoms as well. The whooping crane, peregrine falcon, piping plover, and bald eagle have all been recorded in the area. The protected acreage provided to these and other dependent species is just under 20,000 acres of a 40,000-acre natural land sink. Between the Kansas Department of Wildlife and Parks' efforts in the lower areas and the Nature Conservancy's actions in the upper wetlands, the larger wetland complex is reaping the benefits of coordinated conservation action and promises to be both a migratory and long-term haven for wetland-dependent species.

Further Reading

Leslie, Scott. *Wetland Birds of North America: A Guide to Observation, Understanding, and Conservation.* Toronto, Canada: Key Porter Books, 2007.

Tiner, Ralph W. *Wetland Indicators: A Guide to Wetland Identification, Delineation, Classification, and Mapping.* Grand Rapids, MI: CRC Publications, 1999.

CIMARRON NATIONAL GRASSLAND

In the southwest corner of Kansas, lies the Cimarron National Grassland, the largest expanse of open public land in the state. It contains 108,175 acres of short-grass prairie and sand-sage prairie, which, along with wooded riparian areas, makes this site ecologically diverse. Its location at the junction of eastern and western grasslands allows a variety of species to mingle.

Wildlife includes pronghorn, mule and white-tailed deer, bobwhite and scaled quail, wild turkey, lesser prairie chicken, and dove. The area contains 345 bird species and 31 amphibian and reptile species, including Woodhouse's toads, bullfrogs, northern earless lizards, ornate box turtles, central plains milk snakes, and prairie rattlesnakes. Birding is popular. In fact, Cimarron National Grassland is on the American Birding Association's list of the top 100 locations for observing avian species. It is a famous location to observe lesser prairie chickens that frequent the sand-sage prairie just south of the Cimarron River. The mixed grasses, sagebrush, and yucca fulfill these birds' nutritional and nesting needs. In spring, the lesser prairie chicken performs its courtship display on leks—hilltops or exposed rises. Males establish territory, raise their feathers, dance in small rapid steps, and gobble and cackle.

Before Cimarron was a national grassland, it was farmland. During the 1930s, vast stretches of the Great Plains were blown away in the dust storms of the 1930s. In 1938, the federal government purchased land to prevent farmers from further damaging the soil. The U.S. Soil Conservation Service began experiments to prevent erosion. In 1954, the land was given to the U.S. Forest Service to manage. Cimarron was designated a protected national grassland in 1960. This is not virgin prairie but experimental land the Forest Service uses to learn about erosion control.

Lands are both federal and private. The Cimarron National Grassland's concerns today include wildlife, water conservation, livestock grazing, recreation, and mineral production. It is managed in conjunction with Comanche National Grassland and the Pike & San Isabel National Forests. Livestock grazing is strategically used to maintain the condition of the vegetation. There are 30 allotments, which, depending on the year's precipitation, hold an average of 5,000 head of cattle during the season, from May through November.

Cimarron National Grassland also contains the largest portion of the Santa Fe Trail open to the public—23 miles. Two key landmarks for overland travelers lie along this portion of trail: Point of Rocks, an outcrop towering over the Cimarron River Valley, and Middle Spring, noted as a reliable water source. A 20-mile auto tour allows visitors to observe these landmarks as well as the nature of the landscape. Two blinds allow birdwatchers to observe lesser prairie chicken. The Outdoor Wildlife Learning Site is located at Middle Springs. This site contains nature and signed interpretive trails.

Further Reading

Moul, Francis. *The National Grasslands: A Guide to America's Undiscovered Treasures.* Lincoln: University of Nebraska Press, 2006.

KIRWIN NATIONAL WILDLIFE REFUGE

This north-central Kansas landscape is a transition zone where eastern tall-grass prairie and western short-grass plains meet. The rolling Smoky Hill and the North Fork of the Solomon River shape the terrain. Kirwin National Wildlife Refuge contains 10,778 acres of grassland, wooded riparian, shoreline, open water, wetlands, and croplands. About 4,000 acres are mixed-grass prairie, with 2,000 cultivated acres. The refuge provides habitat for over 300 species—197 birds, 34 mammals, and 31 reptiles and amphibians.

Migratory birds are the key feature at Kirwin National Wildlife Refuge. Twenty-eight birds of conservation concern stop here during migrations along the Central Flyway. Four federal and two state threatened and endangered birds also use the refuge. Thousands of ducks and 85,000 Canada geese migrate through the refuge during November and December. Great blue herons, double-crested cormorants, and interior least terns (endangered) stop here. Native species include greater prairie chickens, wild turkey, yellow-headed blackbirds, and black-billed magpies. Ducks include dabbling (mallard and northern pintail) and diving (redhead and lesser scaup). Double-breasted cormorants and great blue herons nest within refuge land. Burrowing owls, horned larks, kingbirds, meadowlarks, kestrels, and red-tailed hawks all use this habitat. Management priorities ensure food, shelter, and nesting areas for grassland-dependent birds, tree-dwelling neotropicals, waterfowl, and shorebirds.

Birds may be the current focus, but, historically, this landscape was home to herds of bison and predatory wolves. Black-tailed prairie dogs, ground squirrels, black-tailed jackrabbits, and mule and white-tailed deer all still reside on the refuge. During the 1950s, manmade reservoirs were built to control flooding and provide irrigation. Waterfowl soon found this a welcome stopover while migrating. The Bureau of Reclamation built the reservoirs, and they are managed jointly by the bureau and refuge staff. The bureau controls water levels, and the refuge manages all other activities. The Kirwin Reservoir level is low due to recent drought conditions. This low level makes room for invasive plant life that refuge staff works to control.

Set aside as a national wildlife refuge in 1954, Kirwin National Wildlife Refuge was the first such area in the state of Kansas. In 1967, part of the refuge containing bluestem and grama grasses was set aside as a research natural area. Declining bird populations nationwide make restoration of this grassland critical for sustained survival. It is one of the 500 globally important bird areas (designated by the American Bird Conservancy). Management activities include prescribed burns, planned vegetation, and control of invasive plant species. Along streams, nonnative trees are removed, and dense growths of small native trees are thinned out to provide better habitat and prevent fires.

Two thousand acres of cultivated land produce 20,000 bushels of corn and milo, which go to wildlife each year. This land is planted with corn, wheat, and milo by a cooperative of farmers who reap a percentage of the crop, then leave the rest for wildlife. Grazing, brush control, haying, mowing, and controlled burning are other land management techniques used by refuge staff. Green winter wheat is left as browse for geese during winter. Seasonal hunting is permitted for waterfowl and small game, as is fishing for crappie, walleye, and catfish.

Further Reading

Dolin, Eric Jay. *Smithsonian Book of National Wildlife Refuges*. Washington, DC: Smithsonian Institution Press, 2003.

QUIVIRA NATIONAL WILDLIFE REFUGE

Quivira National Wildlife Refuge lies in south-central Kansas at the junction of the lush eastern prairie and the arid western grasslands. This mixture provides nourishment for birds from both sides of the North American continent. Coronado explored this area in his famous search for gold and the Seven Cities of Cibola. The name of the refuge, Quivira, is taken from a group of Native Americans who resided here at that time and hunted waterfowl in these now-protected marshes. The refuge's 22,135 acres include salt marsh, wetlands, and prairie. White-tailed deer, black-tailed prairie dogs, beaver, badgers, coyote, and raccoons find refuge here, but the primary conservation concern is birds.

Quivira National Wildlife Refuge is an important migratory stop for waterfowl, providing food, water, and nesting sites. Birders report more than 300 species sighted at the refuge. Canada geese, ducks, shorebirds, endangered whooping cranes, and sandhill cranes migrate through in the fall; the sandhill cranes roost in the western edge of Big Salt Marsh. In winter, bald and golden eagles rest here, along with ducks and geese that move further south only when extreme cold sets in. These return, along with shorebirds, American white pelicans, and gulls that nest in the spring. Summer sees Swainson's hawks, Mississippi kites, nesting snowy plovers, American avocets, black-necked stilts, white-faced ibis, and endangered least terns. Year-round residents include northern harriers, American kestrels, red-tailed hawks, ring-necked pheasants, bobwhite quail, and wild turkey.

In the 19th century, these marshes became a popular market-hunting location, providing eastern cities and nearby Kansas City with waterfowl for the table. Commercial hunting gave way to recreational hunting. Some of the land at Quivira National Wildlife Refuge was bought and preserved by private hunting clubs. This saved the marshes from development and continued to provide migrating birds the refuge they needed. The Migratory Bird Commission supported the National Wildlife Refuge System's purchase of this land in 1955. The Kansas Department of Wildlife and Parks manages 20,000 acres. The Friends of Quivira, a nonprofit organization founded in 1998, assists the refuge with education and stewardship.

Quivira National Wildlife Refuge. (Jeff Walton)

Quivira National Wildlife Refuge management maintains food, water, and shelter for migrating waterfowl, balancing that with cooperative agriculture, prescribed burns, and water control. Farmers plant on the refuge and share the harvest with each other and the migrating birds. Farmers plant 1,300 acres with winter wheat or milo and occasionally cow peas, which return depleted nutrients to the soil. After farmers take their percentage of the harvest, birds find food and shelter in the remaining milo and wheat.

Controlled cattle grazing and prescribed burns aim to mimic the cycle historically maintained by bison herds, which no longer exist on this grassland. Water is channeled through 21 miles of canals and other structures to create and maintain 34 wetland areas. These structures create control over water levels and vegetation, allowing the refuge to choose the most beneficial plants for bird life.

The refuge maintains interpretive and hands-on exhibits, an educational classroom, a 1.2-mile nature trail, a 1,000-foot accessible trail, a wildlife observation tower, photography blinds, a hunting blind, and two scenic roads. Limited hunting of waterfowl, pheasant, quail, dove, snipe, rails, squirrels, and rabbits is permitted in certain parts of the refuge. Fishing is permitted, and the refuge maintains a fishing pond for kids younger than 15 years of age.

Shorebird species suffered during the mid-20th century, when wetlands throughout the United States fell to development and disappeared. In Kansas, 40 percent of the wetlands disappeared between 1955 and 1978. Quivira National Wildlife Refuge, along with neighboring Cheyenne Bottoms Wildlife Area (owned and maintained by the Kansas Department of Wildlife and Parks and the Nature Conservancy), were recently declared two of the Eight Wonders of Kansas. Together, these sites annually host 45 to 90 percent of all migrating shorebirds in what is the largest interior marsh in the United States at 40,000 acres. Ninety percent of Wilson's phalarope, long-billed dowitcher, white-rumped sandpiper, Baird's sandpiper, and stilt sandpiper stop here. Quivira was also designated a wetland of international importance by the Ramsar Convention on Wetlands and is part of the Wetlands and Wildlife National Scenic Byway.

Further Reading

Dolin, Eric Jay. *Smithsonian Book of National Wildlife Refuges*. Washington, DC: Smithsonian Institution Press, 2003.

TALLGRASS PRAIRIE NATIONAL PRESERVE

When settlers first arrived in the Flint Hills, they hoped the landscape would yield the same benefits as the rest of the Kansas prairie. It did not. Farming was near impossible in the rocky soil of what is now the Tallgrass Prairie National Preserve. Instead, the land became valued for bison and cattle grazing, its year-round supply of spring water, and native plants used for food and medicine.

The Flint Hills contain the only "landscape-level expression of tallgrass prairie," according to the Nature Conservancy, which owns most of the land in a public–private partnership with the National Park Service. Tallgrass Prairie National Preserve is 10,894 acres of that landscape. The ecosystem is balanced to accommodate long-time local ranchers at the WBar Ranch, who were granted a conservation easement in 2007 to restrict development. Nearly 26,000 acres of the Flint Hills are protected through such easements, sought by the Nature Conservancy. The mission is to balance livestock grazing with the restoration of a healthy, diverse grassland.

Prairie ecosystems are second only to the Brazilian rainforest in diversity and complexity. North American prairie was formed some 8,000 to 10,000 years ago and once spread over 170 million acres of the continent. The grasses present include big bluestem, Indian grass, and switch grass. This ecosystem, once the continent's largest continuous natural habitat, was plowed and planted, and now only four percent of the original region remains. The Flint Hills, where the Tallgrass Prairie National Preserve lies, is the largest stretch of this ecosystem, one of the rarest and most endangered in the world. Wildlife in the preserve includes greater prairie chickens, collard lizards, ornate box turtles, upland sandpipers, and coyote.

The 10,984-acre preserve was established in November 1996 and is commissioned to preserve and interpret the prairie ecosystem as well as the history and culture of the Spring Hill Ranch (a national historic landmark in 1997) and the Lower Fox Creek

Tallgrass Prairie National Preserve. (Elizabeth Winterbourne)

School, a one-room schoolhouse from about 1881. The preserve is managed by the National Park Service and is owned by the Nature Conservancy. The goals of this partnership are to maintain and enhance the public's visit to this unique landscape and to preserve local ranching traditions. The Nature Conservancy purchased external mineral and grazing rights and lease grazing rights annually. It also plans to reintroduce bison.

Further Reading

Heat-Moon, William Least. *PrairyErth, a Deep Map*. New York: Houghton Mifflin, 1999.

Klinkenborg, Verlyn. "Splendor of the Grass." *National Geographic*, April 2007. http://ngm.nationalgeographic.com/2007/04/tallgrass-prairie/klinkenborg-text.html.

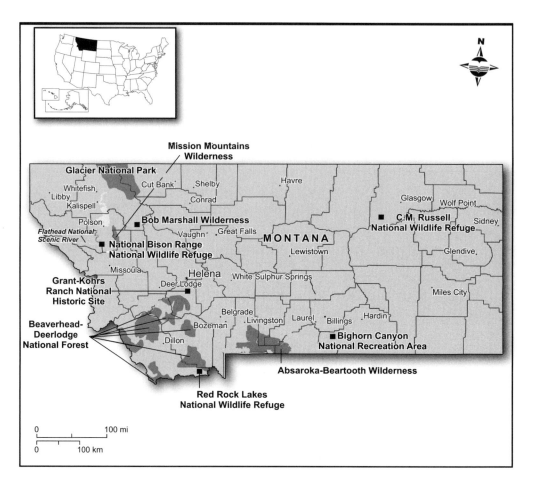

Absaroka-Beartooth Wilderness, 48

Beaverhead-Deerlodge National Forest, 49

Bighorn Canyon National Recreation Area, 50

Bob Marshall Wilderness, 52

C. M. Russell National Wildlife Refuge, 53

Flathead National Scenic River, 54

Glacier National Park, 56

Grant-Kohrs Ranch National Historic Site, 58

Mission Mountains Wilderness Complex, 60

National Bison Range National Wildlife Refuge, 61

Red Rock Lakes National Wildlife Refuge, 62

MONTANA

The expansive arid plains of Montana's eastern two-thirds gives the state its most recognizable nickname—Big Sky Country. Broken in places by canyons and badlands, they slowly rise toward the state's center, where small mountain ranges, rivers, and buttes dominate the landscape. Yet the state is named after its western mountains. Here, the northern Rocky Mountains are dramatically sculpted and checkered with clear blue lakes. Elevation reaches only 12,000 feet above sea level, but the more northern latitude makes these peaks just as foreboding as the southern ranges that rise some 2,000 feet higher. Montana's Rocky Mountains contain the headwaters of two major river systems, the Missouri and the Columbia. Its forests show transition between typical Rocky Mountain species and those common to the northwest region. Pines, firs, and spruces mix with cedar, hemlock, and larch.

Though the mountains have been tapped for minerals such as gold, silver, copper, and zinc, it was closer to the state's center that, at Butte, that extractive industries took their harshest toll on the environment. Once called "the richest hill on Earth," mineral extraction there has left the area with one of the country's largest Superfund sites. Much of Montana's plains was converted to agriculture and ranching in the middle of the nineteenth century. Cattle are the primary livestock, but there is interest in ranching the native bison of the prairie, which are better for the land and potentially more profitable. Oil was tapped, as well, and today the plains are targeted for new sources of energy. Wind power requires open spaces where fields of turbines can operate unobstructed. Scientists working with the Nature Conservancy of Montana have initiated the first scientific study to identify locations for windmills that would minimize threats to avian species, bats, and pollinator agents.

Though humans have changed Montana's landscape, much has been done to preserve, or restore, its natural beauty. The federal government created Glacier National Park in 1910, protecting the scenic mountains of the northern Rockies. But conservation of Montana's environment has farther-reaching impacts than the visual enjoyment of visitors. As the headwaters of two of the nation's largest water systems, the Columbia and the Missouri, minerals or chemicals emitted here can have wide-reaching effects. In 1963, the state protected its streams for wild (not stock) trout. In the 1970s, the state faced two plans to dam the Yellowstone River. In 1978, the Montana Board of Natural Resources and Conservation preserved 5.5 million acre-feet of the Yellowstone's flow, ensuring the river's continued health. Montana lies within the Greater Yellowstone Ecosystem and contains important wildlife corridors. Its international border with Canada was the site of the world's first international peace park. Management of Montana's environment encourages ecosystem conservation across borders of states and nations.

ABSAROKA-BEARTOOTH WILDERNESS

The blue lakes and granite peaks of the Absaroka-Beartooth Wilderness encompass 920,343 acres in Montana and 23,283 acres in Wyoming. The wilderness area is just north of Yellowstone National Park and is included in the 20-million-acre Greater Yellowstone Ecosystem.

The Wilderness gets its name from the two mountain ranges it contains—the Absaroka and the Beartooth ranges. Its highest elevation, Granite Peak (12,799 feet), lies in the Beartooth Range and is comprised mostly of granitic rocks. This is Montana's tallest peak, but it does not stand alone. Many peaks in the Beartooth Range rise above 12,000 feet. Within U.S. borders, only Alaska has as much land above 10,000 feet as the Beartooths. The Beartooth Plateau supports these mountains, where treeless plains, glacial lakes, and deep canyons provide scenery and habitat. Moose, elk, mule deer, and grizzly bear frequent the valleys. Most of the range, however, is harsh, rugged country. Pika live here; mountain goat and bighorn sheep are the only visitors. The alpine environment is sparse, and the weather is unpredictable. This is one of the few places in the United States that sustains vast tundra habitat.

The contrasting darker and bumpier Absaroka Range, formed of volcanic and metamorphic rock, contains active glaciers, tundra plateaus, canyons, and mountain lakes. The Absarokas are more forested than the Beartooths and are more hospitable to wildlife. Lush mountain meadows and streams sustain elk, deer, moose, coyote, wolves, marmots, lynx, and black and grizzly bears. The highest peak here is Mount Cowan (11,206 feet). It and the surrounding rugged elevations provide habitat for bighorn sheep and mountain goats.

The Absaroka-Beartooth Wilderness was formerly national forest land and is still administered by the U.S. Forest Service, which maintains 700 miles of hiking trails and provides permits for traditional outfitter-led pack trips. The wilderness's present boundaries cover the Gallatin, the Custer, and the Shoshone National Forests. At the time of designation, there were proposals to develop a northern entrance to Yellowstone National Park, which would have built a road through the Sough Creek area—vital habitat for wolf, grizzly, and elk.

In 1989, mining giant Noranda, Inc. (through a Canadian subsidiary Crown Butte Mining) applied for a permit to mine claims on land just outside the Absaroka-Beartooth Wilderness—an area it called the New World Mine. The company wanted to access nearly a billion dollars' worth of gold under Henderson Mountain in the Beartooth Range. Although this land is outside wilderness boundaries, extraction activities there would damage the adjacent properties of the wilderness, because waste from extraction releases sulfuric acid into the atmosphere, affecting wildlife and vegetation. At the time, Noranda proposed to submerge waste in an artificial reservoir to be formed by a 90-foot dam. This, however, could lead to potential waste flow down the three streams flowing down Henderson Mountain, all of which are tributaries of the Yellowstone River, the longest free-flowing body in the lower 48 states. Soda Butte Creek leads to Yellowstone National Park, Daisy Creek leads to Absaroka-Beartooth Wilderness, and Clark Fork, a blue-ribbon trout stream, holds a national wild and scenic river designation. With the help of local activism, including the Beartooth Alliance, the Clinton administration approved federal buyouts of Noranda's mining claims—an environmental victory with a $65 million price tag for tax payers. The Beartooth Alliance continues to monitor and fight mining claims in the region. It also works with the U.S. Forest Service cleaning up old mining sites that leak potentially deadly chemicals.

Further Reading

Disilvestro, Roger. "Is This a Bad Deal for Taxpayers?" *National Wildlife*, October/November 1997.

Gellhorn, Joyce. *Song of the Alpine: The Rocky Mountain Tundra through the Seasons*. Boulder, CO: Johnson Books, 2002.

BEAVERHEAD-DEERLODGE NATIONAL FOREST

Beaverhead-Deerlodge National Forest stretches across three million acres of southwestern Montana and over the Continental Divide. It contains three mountain ranges—Centennial, Gravelly, and Snowcrest—as well as the path of two major waterways, the Jefferson and the Madison rivers.

Beaverhead-Deerlodge National Forest is Montana's largest national forest; it was created in 1996, when two holdings (the Beaverhead and the Deerlodge National Forests) were combined. Much of the land was first set aside between 1897 and 1906 as forest reserves known as Hell Gate, Bitter Root, and Big Hole. In 1908, President Theodore Roosevelt consolidated these into two separate national forests under the new U.S. Forest Service.

Beaverhead-Deerlodge National Forest provides a corridor between the Greater Yellowstone and the Selway-Bitterroot ecosystems. Beaverhead-Deerlodge National Forest contains the largest roadless area—nearly two million acres—in the Greater

Yellowstone Ecosystem, of which it is a part. Anaconda-Pintler Wilderness and Lee Metcalf Wilderness comprise 225,147 acres of designated wilderness. In addition, Snowcrest and Mount Jefferson are proposed wilderness areas.

Elk, mule deer, bighorn sheep, grizzly bears, wolves, and lynx share space with upland game birds. Alpine areas host mountain goats and pikas on carpets of bluegrass and lichen. The subalpine forest is populated with hoary marmots, squirrels, and wolverines. Riparian areas provide food and shelter for moose, mallards, and beavers.

Hiking, mountain biking, camping, fishing, horse-packing, climbing, snowmobiling, and cross-country and downhill skiing are allowed in the Beaverhead-Deerlodge National Forest. Gravelly Range is one of the state's most popular hunting areas. Visitors can mine for crystals at Crystal Park. Two scenic roads, Gravelly Range Road and Pioneer Mountains Scenic Byway, meander through the national forest, as does the Nez Perce Historic Trail. Georgetown Lake is managed for recreation, as is Sheepshead Recreation Area, which offers lake fishing and picnicking.

Beaverhead-Deerlodge National Forest contains a wealth of historic sites. Lemhi Pass, at the top of the Continental Divide in the Beaverhead Mountains, is where Lewis and Clark first viewed the Columbia River headwaters and crossed the boundary of U.S. territory. Fur trapper camps, early mines, ranches, and homesteads have left their marks on what is now national forest land. Forest Service staff have stabilized 23 brick beehive kilns from 1881 that were used to make charcoal for lead and silver smelters. The remains of a Civilian Conservation Corps camp, which operated from 1935 to 1941, can be seen at Birch Creek. It is one of only two remaining camps in Montana, which once contained 61.

The most recent national forest management plan recommends 322,000 acres for wilderness designation, 284,000 acres for timber production, and 1.6 million acres for other resource harvesting. It prioritizes preservation of aspen habitats for wildlife, protection of riparian areas for aquatic species, and management of roads and vehicles.

BIGHORN CANYON NATIONAL RECREATION AREA

More than 120,000 acres make up Bighorn Canyon National Recreation Area in northern Wyoming and southern Montana, a part of the Greater Yellowstone Ecosystem. The area contains a variety of habitats characteristic of the region: forest, mountain, upland prairie, canyons and valleys, high desert, lake, and wetlands. Diverse forest types include juniper woodland, mountain mahogany woodland, riparian, and coniferous woodland. Prairies consist of sagebrush steppe, basin grassland, and desert shrubland.

The Bighorn Canyon National Recreation Area manages a small herd of bighorn sheep. Once abundant in the canyon, they were gone by the end of the 19th century due to hunting and settlement. In the 1970s, bighorn sheep were reintroduced near the national recreation area, and they now live mainly on the edge of the canyon. The herd is smaller than an ideal healthy 300 individuals, with an estimated 150 to 200 head, due in part to their susceptibility to livestock diseases. Bighorn Canyon National Recreation Area and the Wyoming Game and Fish Department hope that a relocated herd placed in Devil Canyon will interbreed with those in Bighorn Canyon, increasing the health and diversity of the population.

Wild horses, coyotes, mule deer, mountain lions, bears, and small mammals occupy the Bighorn Canyon's diverse habitats, along with 200 bird species. Bats, amphibians, reptiles, predators, and invertebrates are studied. A 2004 bat inventory discovered 13 species in the national recreation area, making it the densest concentration of bats in the Greater Yellowstone Ecosystem. Wild Pryor Mountain horses have a strong Spanish ancestry (though they are no longer present in Spain) and are protected on the 39,000-acre Pryor Mountain Wild Horse Range, part of which lies within the Bighorn Canyon National Recreation Area. About 160 horses live here. Its land also contains the Yellowtail Wildlife Habitat Management Area, which is managed by Wyoming Game and Fish Department. Below Afterbay Dam, Bighorn River is a world-class trout stream. The upper Bighorn River is the most fished river in Montana, containing trout and whitefish. The lower portion is filled with goldeye, walleye, sauger, smallmouth bass, catfish, and pike. More than 100,000 anglers come here every year; 75 percent of them are from out of state.

Ten thousand years ago, Bighorn Canyon was a Native American thoroughfare, used to access buffalo-rich prairies. It became known as the Bad Pass Trail when mountain men, fur traders, settlers, and ranchers began to use it. The trail was not an easy route,

Devil Canyon, within the Bighorn Canyon National Recreation Area. (Michael J. Scarfo, Jr.)

but it was better than the wild Bighorn River's rapids or rugged mountain crossings. The modern park road follows this route closely so visitors can experience nature as well as history. Historic properties include the Ewing-Snell Ranch, the Caroline Lockhart Ranch, the Mason-Lovell Ranch, and Fort C. F. Smith. Hillsboro was home to a working and then a dude ranch. Most ranchers originally came to the canyon seeking gold. Bighorn Canyon National Recreation Area also contains the site of an 1867 clash of Euro-Americans with Sioux and Northern Cheyenne just northeast of Fort Smith, known as the Hayfield Fight. Archaeological and paleontological research are ongoing, including at the Pretty Creek Archaeological Site (on the National Register of Historic Places). The Bighorn Canyon National Recreation Area hosts visiting researchers at the Bighorn Canyon Research Center on the Ewing-Snell Historic Ranch.

Established October 15, 1966, after construction of the Yellowtail Dam, Bighorn Canyon National Recreation Area contains this dam and its power plant, which provides 250,000 kilowatts of hydroelectricity. The lake formed by the dam, Bighorn Lake, is 71 miles long and ranges in depth from 1,000 feet at Devil Canyon to 2,500 feet at Bull Elk Ridge. There are 27 miles of trails, mostly in the southern portion. Boats, kayaks, and canoes are available for rent; guided tours are also offered.

Further Reading
Mattern, Joanne. *The Bighorn Sheep.* Mankato, MN: Coughlan, 1999.

BOB MARSHALL WILDERNESS

Affectionately known as The Bob, the one-million-acre Bob Marshall Wilderness is the second largest wilderness area in the contiguous United States. (The largest is the Frank Church–River of No Return Wilderness in Idaho.) It borders four national forests: the Lolo, Flathead, Helena, and Lewis and Clark. Not a single road crosses the wilderness area. The Bob Marshall Wilderness Complex includes Scapegoat and Great Bear wildernesses, comprising more than one and a half million total acres. Its mountains, alpine lakes, waterfalls, grassy meadows, streams, coniferous forests, and river valleys comprise what has been called "one of the most completely preserved mountain ecosystems in the world."

Two rivers run through the Bob Marshall Wilderness. The headwaters of the Flathead and the Sun rivers are in its mountains. It encompasses 60 miles of the Continental Divide, including a 22-mile escarpment known as the Chinese Wall. This feature, also known as the Lewis Overthrust, stretches along the Continental Divide, elevated some 1,000 feet above surrounding features. Formed when the earth's crust split open, the west side thrust upward and the east side slid beneath, creating this dramatic structure.

Within the wilderness area, the Continental Divide ranges in elevation from 4,000 to 9,000 feet above sea level. Native forests of Douglas fir, larch, and spruce dominate the landscape. Wilderness staff watches for invasive species such as orange and meadow hawkweed, which displace native mouse-ear hawkweed. The Bob Marshall Wilderness Foundation, park rangers, and the Glacier Raft Company monitor these species in the Castle Lake area. Yellow toadflax, which has taken over five acres here, is pulled or sprayed.

Mammal species in the area include lynx, mountain lion, wolf, black bear, moose, mountain sheep, mountain goat, bighorn sheep, wolverine, elk, white-tailed and mule deer, bobcat, cougar, beaver, river otter, snowshoe hare, and marten. This is possibly the densest grizzly habitat in the United States, except for Alaska. Birds include bald eagles, falcons, hawks, owls, osprey, grouse, woodpeckers, Steller's jay, Clark's nutcrackers, camp robbers, chickadees, nuthatches, trumpeter swans, and pelicans.

Established in 1964, the wilderness was named after conservationist, forester, and Wilderness Society cofounder Bob Marshall (1901–1939). In 1941, most of the region was preserved as South Fork, Pentagon, and Sun River Primitive Areas. Hunting is allowed in season. Over 1,000 miles of trails are maintained, with the assistance of the nonprofit Bob Marshall Wilderness Foundation. Like all wilderness areas, trails are open only to foot travel and stock use. No motorized or mechanical vehicles are allowed. The foundation recently won litigation to prohibit snowmobiles within wilderness boundaries.

Further Reading

Cheek, Roland. *Montana's Bob Marshall Wilderness*. Columbia Falls, MT: Skyline Publishing, 1999.

Graetz, Rick P. *Bob Marshall Country*. Helena, MT: Farcountry Press, 1985.

C. M. RUSSELL NATIONAL WILDLIFE REFUGE

The C.M. Russell National Wildlife Refuge is the largest refuge in Montana, with over one million acres surrounding Fort Peck Reservoir and 125 miles tracing the Missouri River. Native prairies, badlands, river bottoms, and forests abound. The refuge supports the largest population of bighorn sheep outside the Rocky Mountains and one of the largest herds of elk on the prairies. Pronghorn, prairie dog, coyote, mule deer, porcupine, and 235 species of birds (raptors, eagle, hawks, grouse, and quail) share this diverse habitat.

C.M. Russell National Wildlife Refuge is important for hosting the rarest mammal in North America—the black-footed ferret. The last free-roaming black-footed ferret populations in the world live here, fighting back from the brink of extinction. When prairie dog eradication began on the prairies, ferrets fell to disease and effects of the changing landscape. Nine captive ferrets were alive until 1978. When those died, biologists thought the species was extinct. Three years later, however, biologists found 18 wild ferrets in Wyoming. These formed the nucleus of reintroduced colonies, both captive and free roaming.

Other wildlife is closely monitored for deadly chronic wasting disease, which strikes deer and elk. The disease has not yet been detected in Montana but is present in adjacent states. In cooperation with six nearby refuges, the U.S. Fish and Wildlife Service, and the Wetland Management District, the refuge observes and tests animals for the disease and has released a plan to deal with affected animals if they are found.

The refuge has prepared a 15-year comprehensive conservation plan, which is the first such long-range plan since 1986. The plan calls for an assessment of the wilderness qualities of the UL Bend Wilderness Area, a 20,000-acre tract within refuge borders. It also plans for historic preservation, a study of the effects of energy development on pronghorn herds, possibilities of acquiring private and state lands, noxious weed control, wild bison reintroduction, wolf management, impact of livestock, and prescribed burning. It is open for public comment and should be finalized by fall 2011.

Twenty-thousand acres of the National Wildlife Refuge are privately owned; 33,000 acres are state owned. Six-hundred miles of roads are within the refuge borders, with more than 75 percent of the refuge within two miles of a road. Contained on refuge lands is the 245,000-acre Fort Peck Reservoir, created by the Fort Peck Dam on the Missouri River, which provides irrigation and flood control. The Bureau of Land Management recently denied a lease to energy development south of the refuge. There are nearby gas and oil fields, one of which is on pronghorn winter range. But invasive plant species are the greatest threat. Visitors so easily spread them that the refuge stationed a car wash at the entrance in an attempt to rid vehicles of potentially unwanted seeds.

Recreation allows seasonal hunting and fishing. The landscape can be viewed from the 19-mile auto tour route that has stops at interpretive signs. The Upper Missouri River Breaks National Monument is also within the refuge.

Further Reading

Butcher, Russell D. *America's National Wildlife Refuges, 2nd Edition: A Complete Guide.* Lanham, MD: National Book Network, 2008.

Nolt, David. "Revamping the Charles M. Russell Wildlife Refuge Conservation Plan." *New West,* Bozeman, February 22, 2008. http://www.newwest.net/city/article/ charles_m_russell_national_wildlife_refuge_conservation_plan_to_be_revamped/ C396/L396.

U.S. Fish and Wildlife Service. *Chronic Wasting Disease Management on the Charles M. Russell National Wildlife Refuge Complex, Montana: Environmental Assessment,* June 13, 2007, http://www.fws.gov/cmr.

FLATHEAD NATIONAL SCENIC RIVER

The Flathead River begins at the confluence of the North Fork Flathead and the Middle Fork Flathead and joins with the South Fork Flathead just downriver from the headwaters. The river is part of the Columbia River Basin and functions as a tributary of Clark Fork, which in turn is a tributary to Pend Oreille Lake and Pend Oreille

River, which is a tributary to the Columbia River. Because of the far-reaching effects created by this chain of tributaries, the health and stability of the Flathead River are important to much more than just the river and its natural inhabitants. If the Flathead is threatened or damaged, the repercussions of the alterations or pollutants introduced to the system can have a significant and widespread effect across the Columbia River Basin.

In light of this, it is of great concern that in 2009, American Rivers placed the Flathead River on its most endangered rivers list. The major threat to the Flathead River comes from mining activity taking place at the river's headwaters in Canada. Although the U.S. portion is protected as a wild and scenic river, projects in Canada such as a mountaintop removal coal mine and a coal bed methane project pose a threat to the health of the entire river. Not only does the river feed into the Columbia Basin, it also borders Glacier National Park and supports the habitats of a variety of endangered species. The North Fork has seen very little development, which has protected it against human-induced effects. For a long time, it has been considered one of the best protected watersheds in North America. In reaction to the continued mining activity in British Columbia, the National Parks Conservation Association petitioned to have the river put on the 2009 threatened list. American Rivers agreed, and the call now is to urge the Obama administration and the U.S. Departments of State and Interior to actively oppose mining at the North Fork headwaters and to encourage Canada to extend legislative protection to the their portion of the river.

Another issue facing the system is the change in the food chain of Flathead Lake caused by the introduction of nonnative species meant to enhance fishing opportunities. Native fish populations began to decline when landlocked red salmon, or kokanee, lake trout, lake whitefish, and bass were introduced. The native predator, the bull charr, adapted to feeding on the kokanee, but another introduction came to affect them negatively. Mysid shrimp were placed in the lake in the hopes that an abundance of these small shrimp would provide a new food source for the kokanee. This backfired when it was discovered that mysids feed on kokanee food sources; further, the kokanee could not eat the mysids because they were active at night, while the kokanee fed during the day. The new mysid population, however, provided an outstanding feeding ground for lake trout and lake whitefish, causing a significant spike in their numbers. All of these changes resulted in the lake now being dominated by nonnative fish, while native species continue to decline. The nonnative species also emigrated upstream and can be found in lakes throughout Glacier National Park. Native fish are an indispensable part of an ecosystem. When resident populations change, the stability of the entire system is put at risk. Management and mitigation actions taken to preserve the natural state of Flathead water system habitats are important not only in the immediate area but across the region, changing the natural balance and stability of this nationally important watershed.

Further Reading

Hauer, F. Richard, and Gary Anthony Lamberti. *Methods in Stream Ecology.* St. Louis, MO: Academic Press, 2006.

GLACIER NATIONAL PARK

Known as the Crown of the Continent Ecosystem, Glacier National Park preserves land much as Euro-Americans found it, and is considered untouched wilderness. All known historical species—plants and animals—remain in this landscape, with the exception of bison and woodland caribou. As such, it is considered an intact ecosystem and is a valuable research tool for scientists.

The elegant glacier-carved landscape, for which the park was named, contains a diversity of forests, meadows, lakes, peaks, and valleys. Shaping began during the last Ice Age, exposing rocks that now tell paleontologists of ancient seas. Geologic uplifting along faults flipped the earth's crust so that younger layers of rock are beneath older strata, attesting to the power of the area's geologic activity. Since that time, melting alpine glaciers that freeze and thaw have worn away rock, defining the landscape with U-shaped valleys and cirques filled with paternoster lakes or tarns. The scraped sides of mountain peaks are known as horns. When the glacier freezes again and brings debris downhill, terminal and lateral moraines form.

Glacier National Park contains about one million acres. Two mountain ranges, the Lewis and Livingston, mark the landscape. They possess six peaks above 10,000 feet: Stimpson, Kintla, Jackson, Siyeh, Merritt, and the tallest, Mount Cleveland, measuring 10,466 feet. There are 200 waterfalls, 130 named lakes, and about 600 smaller ones. Water in many of these is a striking aquamarine blue. The color is attributed to glacial silt suspended in the water, and the water's clarity is attributed to its cold temperature, which prevents plankton from growing. Atop the Continental Divide, Triple Divide Peak (8,020 feet) features water flowing east, west, and north. This is the only spot in the United States where water flows to three oceans—west to the Columbia River and draining to the Pacific Ocean; east to the Missouri-Mississippi Basin and on to the Atlantic Ocean via the Gulf of Mexico; and north to Hudson Bay and the Arctic Ocean.

Over 1,000 species of plants grow in Glacier National Park. About half of the park is covered in forest, which is primarily coniferous and about 10 percent deciduous, the latter mostly in the eastern portion. In the west, western hemlock and western red cedar reach their eastern limit of the Pacific cedar-hemlock forest type, common to the Pacific Northwest. They mix with Glacier National Park's other flora, such as white spruce, paper birch, white pine, and grand fir. Eastern aspen parklands are open forests that transition from aspen to limber pine on the ridges and grassland. Riparian areas contain black cottonwood (balsam poplar) and white spruce. Dry forests include lodgepole pine, a few ponderosa pines, and Douglas fir. Slightly moister slopes grow western larch, subalpine fir, and Engelmann spruce. At the tree line, alpine larch grows, but whitebark pine has been reduced by white pine blister rust and lack of fire. The tree line on the eastern slopes is much lower than on the west because of its open exposure to the harsh winds of the Great Plains. There are 30 plant species found only in this park and the surrounding national forests. The bold, fluffy heads of beargrass, a tall flowering plant, blooms in mid- to late summer. After it grows, the stalk will not bloom again for 5 to 10 years.

Seventy mammal species, including two threatened species—grizzly bear and Canadian lynx—reside in Glacier National Park along with the endangered bull trout and the rare wolverine. Elk, moose, mule and white-tailed deer, mountain goats, bighorn sheep, beavers, badgers, river otters, porcupines, mink, martens, fishers, bats, black bears, cougars, and a nearly continuous population of wolves make up Glacier's wildlife. The park contains 260 species of birds, including white-tailed ptarmigans, harlequin ducks, dippers, black swifts, Clark's nutcrackers, and golden eagles.

Glacier National Park's sedimentary rocks contain some of the best evidence of life from the Proterozoic era. Well-preserved fossils reveal stromatolites and water indentations from raindrops, ripples, and mud cracks. The Appekunny Formation pushed scientific theories about the time of earth's first animal life back one billion years.

In 1891, the Great Northern Railway ran into the valley, bringing settlers to what was once Native American land. The mountains east of the Continental Divide were taken from the Blackfeet in hopes of finding gold and copper in 1895. Explorer and scientist George Bird Grinnell (1849–1938) advocated for a park in this region, winning a forest preserve designation in 1900. In 1910, the park was created. Early tourism came by rail and boat. Five historic hotels and chalets remain in the park and are national historic landmarks. The National Register of Historic Places contains 350 locales within Glacier National Park. The 52-mile Going-to-the-Sun Highway runs across the park east to west and is one of the nation's premier scenic drives. The road was built between 1916 and 1932; it climbs 3,000 feet, taking visitors through canyons, past waterfalls, and up mountains, topping out at 6,600 feet above sea level. The park maintains over 750 miles of hiking trails.

With the adjacent Bob Marshall Wilderness and the Seeley Swan Valley, the natural space of the Glacier National Park area encompasses three million acres. In 1974, a study proposed some 95 percent of the park for wilderness designation. No action has been taken, but these lands are managed as if they are wilderness areas. To Glacier's north lies a Canadian preserve, Waterton Lakes National Park. In 1932, the two governments established Glacier-Waterton International Peace Park to symbolize international friendship. Because the parks are part of a continuous ecosystem, management is cooperative, especially for migrating wildlife and invasive species. Both parks are world heritage sites and biosphere reserves (designated by the United Nations). Glacier National Park also is adjacent to the Blackfeet Indian Reservation, and nearby are reservations of the Salish and Kootenai.

Glacier National Park's crystalline, plankton-free lakes unfortunately retain pollution longer than other bodies of water. Scientists can easily observe increases of pollutants in these waters. In 2003, the park lost 144,000 acres to wildfire. Hunting is prohibited, but poaching is widely reported. The biggest threat to the park is the loss of its defining feature—glaciers. Although the park will always exhibit a dramatic glacier-carved landscape, the existence of alpine ice is waning. Historic reports cite 150 glaciers here in 1850. Now, there are 26. The area's glaciers are being studied as indicators of global warming trends. Scientists from the U.S. Geological Survey estimate the complete disappearance of the glaciers by 2030. Between 1850 and 1979, glacier acreage at Blackfoot and Jackson Glaciers (once the same body) shrunk by 73 percent. Most famous are photographs taken of Grinnell Glacier between 1939 and 2005.

Further Reading

Guthrie, Carol W. *Glacier National Park: The First 100 Years.* Helena, MT: Farcountry, 2008.

Rockwell, David. *Glacier: A Natural History Guide.* Helena, MT: Falcon Press, 2007.

Sample, Michael. *Glacier on My Mind.* Guilford, CT: Globe Pequot Press, 1997.

Waldt, Ralph. *Crown of the Continent: The Last Great Wilderness of the Rocky Mountains.* Helena, MT: Riverbend, 2004.

Grant-Kohrs Ranch National Historic Site

This 1,600-acre working cattle ranch preserves symbols of the spirit of the West—the cowboy, his horse, and cattle herds. The former owner of this land, Conrad Kohrs, was Montana's "cattle king." His herds grazed over 10 million acres of land from Canada through four U.S. states. Grant-Kohrs Ranch National Historic Site preserves this open range landscape. In addition to the 1,600 acres of the national historic site, 3,675 acres have been preserved as part of a conservation easement.

Conrad Kohrs bought the land in 1866. With his brother he purchased 365 head of cattle and soon expanded the enterprise to lands in eastern Montana, Wyoming, Colorado, and Canada. John Francis Grant built the largest of the remaining houses still standing at the ranch in 1862 and convinced many others to relocate to Deer Lodge Valley, which proved to be a good wintering ground for cattle because the high mountains trapped most harsh winter weather. Homesteaders moved in, parceling land into 160-acre lots and erecting fences with barbed wire. In the 1880s, homesteaders and the effects of overgrazing had changed the landscape. In addition, devastating snowstorms in 1886–1887 killed nearly half of all the cattle on the northern plains.

Grant-Kohrs Ranch National Historic Site preserves not just a landscape, but landscape history. Conrad Kohrs arrived at Deer Lodge Valley in 1862, marveling at its clear, trout-filled waters, abundance of antelope, and cattle. The end of the 20th century brought mining, timbering, ranching, and settlement to the valley. Yet the land preserved in Grant-Kohrs Ranch maintains the 19th-century feel; the ranch preserves a historic state of a landscape, not a wild one.

Wildlife and ranching exist side by side in a seemingly naturally balanced landscape. Livestock grazes on the same land as deer, elk, moose, Columbian ground squirrels, and red foxes. Some native short-grass prairie remains here, with little interruption by ranching activities. The ranch maintains horses, cattle, chickens, and working dogs and cats. It protects native animals and plants and manages livestock health and breeding.

Clark Fork River is home to trout and whitefish. Marshes and streamside habitat allow beaver, muskrat, fox, skunk, raccoon, river otter, and coyote to thrive. Willow, water birch, and cottonwood line the banks of Cottonwood and Fred Burr creeks, tributaries of the Clark Fork River. Pronghorns, black bears, yellow pine chipmunks, northern pocket gophers, badgers, mountain cottontails, porcupines, several species of shrew, mice, voles, and bats are among the 35 mammal species found here. Reptiles and amphibians include western toads, Columbia spotted frogs, long-toed salamanders, common garter snakes, and painted turtles.

This landscape represents the history of nature appreciation as well. Conrad Kohrs's grandson, Conrad Kohrs Warren, was a dedicated birder who kept a personal bird book and hanging birdfeeders on the property. Over 230 species of birds live or migrate through this ranch land, including great blue herons, geese, ducks, chickadees, woodpeckers, magpies, barn swallows, black-headed grosbeaks, bobolinks, red-tailed and rough-legged hawks, sparrows, yellow-headed blackbirds, willow flycatchers, and bald and golden eagles. Warren worked with local agencies to establish state-regulated public livestock auctions, upgraded purebred stock, learned about livestock health and sanitary programs, and mechanized the farm. The site was designated a national historic landmark in 1960. Warren sold the main ranch to the National Park Service in 1972 but lived there until his death in 1993.

The Grant-Kohrs Ranch National Historic Site contains 80 historic structures and 23,000 artifacts. Some of the natural features here are also historic and manmade. Several marshes developed on depressions created by railroad construction or dredging. Wet meadows provide habitat but contain few native species. These grassy areas were formed as a result of agricultural irrigation to produce hay. The ranch maintains walking trails and provides guided tours of the ranch house.

Due to dangerous chemical concentrations, the U.S. Environmental Protection Agency (EPA) declared the Upper Clark Fork River a superfund site in 1992. A portion of the ranch lies within this superfund, known as the Clark Fork River Operable Unit of the Milltown Reservoir/Clark Fork River National Priorities List Site. Arsenic, copper, lead, zinc, and cadmium lie within the floodplain. In 2008, a responsible mining company, the Atlantic Richfield Company, agreed to work with the EPA, the Department of the Interior, and the state of Montana to clean up and restore the landscape.

Further Reading

Swant, Gary. *A Field Guide to the Wildlife and Habitats of the Grant-Kohrs Ranch.* Deer Lodge, MT: National Park Service.
http://www.nps.gov/grko/naturescience/animals.htm

MISSION MOUNTAINS WILDERNESS COMPLEX

Mission Mountains Wilderness is in the Flathead National Forest, bordering the Mission Mountains Tribal Wilderness, owned by the Confederated Salish and Kootenai Tribes, and the Flathead Indian Reservation. In 1979, the tribes designated 89,500 acres of their private reservation part of the wilderness area. Mission Mountains is the only wilderness area on an Indian reservation established by the tribes themselves.

Mission Mountain Wilderness was designated in 1975 and contains 73,877 acres. These mountains were traditional hunting, gathering, and spiritual landscape for the Flathead and Pend Oreille Indians. Euro-Americans did not explore here until 1922. Less then a decade later, the region was designated the Mission Mountains Primitive Area. In 1931, it encompassed 67,000 acres to the east of Mission Divide. In 1939, 8,500 acres were added from Piper to Fatty Lakes. The Northern Pacific Railway Company owned a portion of this land at the time and sold its high-elevation holdings in exchange for land in the Swan Valley. These negotiations took place until the 1950s.

Snow-capped peaks, glaciers, alpine lakes, mountain meadows, and streams mark this landscape. Glaciers melt into tarns, creating one of the northern Rockies' highest concentrations of alpine lakes as well as two striking waterfalls—Elizabeth and Mission Falls—which drop 1,000 feet. The Mission Mountain Range's jagged precipices rise some 7,000 feet above the valley. McDonald Peak is the tallest at 9,280 feet, and 12 others rise above 9,000 feet. Forests are populated with western white, lodgepole, whitebark, and limber pines; Engelmann spruce; alpine, grand, and Douglas firs; alpine and western larches; western red cedars; quaking aspen; alder; and Rocky Mountain maple. Mountain meadows and basins contain many summer wildflowers.

Elk, mule and white-tailed deer, black and grizzly bears, mountain goats, mountain lions, gray wolves, martens, mink, bobcats, coyote, badgers, skunks, beavers, muskrats, porcupines, chipmunks, pika, squirrels, snowshoe rabbits, yellow-bellied and hoary marmots, lynx, weasels, wolverines, and smaller mammals call Mission Mountains Wilderness home. Fifty species of birds find food and shelter in the mountains; they include bald and golden eagles, common loons, red-tailed hawks, osprey, mallards, great blue herons, ruffed grouse, killdeer, great horned and saw-whet owls, common goldeneyes, rufous hummingbirds, common flickers, Steller's and gray jays, belted kingfishers, black-capped and mountain chickadees, western tanagers, American robins, dippers, and hairy and pileated woodpeckers.

Sheer cliffs, large boulders, talus slopes, and thin, gravelly soil comprise Mission Mountains Wilderness's rough landscape, and the area is largely unsuitable for travel by anything other than foot. Forty-five hiking trails are maintained. Lakes are stocked with cutthroat trout, which are native to the area. Nonnative fish include rainbow, golden, Dolly Varden, and hybrid trout, and mountain whitefish.

In 1952, spruce bark beetles infested the forest when blown down trees from a wind storm in November 1949 were not removed, despite the Forest Service's permission to collect the trees (salvage logging) over 1,000 damaged acres of the wilderness area.

Because of the beetle infestation, the Forest Service allowed logging on adjacent tracts in hopes of preventing the spread of the spruce bark beetles. This logging resulted in eight roads and a loss of about 2,000 acres of trees. The tribal wilderness gives priority to wildlife, closing 12,000 acres to public use between mid-July and October, when grizzly bears live on and near McDonald Peak. At other times of the year, all visitors must obtain a recreation permit to enter the tribal portion of the wilderness area.

NATIONAL BISON RANGE NATIONAL WILDLIFE REFUGE

The National Bison Range National Wildlife Refuge is among the oldest wildlife refuges in the National Wildlife Refuge System. By the end of the 19th century, bison that once roamed throughout the United States were nearly extinct. Westward settlement and federal plans to eliminate Plains Indians forced hunting of these large mammals. Cattle were considered superior food, and bison were pushed off grasslands for the newcomers. By 1890, only a few wild bison remained, mostly in Yellowstone National Park. In 1908, President Theodore Roosevelt set this land aside as a game reserve, and the American Bison Society placed the founding herd of American bison here.

Today, the U.S. Fish and Wildlife Service manages 350 to 500 bison on 18,500 acres of land. If too many bison are present to maintain a healthy herd and productive grasslands, they are donated to public herds, including the InterTribal Bison Cooperative, which raises bison on land belonging to Native Americans. Some are sold to private herds. Research is done on the bison herd, examining health and DNA structure. Bison have now been preserved and raised by the federal government on several public lands, resulting in a population of 250,000 bison living on federal, state, and private land.

Grasslands also support elk, white-tailed and mule deer, pronghorns, bighorn sheep, and black bears. Eagles, hawks, meadowlarks, bluebirds, ducks, and geese are among the 200 species of birds. Scientific research by private parties involves bighorn sheep, pronghorns, grasshoppers, weed control, and water quality. Native prairie is watched for invasive vegetation. Insects are used to keep this balance in a management program known as integrated pest management. This management strategy has been in place here since 1948, using 24 species of insects.

The National Bison Range Complex includes Ninepipe and Pablo National Wildlife Refuges and the Northwest Montana Wetlands Management Area. These are prime bird-watching wetlands, managed by National Bison Range National Wildlife Refuge staff. The National Bison Range sees some 250,000 visitors per year. Interpretive exhibits at the visitor center lead to two scenic roads, including a 19-mile auto tour loop. A nature trail and the one-quarter-mile Grassland Trail are also near the visitor center. Two other short trails can be accessed along Red Sleep Mountain Drive.

Further Reading

Dolin, Eric Jay. *Smithsonian Book of National Wildlife Refuges.* Washington, DC: Smithsonian Institution Press, 2003.

Isenberg, Andrew. *Destruction of the Bison: An Environmental History, 1750–1920.* Cambridge, UK: Cambridge University Press, 2000.

RED ROCK LAKES NATIONAL WILDLIFE REFUGE

At the top end of Centennial Valley, mountain wetlands and riparian areas comprise the protected landscape of Red Rock Lakes National Wildlife Refuge. Although the land was homesteaded in the late 19th century, refuge staff restored the natural conditions, creating one of the nation's few marshlands with wilderness designation. These high-elevation wetlands, at 6,600 feet above sea level, are some of the country's most diverse and productive. The management priority is natural diversity. Hiking trails are not formally maintained, and visitors are asked to follow game trails in keeping with "the wilderness spirit."

The Red Rock Lakes National Wildlife Refuge provides food and shelter to 232 bird species, including trumpeter swans, Canada goose, mallards, common and Barrow's goldeneyes, American wigeons, buffleheads, hooded mergansers, white-faced ibises, sandhill cranes, curlews, peregrine falcons, eagles, hawks, owls, American dippers, northern goshawks, belted kingfishers, dusky and ruffed grouse, Steller's jay, black-billed magpies, Clark's nutcrackers, common raves, black-capped and mountain chickadees, white-breasted and red-breasted nuthatches, pine grosbeaks, red crossbills, pine siskins, great gray and great horned owls, and hairy and downy woodpeckers. Winter visitors include northern shrikes, rough-legged hawks, snow buntings, common redpolls, rosy finches, and American tree sparrows. The refuge contains 53 rare or accidental birds. Species that have been sighted here—even though it is outside their normal range—include the great egret, whooping crane, woody duck, turkey vulture, dunlin, northern mockingbird, black-and-white warbler, northern oriole, northern parula, grasshopper sparrow, rock dove, and rose-breasted grosbeak. Mammals include badgers, wolverines, coyotes, foxes, rodents, bears, wolves, moose, and pronghorns.

Trumpeter swans are the largest North American waterfowl and the only continental swan species. They can weigh up to 30 pounds, stand four feet tall, and have an eight-foot wingspan. In the early 19th century, they were hunted for meat, feathers, and skins, until they were on the brink of extinction in 1932, with only 68 individuals remaining in the Greater Yellowstone Ecosystem. Recently, counts have been as high as 500. Another 4,000 have been known to stop at Red Rock Lakes National Wildlife Refuge during winter, escaping Canada's colder temperatures. Trumpeter swans consume primarily pond and lake vegetation such as waterweed, water milfoil, duck potato, and pondweed. Much of the open water of Yellowstone National Park remains unfrozen throughout the winter, providing constant nourishment. Trumpeter swans may abandon their nests and eggs if their environment is disturbed. They will abandon habitat areas because of recreational and logging activities as well as housing and road development. Survival can only be ensured by curtailing development, keeping open water unfrozen, and controlling human use of trumpeter swan habitat. There are three populations of trumpeter swans today; the largest are in Alaska and western Canada. Rocky Mountain and interior populations are smaller, but together all three have reached a high of 34,000 individuals, thanks to reintroduction programs initiated in the 1980s.

The American peregrine falcon population suffered at mid-century. Due to the use of DDT (dichlorodiphenyl trichloroethane) as an agricultural insecticide, numbers fell in the 1950s and continued to fall until the species was listed as endangered in the mid-1970s. DDT was ingested by birds and responsible for thinner eggshells and fewer births. Montana reintroduced the species in the 1980s, beginning in the Centennial Valley. Reintroductions ceased in 1997. In 1999, American peregrine falcons were removed from the federal endangered species list.

Red Rock Lakes National Wildlife Refuge manages natural habitat for migratory birds and endangered species. Waterfowl nesting habitat and native wildlife are the top priorities. Grazing for big game is controlled through prescribed burns. Willow habitats are maintained to encourage bird diversity and to provide forage for moose. Bird-watchers enjoy the variety of habitats, especially at places like Upper Red Rock Lake Campground, where open water, mudflats, willows, aspens, grasses, sagebrush, and evergreen forests grow in close proximity.

Further Reading

Kaufman, Kenn. *Lives of North American Birds*. New York: Houghton Mifflin, 1996.

Kortright, Francis H. *The Ducks, Geese and Swans of North America*. Washington, DC: American Wildlife Institute, 1943.

Mitchell, C. D. *The Birds of North America*. Philadelphia: Academy of Natural Sciences, 1994.

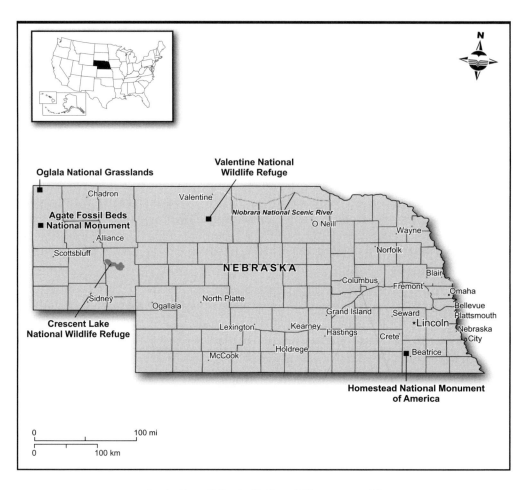

Agate Fossil Beds National Monument, 66

Crescent Lake National Wildlife Refuge, 67

Homestead National Monument of America, 68

Niobrara National Scenic River, 70

Oglala National Grassland, 71

Valentine National Wildlife Refuge, 72

Nebraska

Typical of the Great Plains, grasslands and wetlands make up most of the Nebraskan landscape. But the state's most unusual feature are its 20,000 miles of sand dunes. The Sandhills region's grass-covered hills provide habitat for 700 plant species and 300 land species. Nebraska's wetlands vary from marshes and forested swamps to wet meadows and fens. Lakes, rivers, and streams round out the state's wetland diversity.

Situated in the heart of the Great Plains, Nebraska exemplifies agricultural America in its wide open spaces, rich fertile soil, and sparse but friendly communities. Corn is the foundation of Nebraska's economy. Nebraska's farmers have benefited by recent developments that put corn at the center of many consumer products, such as high-fructose corn syrup and ethanol. Fully 25 percent of the state's crop is grown for ethanol production. The largest percentage, though, is used as feed corn, fueling the livestock industry throughout the United States. Soybeans, grains, pork, and beef also play a significant part in the state's agricultural production, and these commodities provide a strong foundation for economic stability. These resource-intensive activities have altered the Nebraskan landscape. Many prairie and plains environments were converted to cultivate commercial crops or grazing herds. Finding a balance between maintaining the land's natural character and supporting human habitation and economic endeavors is a difficult task. Nebraska struggles to achieve that balance of restoration and protection.

Nebraska recognizes that a strong, sustainable future depends on a sound natural environment. Habitats are often the most obvious focus of restoration and preservation efforts, but surface and ground water quality, important to wildlife and agriculture, are also addressed. Soil management and air quality directly affect human communities, industrial pursuits, and ecosystems. State agencies and private organizations combine efforts to work on this wide variety of issues and concerns. As a state dotted with many small communities, special attention is paid to developing partnerships to bolster communities' abilities to combat their own environmental issues. Nebraska is constantly adapting to the special challenges posed by having a small, widely dispersed population that must address the state's many important environmental issues. Here the balance of economic stability and environmental health is constantly pursued through a dynamic dance of community participation, private interest support, and public funding and coordination.

AGATE FOSSIL BEDS NATIONAL MONUMENT

In the Niobrara River Valley, the landscape of Agate Fossil Beds National Monument is unglaciated—a rarity in high plains geography. This national monument is only 2,700 acres, but it contains a wealth of information in its fossil record. River and wetland habitats lead to buttes, which contain fossils of the former landscape. During the Miocene era (20 million years ago), this land was a grass savanna feeding the ancestors of modern mammals. Dinohyus (a giant pig), stenomylus (a small gazelle-camel), paleocastor (a land beaver), amphicyon (beardogs), and menoceras (a small rhinoceros) fossils have been found at Agate Fossil Beds National Monument. Evidence of this former life is found in hoofprints preserved in sediment as well as fossilized bone. Researchers believe that this landscape was a gathering place for a variety of animals during a period of sustained drought. As animals began to die, they simply collapsed in the moist soil of the savanna, preserving them as fossils.

The landscape today consists of mixed-grass prairie with a variety of grasses. Buttes and hills contain bluestem grass, threadleaf sedge, and needle-and-thread. Riparian areas support cottonwoods, foxtail barley, cattails, reeds, sedges, yellow Siberian irises, and blue flag irises. Monument staff seeks to control invasive Canada thistle. Nebraska has long sought to control this noxious weed. It affects prairie as well as crops, decreasing the yield of wheat and corn. Cattle avoid it. Staff mows, sprays herbicide, and has introduced biological control in the form of stem mining weevils that inject eggs into thistle shoots, robbing the plant of nutrients. Another concern for the park is water contamination from neighboring ranches and farms.

The land was originally a cattle ranch, and the monument houses the owner's collection of artifacts, the Cook Collection of Plains Indians artifacts. A new management plan for the monument—the first in some 50 years—is being drawn up. It includes preserving short-grass prairie, riparian zones, and the cultural landscape of ranching.

Further Reading
National Park Service. *Agate Fossil Beds National Monument, Nebraska.* Washington, DC: U.S. Department of the Interior, 1989.

CRESCENT LAKE NATIONAL WILDLIFE REFUGE

Crescent Lake National Wildlife Refuge sits on the southwestern edge of Nebraska's 12-million-acre Sandhills—the largest continuous sand dunes in the United States. Created by winds blowing off an ancient sea, these dunes and swales are one of the world's largest bodies of sand not located in a desert. Crescent Lake National Wildlife Refuge encompasses some 45,818 acres of grassland and wetlands in the Nebraska panhandle.

Sand dunes are covered with grasses and forbs. The landscape has been restored with native grasses that control erosion with their extensive and deep root systems. Introduced species establish themselves quicker, but one stable, native grassland prevents competing species on its own. Lush meadows and choppies—sparsely covered land—contain cottonwood trees, big bluestem, spiderwort, yucca, prickly pear, and endangered blowout or Hayden's penstemon—Nebraska's rarest plant. Blowout penstemon thrives on sand surfaces. The Crescent Lake National Wildlife Refuge, along with the University of Nebraska, is seeding new areas that had historic populations of this rare plant.

Much of this land is irrigated, creating 8,251 acres of wetland habitat, 21 lakes, and many ponds swimming with bluegill, yellow perch, largemouth bass, and carp. An aquifer lies below the refuge. Fall bird migration counts record over 200,000 waterfowl and

Crescent Lake National Wildlife Refuge. (Murray Eatherton)

20 bald eagles. About 275 bird species make use of Crescent Lake National Wildlife Refuge and are its primary management concern. Refuge staff maintains areas for waterfowl rookeries, as well as habitat and nesting for bald eagles. Other birds using this land are ducks and geese, red-tailed hawks, northern harriers, golden eagles, sandhill cranes, Wilson's phalaropes, cormorants, grebes, and blue-winged teals. Pheasants and grouse are full-time residents. Bird species that breed in the wetlands include eared grebes, American bitterns, willets, Forster's and black terns, Wilson's phalaropes, and Baird's sandpipers. On the prairie, species need large, unbroken areas for breeding. Species that breed on the prairie include long-billed curlews, upland sandpipers, loggerhead shrikes, dickcissels, grasshopper sparrows, bobolinks, and northern harriers. The Audubon Society calls it the best bird site in the state of Nebraska. Other wildlife consists of raccoons, opossums, blacktail jackrabbits, pronghorns, coyote, eastern cottontails, and mule and white-tailed deer.

Recreation is managed in harmony with the primary goal of protecting spaces for migrating birds. Crescent Lake National Wildlife Refuge is managed with the nearby North Platte National Wildlife Refuge, both in the Platte Kansas Rivers watershed. The U.S. Fish and Wildlife Service uses an ecosystem approach to managing lands, considering not the existence of a single species but the health of the ecosystem as a whole, its watershed, and the economic welfare of communities. Nearby North Platte National Wildlife Refuge contains four Bureau of Reclamation irrigation projects: Lake Minatare, Winters Creek Lake, Lake Alice, and Stateline Island. Crescent Lake National Wildlife Refuge was established in 1931. In 1972, about half the refuge land was proposed for wilderness designation. This proposal remains in front of Congress, and the land is managed as if it were designated wilderness.

Further Reading

Dolin, Eric Jay. *Smithsonian Book of National Wildlife Refuges*. Washington, DC: Smithsonian Institution Press, 2003.

Johnsgard, Paul A. *The Nature of Nebraska: Ecology and Biodiversity*. Lincoln: University of Nebraska Press, 2005.

Jones, Stephen R. *The Last Prairie: A Sandhills Journey*. Lincoln: University of Nebraska Press, 2006.

Sharpe, Roger S., W. Ross Silcock, and Joel G. Jorgensen. *Birds of Nebraska: Their Distribution and Temporal Occurrence*. Lincoln: University of Nebraska Press, 2001.

HOMESTEAD NATIONAL MONUMENT OF AMERICA

Homestead National Monument of America commemorates the lives and accomplishments of pioneers, and the changes brought to the land by the Homestead Act of 1862. It preserves the landscape they found and the changes they made. Originally, this whole landscape was tall-grass prairie—a moist and diverse ecosystem. The soil was made fertile by years of decaying vegetation. This fertile soil drew agricultural interests to this region—and to prairies across the world. Fewer than one percent of native prairie remains today. Homestead National Monument contains 100 acres of restored tallgrass prairie.

The national monument contains one tract of never-plowed tallgrass prairie. This was the playground for the Freeman School for nearly a century, from 1872 until 1967. It is only three-fourths of an acre yet has the most diversity of any area in the monument. The majority of land here is restored tall-grass prairie. Homestead National Monument's program is the second-oldest prairie restoration program in the United States. After decades of agriculture and grazing, the National Park Service began to restore this land to reduce soil erosion and to re-create the landscape seen by homesteaders. Tall-grass prairie was restored through seeding with native grasses, moving sod from unplowed land, and eradicating exotic species by mowing, spraying, or burning. Today, big and little bluestem, Indian grass, switchgrass, goldenrod, field pussytoes, and leadplant thrive. Shrub species include sumac, wild plum, and dogwood.

These habitats support insects, birds, and mammals. The prairie and forest contain more than 100 species of birds. Prairie birds are declining in numbers, and the monument is overseeing a count performed by the Heartland Network and Prairie Cluster Prototype to assist in management strategies. The count was begun in 2008 and will be performed each May and June until 2012. Mammals include white-tailed deer, coyote, red foxes, otters, weasels, eastern cottontails, badgers, raccoons, shrews, bats, and rodents.

Forested Cub Creek runs through the monument, watering a mesic bur oak forest—a rare landscape in Nebraska, even at the time of homesteading. This lowland plant community contains 116 types of plants. Trees grow up to 60 feet tall, providing shade on the open prairie and habitat for barred owls. Research into the forest's past shows it is actually denser and bigger than it was in the 19th century due to historic logging and grazing and lack of wildfires.

Beginning in 1909, Nebraskans began to lobby for a national park on this site, known as the Freeman property, after the original homesteader, Daniel Freeman. This was one of the first parcels claimed under the Homestead Act. With the support of Nebraska Senator George W. Norris and the Homestead National Park Association (formed in 1934), a proposal was put before the House of Representatives in 1935. In 1936, President Franklin D. Roosevelt created Homestead National Monument of America.

Further Reading

Madson, John, and Dycie Madson. *Where the Sky Began: Land of the Tallgrass Prairie.* Iowa City: University of Iowa Press, 2004.

Niobrara National Scenic River

Seventy-six miles of the Niobrara River were designated a national scenic river in 1991. It scenic waterfalls cascade from high canyon walls and lush vegetation unique in the area to the river's shore. Some 90 waterfalls drop into the river in its western portion, and 200 waterfalls are in the Niobrara River Valley. Smith Falls drops 63 feet; it is the tallest waterfall in the state.

The Niobrara River drains Nebraska's Sandhills. It begins in eastern Wyoming's high plains and flows for 535 miles, until it meets the Missouri River in northeastern Nebraska. The river courses through rock, revealing paleontological treasures in the form of beaver, horse, fish, alligator, turtle, rhinoceros, and mastodon fossils. The Niobrara National Scenic River in this portion of northeastern Nebraska is at the edge of changing environments. Due to the unbroken riparian east-west corridor, plants from the humid prairie mix with those from the drier west. Six ecosystems meet: northern boreal forest, ponderosa pine forest, eastern deciduous forest, and tall-grass, mixed-grass, and short-grass prairies. This is an edge community for 160 species, including indigo and lazuli buntings, yellow and red-shafter flickers, and Baltimore and Bullock's orioles. Because of cooler, north-facing branch canyons, many plants that have disappeared with climate change on adjacent lands still grow in the river valley.

Grasslands grow a mix of grasses, including needle-and-thread, grama, little and big bluestem, and switchgrass, as well as common milkweed, yucca, sunflowers, coneflowers, and wild rose. Ponderosa pine forest grows on the eastern valley, with the nearest larger forest in South Dakota's Black Hills. Eastern deciduous forest of bur oak, American elm, green ash, basswood, black walnut, and hackberry grows through the valley. This community includes a variety of shrubs and vines as well as tree species including sumac, western snowberry, wild plum, wild grape, and gooseberry. North-facing slopes contain the northern boreal forest ecosystem, which is characterized by paper birch, ferns, mosses, and a unique hybrid of quaking and bigtooth aspen. Scientists believe this latter community is a preserved remnant of the Pleistocene ecosystem of the Great Plains.

Invasive species include leafy spurge, purple loosestrife, Canada thistle, and spotted knapweed. The Nature Conservancy, which owns 25 miles of land along the scenic river called the Niobrara Valley Preserve, is working to control these plants. The University of Nebraska-Lincoln maintains an experimental ground where it researches techniques for eradicating purple loosestrife. The National Park Service has sprayed to control that species as well as Canada thistle and leafy spurge. It also works with private landowners to help them control invasive species on their land.

This biological crossroads provides habitat for mule deer, elk, pronghorn, bison, beaver, mink, and coyote. Herons and kingfishers roam the river shores. Overall, 581 plants, 213 birds, 86 lichen, 70 butterfly, 44 mammal, 25 fish, 17 reptile, and 8 amphibian species live here. Along the river is the Fort Niobrara National Wildlife Refuge that maintains habitat for elk and some 400 bison. After a five-year monitoring program, the eastern stretch of the scenic river was designated critical habitat for piping plover (threatened), least tern (endangered), western prairie-fringed orchid (threatened), and blowout penstemon (endangered).

The area is managed jointly by the National Park Service, the U.S. Fish and Wildlife Service, state agencies, and the Nature Conservancy. Canoeing, kayaking, and tubing are popular here, with Class I and II rapids. Fishing is also permitted. One dam, the Cornell Dam on the Fort Niobrara National Wildlife Refuge, interrupts the scenic stretch of river. Although the dam is no longer in operation, it prevents the upstream migration of species as well as the hydrology of the upper stretch of the river. Staff monitors water quality, looking for chemicals, dissolved oxygen, pH, turbidity, and conductivity.

Further Reading
Johnsgard, Paul A. *The Niobrara: A River Running through Time*. Lincoln: University of Nebraska Press, 2007.

OGLALA NATIONAL GRASSLAND

Oglala National Grassland covers 94,520 acres in the northwest corner of the state known as the high plains of Nebraska. The area is administered by the U.S. Forest Service, which manages it jointly with the Nebraska National Forest, the Samuel R. McKelvie National Forest, and Buffalo Gap and Fort Pierre National Grasslands. Collectively, this area is called the Nebraska National Forest and stretches across central and western Nebraska and central and western South Dakota. Native ponderosa pine and mixed-grass prairies combine in an unusual array of landscapes. Three reservoirs—Agate, Bordgate, and Rock Bass—provide open-water habitat. Meanwhile, human-planted forests in the Sandhills region of the McKelvie National Forest and Bessey Ranger District are an unusual feature to the U.S. Forest Service. The Charles E. Bessey Nursery is an important historical center for ecological studies, as well as the oldest federal tree nursery in the United States.

Wildlife includes the black-footed ferret, North America's most endangered mammal. Few tree species exist here, but over 250 species of grasses thrive. Badland formations and fossils are located in Toadstool Geologic Park. A one-mile loop interpretive trail explains erosion processes at work here. The entire acreage of Oglala National Grassland is open to off-road vehicles. Rock hounding is permitted. Visitors may collect rocks, minerals, gemstones, and fossils, with the exception of vertebrate fossils.

Archaeological excavations at Hudson-Meng Bison Kill unveiled the largest Alberta-culture bison kill site, dated to 10,000 years ago. They found more than 600 bison remains here; some bones contained stone tools, though this information remains controversial. The grassland maintains a museum with this collection of artifacts.

Oglala National Grassland. (Kevin Saff)

Further Reading

Worster, Donald. *Nature's Economy: A History of Ecological Ideas*. New York: Cambridge
    University Press, 1994.

VALENTINE NATIONAL WILDLIFE REFUGE

Established in 1935, Valentine National Wildlife Refuge preserves 71,516 acres of the
Nebraska Sandhills—the largest single expanse of mid- and tall-grass prairie in the
United States. Tall-grass prairie, marshes, and lakes provide refuge for migrating birds.
Blue-winged teal, pintails, gadwalls, redheads, mallards, shovelers, ruddy ducks, herons,
terns, shorebirds, and pelicans nest here, while many other ducks stop for food and rest.
Ducks can number 150,000 during migration peaks. Sandhill cranes migrate through,
and bald and golden eagles winter here. Grasslands host prairie chickens and sharp-
tailed grouse. In all, over 260 species of birds have been recorded at Valentine National
Wildlife Refuge.

Nebraska's Sandhills were the bed of an ancient sea located west of what is now the
state line. Winds from the west blew the sand to its current location, forming a series of
rolling dunes. Grasses established in the dunes and hold the dunes together. Natural pools
and lakes formed from precipitation, while the rising water table irrigated lush meadows.

Valentine National Wildlife Refuge is managed along with Fort Niobrara National Wildlife Refuge. Staff manages grasslands and wetlands for wildlife, using cattle grazing and prescribed fire to maintain healthy growth. Mule and white-tailed deer, muskrats, beaver, mink, weasels, and raccoon find food and shelter in refuge habitats.

Further Reading

Jones, Stephen R. *The Last Prairie: A Sandhills Journey.* Lincoln: University of Nebraska Press, 2006.

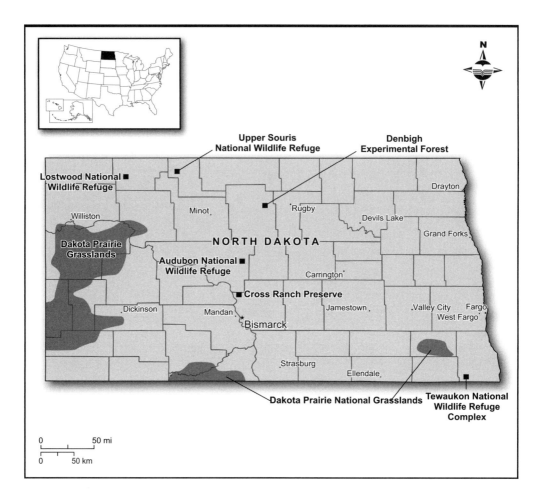

Audubon National Wildlife Refuge, 76
Cross Ranch Preserve, 77
Dakota Prairie National Grasslands, 78
Denbigh Experimental Forest, 79
Lostwood National Wildlife Refuge, 80
Tewaukon National Wildlife Refuge Complex, 81
Upper Souris National Wildlife Refuge, 82

NORTH DAKOTA

From the Red River Valley in the east, through the Drift Prairie's rolling hills, to the southwestern badlands, North Dakota's landscape reflects the transition from Midwest to the Great Plains. North Dakota is reputedly the least-visited of the 50 United States, but its wetlands lure millions of migrating birds along the central fly zone. It was also among President Theodore Roosevelt's inspirations to create federal protection for natural places.

Like most Great Plains states, agriculture directs North Dakota's economy. Over 90 percent of the state's land area is farmland, rendering the population of barely 700,000 largely rural in character. It is the country's largest producer of barley, sunflowers, and durum wheat and also has significant cattle, soybean, and corn industries. Underground stores of oil and coal add the promise of great economic potential. In the late 1980s and early 1990s the energy industry sought North Dakota's coal deposits, resulting in air pollution from a growing number of coal-fired plants.

Extraction of North Dakota's rich natural resources have disturbed much of its land. Its remaining natural places are the focus of protection efforts, and restoration and mitigation projects, aimed at stabilizing and minimizing human impact. Projects currently underway across the state involve plains habitat restoration, watershed stability, and ecosystem support. The state of North Dakota maintains nature preserves and has created wetlands in the southwestern region to provide habitat for resident and migrating avian species. They organize wildlife concerns and agricultural interests toward common goals. Supported by legislation such as the North American Wetlands Conservation Act, several programs across the state have successfully established and reintroduced native wildlife. Wetlands act as a filter and improve water quality.

AUDUBON NATIONAL WILDLIFE REFUGE

In 1955, the U.S. Fish and Wildlife Service set aside the land that is now Audubon National Wildlife Refuge as Snake Creek National Wildlife Refuge. They renamed it in 1967, honoring 19th-century naturalist and artist John James Audubon, who came to this area in the summer of 1843. Wetlands, native prairie, and planted grasslands combine here to create habitat for native and migratory birds, including various endangered and threatened species. On the refuge lands, 243 avian species have been recorded, along with 34 species of mammal, 5 of reptile, 4 amphibian, and 37 fish species. Sharp-tailed grouse, fox, coyote, and white-tailed deer reside in over 3,000 acres of wetlands.

The wetlands of the Audubon National Wildlife Refuge were formed over 10,000 years ago by melting glaciers, creating what are known as prairie potholes. This area is part of a larger Prairie Pothole Region that runs from Canada through South Dakota, eastern Montana, and east to Minnesota and western Iowa.

The Audubon National Wildlife Refuge contains 14,735 acres. Audubon Lake is the centerpiece of the refuge and is owned by the U.S. Army Corps of Engineers. The lake is managed through a system of pumps and siphons that move water from the lake to wetland areas if needed. One hundred islands form 450 acres of nesting ground for geese and ducks, as well as Baird and Le Conte's sparrows. Threatened piping plovers nest here as well. Shorebirds, marbled godwits, upland sandpipers, northern harriers, bobolinks, western meadowlarks, gulls, terns, rails, and sandhill and whooping cranes (endangered) use this habitat. Short-eared owls and silver-haired bats come out at night, eating moths and flies.

The Audubon National Wildlife Refuge is managed primarily for waterfowl. Staff members ensure an abundance of food and cover. Locals plant crops on refuge land, harvesting a percentage and leaving the rest for wildlife. Haying and grazing revives grass and soil. Prescribed burning controls invasive species while spurring the growth of native plants and enriching the soil.

Part of the Audubon National Wildlife Refuge Complex, this conglomeration of land includes U.S. Fish and Wildlife Service and private lands and easement refuges, on which landowners agree to management by the U.S. Fish and Wildlife Service. Easement areas include Camp Lake, Hiddenwood, Lake Nettie, Lake Otis, Lake Patricia, Lost Lake, McLean, Pretty Rock, Sheyenne Lake, Stewart Lake, and White Lake National Wildlife Refuges. Federally owned land is found at Lake Ilo and Audubon Wetland Management District.

Interpretive displays explain the ecology of wetlands and prairie. There is a one-mile interpretive trail and a seven-and-a-half-mile auto tour route. The National Wildlife Refuge leads environmental education programs, bird-watching classes, and boat tours. Ice fishing in Lake Audubon can yield walleye, perch, and northern pike. Hunting for deer, pheasant, grouse, and partridge is regulated and permitted in season.

Further Reading
Butcher, Russell D. *America's National Wildlife Refuges, 2nd Edition: A Complete Guide*. Lanham, MD: Rowman and Littlefield, 2008.

Dolin, Eric Jay. *Smithsonian Book of National Wildlife Refuges*. Washington, DC: Smithsonian Institution Press, 2003.

CROSS RANCH PRESERVE

The 5,593-acre Cross Ranch Preserve, managed by the Nature Conservancy, lies along the only free-flowing section of the Missouri River in North Dakota. It protects increasingly rare floodplain forests along the river and is the largest such stretch in the state. Adjacent hillsides are filled with upland mixed-grass prairie, one of the world's most threatened habitats.

Three ecological communities coexist within the preserve: riparian woodlands and forest, ravine woodlands, and mixed-grass prairie. Riparian woodlands and forest where cottonwoods and willows used to thrive are seeing these species replaced with green ash, boxelder, and American elm. Flooding of the Missouri River is managed further upstream, allowing only spring floods. Cottonwoods and willows require such moisture throughout the year. Ravine woodlands are important habitats, providing enough moisture for burr oaks, buffaloberry, hawthorn, box elder, quaking aspen, American elm, and basswood. The preserve's mixed-grass prairie contains needle-and-thread, blue grama, junegrass, little bluestem, and buffalo grass. Nonnative species include smooth brome, crested wheatgrass, and Kentucky bluegrass.

White-tailed and mule deer graze on these lands. Coyote, badger, and raccoon are also common. Nearly 100 bird species use Cross Ranch Preserve, including rare Baird's sparrows and Sprague's pipits. Three rare butterflies have been recorded here: regal fritillary, Dakota skipper, and Ottoe skipper. Bison were original natives and were returned in 1986 to restore the native wildlife and landscape. Fish and bird populations dependent upon the river have suffered in numbers due to human management of the river, which changed its course. Local endangered species include least terns, piping plovers, migrating whooping cranes, pallid sturgeon, and bald eagles.

Cross Ranch Preserve and the adjacent Cross Ranch State Park are listed as an archaeological district on the National Register of Historic Places, ensuring preservation of Archaic period artifacts, as well as the remains of a pioneer homestead, including a family cemetery. The Nature Conservancy manages the land, using prescribed fire and rotational grazing of both bison and cattle. It controls invasive species and restores prairie and wetland ecosystems. Nearly 600 acres are owned by private (farmers, ranchers, landowners) or state (North Dakota Parks and Recreation) entities, who partner with the Nature Conservancy to ensure the continued health of these ecosystems. Cross Ranch Preserve was the Nature Conservancy's first site in North Dakota, established in 1982.

Further Reading
Birchard, Bill. *Nature's Keepers: The Remarkable Story of How the Nature Conservancy Became the Largest Environmental Group in the World*. Hoboken, NJ: Jossey-Bass, 2005.
Mork, Andy. *North Dakota's Missouri River*. Mandan, ND: Crain Grosinger, 2003.

DAKOTA PRAIRIE NATIONAL GRASSLANDS

Over one million acres make up of a patchwork of federal, state, and private lands known collectively as the Dakota Prairie National Grasslands. The Sheyenne National Grassland features rolling hills and tall-grass prairie, and Little Missouri National Grassland is a dramatic badland. Cedar River and Grand River National Grasslands are comprised of mixed-grass prairie, cottonwood riparian, and woody draws. Three other preserved grasslands are administered by the Department of Agriculture in North Dakota. This region preserves the distinctive character of the northern Great Plains and is a paradise for plant lovers, with 470 plant species from 78 families.

In western North Dakota, Little Missouri National Grasslands' one million acres contain colorful and strange badlands surrounding the Little Missouri River. Badlands are rugged rock formations caused by wind and water. They create a landscape that is difficult for both travel and settlement. The state's highest elevation, White Butte, lies here. Also within this the largest grassland is Theodore Roosevelt National Park, where the former president maintained a ranch. He lived there for the better part of two years from 1884 to 1886 and wrote essays on his experiences for eastern publications. He boldly declared: "I never would have been President if it had not been for my experiences in North Dakota." This area was set aside in 1935 and achieved national park designation in 1978. Nearly 30,000 acres of the park are set aside as the Theodore Roosevelt Wilderness. Roosevelt's Elkhorn Ranch is long gone, but fences mark the outlines of the buildings.

Dakota Prairie National Grasslands. (Niels Batke)

Elk, pronghorn, white-tailed and mule deer, bighorn sheep, coyote, 100 wild horses, and prairie dogs reside within Dakota Prairie National Grasslands. Birds include sharp-tailed grouse, pheasants, wild turkeys, eagles, and falcons. Rattlesnakes and black snakes crawl in the grasslands. About 500 bison graze along the park's two scenic drives. Though gone from this landscape since the early 1880s, bison were reintroduced in the 1950s, when the grassland accepted 29 bison from Nebraska's Fort Niobrara National Wildlife Refuge. Grassland staff keeps bison from wandering onto nearby livestock grazing plots by a wire fence surrounding their allotment. The U.S. Forest Service reintroduced bighorn sheep in the 1950s.

In this sagebrush country, there is little water. Summer temperatures rise to 95° F, and winter is just as harsh, in the opposite extreme, with temperatures below negative 20° F. A significant deposit of petrified wood lies within the national grasslands. Stars and northern lights are visible in the dark skies. Hiking and camping, horseback riding, backpacking, canoeing, fishing, and hunting are allowed. The U.S. Forest Service manages the Dakota Prairie National Grasslands for diverse uses, from scientific investigations of paleontologists and archeologists to livestock grazing, energy production, and recreation.

Further Reading

Jenkinson, Clay S. *Theodore Roosevelt in the Dakota Badlands*. Dickinson, ND: Dickinson State University Press, 2006.

Moul, Francis. *The National Grasslands: A Guide to America's Undiscovered Treasures*. Lincoln: University of Nebraska Press, 2006.

Roosevelt, Theodore. *Big Game Hunting in the Rockies and on the Great Plains, Comprising "Hunting Trips of a Ranchman" and "The Wilderness Hunter."* London: G. P. Putnam's Sons, 1899.

DENBIGH EXPERIMENTAL FOREST

Established in 1931 on land depleted by agricultural and ranching practices, Denbigh Experimental Forest was former prairie turned to sand dunes. President Franklin Delano Roosevelt and the federal government hoped federal management by the U.S. Forest Service and Department of Agriculture of this land would lessen the effects of the Dust Bowl. They planned to build a 100-mile wide "shelterbelt zone" stretching from North Dakota to Texas. The forest shelter would, they hoped, reduce soil erosion and end the debilitating dust storms. They planned a 480,000-acre forest, but these plans were never completed. The U.S. Forest Service purchased 636 acres. North Dakota held an additional 596 acres. In 1971, these two parcels became one, under the management of the U.S. Forest Service.

Denbigh staff members test the success of different tree types in the environment of the northern Great Plains. Of the 40 species planted—specimens from the United States, Europe, and Asia—30 species have succeeded. Among the most prosperous are Scots pine, ponderosa pine, Siberian larch, Black Hills spruce, elaeagnus, and Rocky Mountain juniper. Wildlife has made its home among these trees, including deer, wild turkey, porcupine, elk, and moose.

Experiments at Denbigh have found effective wind-blocking trees. Denbigh Experimental Forest provides 500,000 seedlings each year to communities in need of wind protection for crops. The forest is being put under the administration of Custer National Forest.

LOSTWOOD NATIONAL WILDLIFE REFUGE

In Lostwood National Wildlife Refuge, short- and mixed-grass prairies roll over gentle hills dotted with 4,100 wetlands and hundreds of ponds and potholes. Part of the Prairie Pothole Region, this area has more ducks than any other place in the contiguous United States. Lostwood National Wildlife Refuge is the largest single prairie pothole habitat in the national system. It is a globally important bird area, providing critical breeding ground for the threatened piping plover.

Lostwood National Wildlife Refuge's 26,900 acres hosts aspen groves, western snowberry, needlegrasses, wheatgrasses, gramas, and muhly. The landscape here is an ice moraine feature in the Missouri Coteau. The refuge's wetland habitats provide nesting grounds for an astonishing number of ducks—more than half the U.S. population.

Drought is a serious threat to this landscape, and to all of the northern plains. Environmental Protection Agency scientists report an increase of 1° F in North Dakota over the past century, and they predict a more rapid increase over the next 100 years. Increased evaporation would reduce potholes nationwide to an estimated 800,000 by mid-century. Waterfowl would find less ground for nesting and produce fewer offspring. Refuge staff manages invasive species through prescribed burning and grazing. The refuge established a 5,577-acre wilderness area here in 1975. Recreation includes bird-watching, hiking, and Nordic activities.

Further Reading

Dolin, Eric Jay. *Smithsonian Book of National Wildlife Refuges*. Washington, DC: Smithsonian Institution Press, 2003.

Galatowitsch, Susan M., and Arnold G. Van der Valk. *Restoring Prairie Wetlands: An Ecological Approach*. Hoboken, NJ: John Wiley, 1994.

TEWAUKON NATIONAL WILDLIFE REFUGE COMPLEX

Tewaukon National Wildlife Refuge Complex lies in the Prairie Pothole Region of southeastern North Dakota, along the Red River of the North Valley. The rolling plain is broken by various and diverse wetlands preserved as Tewaukon Wetland Management District. The complex and wetland have served as a safe haven for migratory and nesting birds since 1945. The National Wildlife Refuge Complex protects 35,000 acres of wetlands and 10,000 acres of grasslands. Fourteen thousand acres are designated waterfowl production areas, and 45,581 acres of wetland and grassland on private land have been preserved through conservation easements.

The Tewaukon National Wildlife Refuge Complex is located on the western extreme of the northern tall-grass prairie. Only the Wild Rice River flows through it. Tewaukon sits on the edge of habitats, adding to its diversity. Eastern woodland birds mix with midwestern grassland birds. In all, more than 243 birds use refuge lands. Wetlands are one of the continent's most biologically productive systems, giving food, water, and shelter to waterfowl, shorebirds, leopard frogs, painted turtles, mink, muskrats, tiger salamanders, raccoons, and aquatic vertebrates. Deep-water wetlands host diving ducks such as redheads, ruddy ducks, and canvasbacks, as well as American white pelicans, grebes, and cormorants. The tall-grass prairie provides protection for migrating and nesting birds and butterflies. Indigenous prairie birds include upland sandpiper, bobolink, northern harrier, and short-eared owl. Riparian habitat along the Wild Rice, the Sheyenne, and the Red rivers creates breeding and shelter for birds and mammals. Riparian and lakeside areas are wooded with willows, cottonwoods, bur oaks, and ash. Nesters here include warblers, orioles, woodpeckers, flycatchers, and songbirds. White-tailed deer find cover here to give birth to and nurture newborn fawns. Seasonal residents of the complex include snow buntings, snowy owls, common goldeneyes, buffleheads, and bald eagles in winter; snow and Canada geese, pintails, mallards, golden plovers, lesser yellowlegs, and shorebirds in spring; blue-winged teals, shovelers, gadwalls, western meadowlarks, bobolinks, grasshopper sparrows, regal fritillaries, skippers, and monarch butterflies in summer; red-tailed and rough-legged hawks, peregrine falcons, white snow geese, ducks, and tundra swans in fall.

Much of the land around the complex was farmed beginning in the late 19th century. Local sportsmen organized to preserve and restore land as a refuge for wildlife. Refuge staff has reseeded formerly farmed land with grassland flora. Corn, millet, wheat, and winter rye are still farmed on 500 acres, feeding white-tailed deer and migrating waterfowl. Local farmers who plant the crops harvest a portion, then leave the rest for wildlife. The refuge complex maintains planted grasslands to provide dense cover for nesting mallards, gadwalls, bobolinks, and grasshopper sparrows. Remnants of native tall-grass prairie remain on the landscape in the form of porcupine grass, Indian grass, big bluestem, switchgrass, cordgrass, purple coneflower, Maximillian sunflower, prairie lily, blazing stars, and ladies tresses. Plants here include alfalfa, sweet clover, and wheatgrass. In the 1960s, four dams were built to control the Wild Rice River. The refuge has created hundreds of acres of lakes and marshes, adding nesting areas and shelter for migrating and local waterfowl.

The mission of the Tewaukon National Wildlife Refuge Complex is to "preserve, restore, and enhance the ecological diversity" of native prairie and wetland plants, migratory birds (especially waterfowl), and other native wildlife. It also aims to protect all remaining tall-grass prairie in the region through cooperative agreements, conservation easements, or fee title acquisitions. In addition to reducing nonnative plants, staff members control fires on 5,000 acres of grassland and 200 acres of wetlands to mimic and restore natural conditions. Tewaukon maintains 135 acres of croplands for birds and wildlife. Two lakes—Lake Tewaukon and Sprague Lake—are managed for nonmotorized boating, fishing, and migratory bird habitat. Hunting, wildlife observation, and photography are permitted. The eight-mile Prairie Lake Auto Tour provides a view of this diverse landscape.

Further Reading

Dolin, Eric Jay. *Smithsonian Book of National Wildlife Refuges*. Washington, DC: Smithsonian Institution Press, 2003.

Moul, Francis. *The National Grasslands: A Guide to America's Undiscovered Treasures*. Lincoln: University of Nebraska Press, 2006.

UPPER SOURIS NATIONAL WILDLIFE REFUGE

The 32,000-acre Upper Souris National Wildlife Refuge lies in the Souris River Valley along the Central Flyway migration route of countless waterfowl. Thirty miles of the Souris River are contained within this refuge. The mixture of habitat—from riparian woodlands, floodplains, grasslands, and coulees—has earned it the American Bird Conservancy's designation of globally important bird area.

The 10,000-acre Lake Darling is a dam-created water impoundment, which regulates water flow to marshes here and on the J. Clark Salyer National Wildlife Refuge. Lake Darling holds two years' worth of water to protect the area and its residents from drought. Fishermen catch walleye, yellow perch, northern pike, and smallmouth bass here and in the Souris River. Waterfowl are the highlight of the refuge. During spring and fall migrations, they number 350,000. These include lesser snow geese, pintails, canvasbacks, redheads, buffleheads, tundra swans, grebes, pelicans, Sprague's pipit, and Baird's, Le Conte's, and sharp-tailed sparrows. Cormorants and great blue herons nest near the lake. Endangered piping plovers also find refuge around Lake Darling. A reestablished population of Canada geese has suffered from development and lack of available land suitable to their needs. In all, about 250 avian species use the refuge.

Upper Souris National Wildlife Refuge was established in 1935 by J. Clark Salyer (of the Bureau of Biological Survey), who purchased this land and that of three other

Upper Souris National Wildlife Refuge. (Johnida Dockens)

refuges, all on the Souris River. Waterfowl of the Great Plains were devastated as much by the dry conditions of the Dust Bowl as were its human residents. In 1934, the Bureau of Biological Survey, headed by Jay N. "Ding" Darling, established a program to raise money for refuges. Each hunter of waterfowl was required to purchase a federal duck stamp, and the money was used to protect land for waterfowl survival.

Today the U.S. Fish and Wildlife Service manages the refuge. The primary goal is to provide habitat for migrating and breeding birds. It also grazes, hays, and burns grasslands for grazing mammals, such as white-tailed deer, pronghorn, and occasional elk and moose. Small mammals live in this habitat as well, including muskrats, raccoons, and mink. Visitors can take in the scenery and wildlife from the three-and-a-half-mile Prairie-Marsh Scenic Drive. Hiking, canoeing, and cross-country skiing are popular. Hunters come for deer, sharp-tailed grouse, ring-necked pheasant, and Hungarian partridge.

Further Reading

Sullivan, Noelle, and Nicholas Peterson Vrooman. *M-e Ecci Aashi Awadi: The Knife River Indian Villages*. Medora, ND: Theodore Roosevelt Nature & History Association, 1995.

Tekiela, Stan. *Birds of the Dakotas Field Guide*. Cambridge, MN: Adventure Publications, 2003.

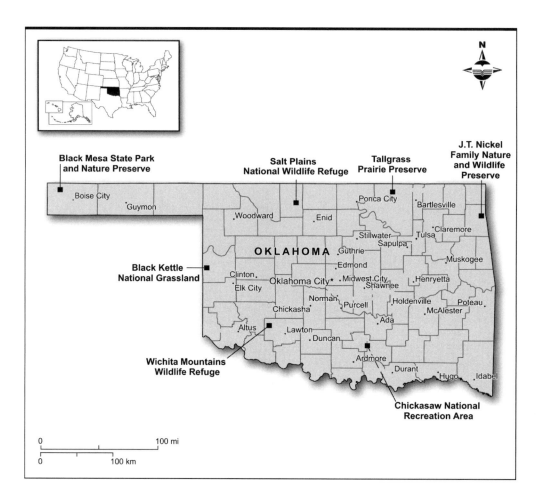

Black Kettle National Grassland, 86

Black Mesa State Park and Nature Preserve, 87

Chickasaw National Recreation Area, 88

J. T. Nickel Family Nature and Wildlife Preserve, 89

Salt Plains National Wildlife Refuge, 90

Tallgrass Prairie Preserve, 92

Wichita Mountains Wildlife Refuge, 92

OKLAHOMA

Oklahoma is among the nation's most geographically diverse states. It contains 11 ecological regions. Four mountain ranges, semi-arid high plains, canyon and mesa landscapes, prairie, and woodlands mark this diversity. Although much of Oklahoma's native prairies have been converted to agriculture, the Tallgrass Prairie Preserve is the world's largest preserved tallgrass prairie.

Oklahoma was initially devalued by Euro-American settlers. In the 1830s, the federal government set it aside for the relocation of Native American peoples, primarily those in the South—the Chocktaw, Cherokee, Chickasaw, Creek, and Seminole. By the end of the 19th century, cattle trails and railroads cut through the landscape. The U.S. government opened the region for settlement in 1889. Oklahoma's thin but fertile soils were severely affected by the Dust Bowl of the 1930s. Conservation efforts in the years that followed helped the soil recover, but drought concerns led to the construction of hundreds of dams, disturbing natural waterways. Oklahoma is still a top producer of wheat and cattle, but it t was oil that put Oklahoma on the map again economically. More recently, the state has focused on developing and harnessing wind power technology. But debate rages on this issue; while wind power is a clean technology, there are drawbacks to this natural resource. Turbines and wind farms endanger migrating fowl and threaten ground-nesting native birds. Transmission lines necessary to carry energy interrupt scenic landscapes.

As do many other states, Oklahoma directs a great deal of energy and effort toward ecosystem restoration with the ultimate goal of providing safe, sustainable habitat for rare and endangered species. The prairie expanses that used to cover Oklahoma were home to many species important to their natural environments and to the human populations that now inhabit these areas. State programs support habitats of every type in the effort to reestablish the natural health and character of Oklahoma. Wetlands, prairies, forests, and watersheds across the state benefit from public and private interest creating a cleaner environment.

Black Kettle National Grassland

Black Kettle National Grassland encompasses 31,300 acres, all but 576 of which are in Oklahoma. Texas's Lake Marvin Recreation Area contains those acres, as well as the 1,449-acre McClellan Creek National Grassland, administered along with the Black Kettle National Grassland as part of the Cibola National Forest, a 1.6-million acre interrupted landscape with land in New Mexico, Texas, and Oklahoma. The U.S. Department of Agriculture (USDA) acquired land here in the late 1930s to restore damage from the Dust Bowl. In the 1950s, the land passed to the U.S. Forest Service. Black Kettle was designated a national grassland in 1960.

The lands here were opened to homesteading in 1892, followed by a few decades of agricultural success. By the 1930s, however, the region was depleted. Drought and wind swept away soil. With nothing growing in it, loose topsoil flooded away when rains came. In 1938, the USDA's Soil Conservation Service began to reseed, plant trees, install fences and windmills, and construct structures for flood control.

Upland mixed-grass prairie blooms with big bluestem, Indian grass, little bluestem, side-oats grama, buffalo grass, shinnery oak, sagebrush, and sand plum. In the hills, short-grass prairie, sagebrush, and mesquite grow. Bottoms are home to cottonwood, elm, and hackberry. Water covers 10 percent of the landscape, making this the wettest grassland, with four manmade lakes, hundreds of stock ponds, springs, streams, and the Washita River. A rare shinnery oak community is here; these environments are shrinking across the United States.

This area is a transition zone between east-west and north-south species, creating a great diversity of flora and fauna, including white-tailed and mule deer, Rio Grande wild turkey, cottontail and jack rabbits, coyote, bobcat, porcupine, armadillo, raccoon, beaver, bald eagles, doves, waterfowl, hawks, owls, Mississippi kite, scissor-tailed flycatcher, monarch butterflies, and bobwhite quail. Waters are filled with catfish, saugeye, black bass, and pan fish.

Staff maintains food for native wildlife by planting a few agricultural plots each year of ragweed and sunflower. The grasslands are also used for cattle range, and 60 permits are granted for cattle grazing on the grassland. Windmills provide water for the herds. The Black Kettle National Grassland sits in the Anadarko Basin, which has provided oil and gas since the 1950s. Twenty-one wells exist on the Grassland. Old wells are plugged and staff members revegetate these sites. Prescribed burns regenerate native grasses and keep out eastern red cedar, an invasive species. Other unwanted vegetation, including scotch thistle, is sprayed or dug out. Recreation is managed at the Black Kettle Recreation Area, Skipout Lake, and Spring Creek Lake, and the opportunities include camping, boating, hunting, picnicking, hiking, fishing, and wildlife viewing.

Further Reading

Butcher, Russell D. *America's National Wildlife Refuges, 2nd Edition: A Complete Guide*. Lanham, MD: Rowman and Littlefield, 2008.

Moul, Francis. *The National Grasslands: A Guide to America's Undiscovered Treasures*. Lincoln: University of Nebraska Press, 2006.

BLACK MESA STATE PARK AND NATURE PRESERVE

Black Mesa is the highest point in the state of Oklahoma, standing 4,973 feet above sea level. Black Mesa State Park and Nature Preserve protects 1,600 acres, just over half of the mesa top, along with talus slopes and short-grass prairie habitat. Twenty-three rare plant species and eight rare animal species exist in four ecological communities. Bluestem grama grows on top of the mesa, while talus slopes are covered with one-seed juniper–shrub oak community; other buttes have juniper-piñon forest.

Black Mesa State Park and Nature Preserve represents a transition zone between plains and mountain, marking the edge for short-grass prairie and Rocky Mountain species. Black bears, bobcats, mountain lions, mule deer, swift foxes, pronghorns, rock squirrels, and Texas horned lizards use this habitat. Prairie dogs roam the short-grass prairie. Birds include golden eagles, Chihuahuan ravens, curve-billed thrashers, common bushtits, scaled quails, black-billed magpies, piñon jays, burrowing owls, long-billed curlews, and ferruginous hawks.

The fossilized skeleton of a 65-foot long brontosaurus, dinosaur footprint fossils, and petrified trees (possibly sequoia relatives) have been found at Black Mesa State Park and Nature Preserve. Human use dates to cliff dwellers some 15,000 to 20,000 years ago. Archaeologists have found pictographs and uncovered evidence of pumpkin and corn propagation, which could make this one of the earliest agricultural sites in the United States. A remarkable historic artifact is an inscription on a canyon wall stating, "Coronatto, 1541," made by Spanish explorer Frances Vasquez de Coronado, one of the first Europeans to explore the continent.

Black Mesa State Park Nature Preserve. (Steven Wagner)

Black Mesa extends into neighboring New Mexico and Colorado for 45 miles. Basaltic lava rock sits atop mesas; its dark color gives the preserve its name. The Cimarron River cuts through the landscape. The Nature Conservancy formerly managed the preserved land and transferred it to the Oklahoma Tourism and Recreation Department in 1991. This transfer included restrictions on use and development meant to maintain the area's natural state. Lake Carl Etling, a 200-acre manmade lake created by a dam on Carrizzo Creek, is popular for boating and fishing.

Further Reading

Day, Arthur Grove. *Coronado's Quest: The Discovery of the Southwestern States*. Westport, CT: Greenwood, 1982.

CHICKASAW NATIONAL RECREATION AREA

First created in 1902 as Sulphur Springs Reservation, renamed Platt National Park four years later, this land was combined with Arbuckle National Recreation Area in 1976 to create its current entity—Chickasaw National Recreation Area. The recreation area was first reserved when the Chickasaw tribe sold it to the U.S. government in order to protect the water resources from private development.

The Chickasaw called the place "peaceful valley of rippling waters." The landscape is a transition zone between eastern deciduous forests and western prairies. Sycamore, willows, and cottonwoods line the rivers. Prairie grasses, prickly pear cacti, and yucca decorate prairies. Small mammals such as mice, rats, shrews, squirrels, bats, and voles live here, along with badgers, opossums, weasels, rabbits, armadillos, beavers, foxes, raccoons, mink, skunks, bobcats, bison, wild turkeys, and white-tailed deer. Six species of toads and eight species of frogs occupy this moist environment, along with salamanders, lizards, nine species of turtles, and more than 30 species of snakes. Six bison were brought here from the Wichita Mountains National Wildlife Refuge in 1920. Chickasaw National Recreation Area maintains a pasture for this herd, representing the original herds that were eliminated by the end of the 19th century.

Mineral springs, cool water, and shade have long made Chickasaw National Recreation Area a place of respite for humans and wildlife. The calcium carbonate–rich waters of Travertine Creek form their own rock. When the mineral is exposed to air, it precipitates into deposits that form travertine rock. The largest stream, Rock Creek, drains 170 square miles and provides habitat for fish. The cold-water mineral springs of Chickasaw National Recreation Area contain sulfer, bromide, and iron. The park has constructed pools and pavilions for soaking in these mineral waters. Sulfer springs include Hillside Spring, Pavilion Spring, and Black Sulphur Spring; Medicine and Bromide springs are bromide waters; Flower Park has muddy pools of sulfer water.

Two springs in the eastern portion feed the rest of the Chickasaw National Recreation Area's waterways: Buffalo Spring and Antelope Spring. A 67-acre manmade lake,

Chickasaw National Recreation Area. (Topheth)

Veterans Lake, hosts Canada geese during their migrations, and fish include largemouth, spotted, and white bass; shiners, sunfish, catfish, dace, carp, shad, and minnows. Boating, swimming, fishing, hiking, hunting, horseback riding, and mountain biking are some of the recreational activities available. Early examples of National Park Service rustic-style buildings created by the Civilian Conservation Corps are still here. Between 1933 and 1940 the corps and the National Park Service built pavilions, campgrounds, picnic areas, dams, waterfalls, roads, and trails. They also planted over half a million trees and shrubs.

J. T. Nickel Family Nature and Wildlife Preserve

This young preserve is the largest private preserve in the Ozarks, with 17,000 acres overlooking the Illinois River. Owned and maintained by the Nature Conservancy, the J. T. Nickel Family Nature and Wildlife Preserve may be the last tract of preservable Oklahoma-Ozarks environments. Many of the plants here do not exist outside the Ozark Mountains. It is a key conservation area for the ensured future of biodiversity in the Ozarks Ecoregion.

Nickel Preserve is primarily managed for bird habitat. Fragmentation of habitat can be as damaging for bird numbers as complete loss of habitat, so the goal is to provide consistent expanses. The Ozarks contain a few endemic and rare species of salamanders, including ringed, western slimy, Oklahoma gray-bellied, Ozark zigzag, grotto, and dark-sided salamanders. Nickel Preserve monitors these species, which are indicator species of the health of the larger ecosystem. It studies populations in different areas of the forest to learn which management practices best suit these species' needs. Caves contain threatened Ozark big-eared bats as well as unique invertebrates like Ozark cave amphipods, Ozark cavefish, and Hensley's cave isopods. After a few years of fire management to create suitable grazing land, 20 elk were reintroduced to the preserve in 2005. Historically, elk are thought to have helped ecological diversity through their grazing practices. The original native subspecies, North American elk, are extinct, so Rocky Mountain elk were chosen for the reintroduction. Deer and turkey also live in the preserve.

Riparian forests consist of Shumard oak, sycamore, cottonwood, hackberry, elm, hickory, vines, and ground cover. Most of Nickel Preserve is a former cattle ranch with Bermuda and fescue grasses now being replaced by the Nature Conservancy with tallgrass prairie and woodland. One hundred acres have been planted every year with six native grasses and several wildflowers. Prescribed burns have restored woodlands and diversity. Wildfire suppression had reduced plant diversity and allowed invasive species such as sericea lespendeza, Johnsongrass, thistles, multiflora rose, privet, and Nepalese browntop to flourish. Water contamination is a threat to the region's biodiversity, caused by bad land management practices elsewhere and in the past. The Nature Conservancy brings in private landowners to learn land management practices compatible with conservation of the region. The Ozark chinquapin, a small chestnut tree, has been devastated by chestnut blight. Long a staple in Ozark folklore, it used to be found throughout the region. Scientists are developing a blight-resistant tree by crossing Ozark chinquapin with Chinese chestnut. The breeding process takes years to propagate. The Nature Conservancy imagines it will have a blight-resistant tree in 20 or 30 years.

Further Reading

Freinkel, Susan. *American Chestnut: The Life, Death, and Rebirth of a Perfect Tree*. Berkeley: University of California Press, 2007.

Salt Plains National Wildlife Refuge

Salt Plains National Wildlife Refuge is 32,000 acres of nearly equal parts barren salt flat, open water, and vegetated stretches of wetland, prairie, woodland, and farm. The salt flat is a 10,000-acre stretch of barren land created by deposits from an ancient body of water. Millions of years ago, the water was cut off from the sea. Salinized water evaporated, leaving a thick crust of salt in its place. The salt plains are extremely flat, with a slope of only four to eight feet leading down to the reservoir. Vegetation is scarce.

Groundwater picks up saline and, in one area, combines with gypsum, creating selenite crystals just beneath the surface. These crystals are brown from iron oxide in the soil and contain unique hourglass-shaped clay particles from being formed in wet soil.

Some 312 species of birds use Salt Plains National Wildlife Refuge for habitat, migration stops, or nesting. It provides critical habitat for whooping cranes that migrate through in fall and spring and is a member of the Western Hemisphere Shorebird Reserve Network—an international alliance protecting over 22 million acres of habitat. It is an important nesting site for American avocets, endangered interior least terns, and threatened western snowy plovers. At its peak, the refuge hosts 100,000 migrating geese and 70,000 migrating ducks, along with American white pelicans, whooping and sandhill cranes, and bald eagles. The ivory-colored salt flats provide camouflage for eggs, which some birds lay directly on the ground. Whooping cranes enjoy the lack of vegetation at water's edge that prevents hidden predators.

Salt Plains National Wildlife Refuge is managed to provide water and vegetation for birds. American lotus, cattails, and cottonwood trees provide natural food and shelter. In one 70-acre pond, cattails and young cottonwood are too dense for ducks to use, so refuge staff controls this vegetation with disking, mowing, and burning. The refuge manages farming, grazing, water, and fire on its land. There are 15 managed agricultural fields. Puterbaugh Field is planted with wheat and cowpeas to provide feed for deer, turkey, and quail. Manmade ponds and marshes are filled with wild millet, alkali bulrush, and smartweed. Water management mimics the natural precipitation cycle while ensuring proper feed for migrating waterfowl. School Marsh Overlook is drained in spring, bringing herons, egrets, and white-faced ibis in to feed on the crayfish, minnows, and insects. The marsh is then planted with Japanese millet that nourishes mallards and green-winged teal in the fall. Thirty species of mammals also use the refuge, including white-tailed deer, opossums, beavers, raccoons, coyote, and bobcats.

In 1811, Indian Agent Major George C. Sibley was the first white to see the Salt Plains. Osage Indians guided him here. Many tribes, including the Cherokee, gathered salt from these plains, which was valuable for meat preservation. The U.S. government gave ownership of the area to the Cherokee, and they gave it back in 1890, when it was opened to homesteading. Not unsurprisingly, no one settled here and it remained public land, with people—mostly cattlemen—gathering salt by the wagonload. It was also good hunting ground for waterfowl and grazing game like deer and bison. The National Wildlife Refuge was established in 1930. Great Salt Plains Lake was created in 1940. The artificial Ralstin Island is a nesting ground for heron, egret, and ibis. In 1941, the U.S. Army Corps of Engineers constructed a dam on the Salt Fork of the Arkansas River, creating the Great Salt Plains Reservoir. During World War II, the expanse of the plains was used for target practice. A one-mile nature trail and a two-and-a-half-mile auto tour route allow access to the Salt Plains National Wildlife Refuge. Crystal collecting in the region is popular.

Further Reading

Dolin, Eric Jay. *Smithsonian Book of National Wildlife Refuges*. Washington, DC: Smithsonian Institution Press, 2003.

TALLGRASS PRAIRIE PRESERVE

Oklahoma's Tallgrass Prairie Preserve is the largest expanse of remaining tall-grass prairie in the world. The Nature Conservancy owns 39,000 acres and has restored the land to near-native conditions with big bluestem, wild rye, and other native grasses, some of which can grow up to 10 feet tall. The Nature Conservancy began restoration in 1989, when it purchased the land; now, more than 300 species of grasses, forbs, and flowers grow here. Over 400 total plant species occupy the preserve.

Conservancy management includes mimicking natural processes of prairie renewal; prescribed fires and buffalo grazing keep shrubs and trees at bay. About one-third of the rangeland is burned each year in a practice called patch burn, which allows diversity of species in a patchwork of vegetation. Invasive species such as sericea lespedeza and eastern red cedar threaten the restoration project. Erosion and stream degradation are also problems.

The conservancy reintroduced bison here in 1993. A ranch donated 300 individuals; the herd has grown as planned and fluctuates between 2,000 and 2,600 individual free-range bison. Staff vaccinates calves for brucellosis, new animals are tested to prevent the spread of brucellosis and tuberculosis, and the entire herd is vaccinated and treated for parasites annually. The Nature Conservancy provides salt and minerals to supplement bison diet, but no other food or water. It sells mature bulls and cows.

The Nature Conservancy views its restoration as a model for future ranchers to practice grazing techniques in tune with the natural landscape where cattle and wildlife coexist. It offers conservation easements for cooperating landowners. In 2004, the conservancy completed the Tallgrass Prairie Ecological Research Station to encourage further scientific investigations. There are more than 30 ongoing research projects, some in coordination with Oklahoma State University. The preserve maintains driving tours and hiking trails for visitors.

WICHITA MOUNTAINS WILDLIFE REFUGE

Southwestern Oklahoma is home to the oldest wildlife program managed by the U.S. Fish and Wildlife Service: Wichita Mountains Wildlife Refuge. Its 59,020 acres represent mixed-grass prairie, which, because of the rocky soil, was largely spared the damaging effects of the plow. The refuge is managed primarily for the survival of big game herds—American bison, Rocky Mountain elk, white-tailed deer, and Texas longhorn cattle.

The Wichita Mountains are 500 million years old. They were formed when silt deposits grew into mountains and then were eroded to knobs and domes. In its prairie, ravine, and mountain environments grow 806 plant species. Bunchgrasses proliferate on the prairie. Mixedoak forest includes post and blackjack oaks, as well as a disjunctive population of bigtooth maple—the nearest population is 400 miles away in western Texas. Fifty mammal species, 240 species of birds, 36 of fish, and 64 of reptiles and amphibians live in the habitats at Wichita Mountains Wildlife Refuge. Nine-banded armadillos, black-tailed prairie dogs, wild turkeys, raccoons, opossums, and red-tailed hawks are common. One endangered bird, the black-capped vireo, breeds only in the south-central United States and north-central Mexico. Loss of habitat and attacks on nests by brown-headed cowbirds (nest parasitism) has reduced numbers drastically; in neighboring Kansas, the bird had disappeared by the 1930s. Refuge staff conducts surveys, listens for their distinctive song, and records visual sightings. In 2005, studies estimated 1,250 birds on the refuge, which indicates a rise due to successful habitat management.

Bison, elk, and white-tailed deer share range with Texas longhorn cattle. The refuge reintroduced these wild species after their local disappearances. The original elk subspecies, Merriam's elk, were extinct by 1875. (Some say it was the Manitoban elk subspecies, which is also extinct.) In 1911, the refuge reintroduced five Rocky Mountain elk from the National Elk Refuge in Jackson, Wyoming in place of these former natives. The following year, 15 more arrived. Now the herd numbers 800. Staff manages native white-tailed deer through public hunting to maintain a herd of 450. More than this number would cause competition for other grazers, and the refuge prioritizes species diversity.

Bison were locally extinct but reintroduced in 1907. The American Bison Society, formed in 1905 to save the nearly extinct species, transported 15 head to the then-named Wichita National Forest and Game Preserve from the New York Zoological Park. Today, 650 bison are currently in the herd. U.S. Fish and Wildlife staff monitor, test, and vaccinate the herd for diseases; they auction excess animals to support the refuge. Texas longhorn cattle were introduced in 1927 to represent historic cattle populations. The subspecies was first introduced to North America (via Mexico) in 1521. It was once the main beef source in the United States, but breeding has made them rare. These longhorn represent a historic introduction. More recent reintroductions to Wichita Mountains Wildlife Refuge include river otters, burrowing owls, and prairie dogs.

In 1901, this land, which was originally part of the Comanche-Kiowa-Apache Indian Reservation, was set aside as the Wichita Forest Reserve. In 1905, President Theodore Roosevelt renamed it the Wichita Game Preserve. Roosevelt hunted wolf here, staying at Camp Doris, now a public campground. The area earned its current name and designation as a national wildlife refuge in 1936. Rock climbing, hiking, fishing, wildlife watching, and photography are common visitor activities. Popular rock climbing routes are Mount Scott, the Narrows, Elk Mountain, Crab Eyes, and Lost Dome. The refuge did not regulate climbing until 1996, when the sport's increasing popularity brought more climbers, causing soil erosion, trail degradation, litter, and controversy over fixed anchors and bolts. The Wichita Mountains Climbers Coalition now advises the refuge on any new anchor placement, and climbers are prohibited from placing or removing these fixtures. Wichita Mountains is the second most visited national wildlife refuge in the system. More than 22,000 acres are designated for public use, including the 5,700-acre Charons Garden Wilderness Area.

Further Reading

Dolin, Eric Jay. *Smithsonian Book of National Wildlife Refuges*. Washington, DC: Smithsonian Institution Press, 2003.

Worcester, Don. *Texas Longhorn: Relic of the Past, Asset for the Future*. College Station: Texas A&M University Press, 1994.

SOUTH DAKOTA

Ninety percent of South Dakota is covered with grass and farm land. Some of the state's most well-known scenic areas, however, are those that break away from the monotonous prairie—the Black Hills and the Badlands. Both became iconic landscapes of the Wild West after an 1874 expedition led by General Custer found gold in the Black Hills. The landscape became dotted with gold rush towns. The legacy of South Dakota's industrial history provides some interesting challenges to environmental conservation efforts.

The Badlands of south-central South Dakota encompass 250,000 acres of the planet's richest Oligocene fossil bed, dating back 30 million years. It is also home to wide variety of plant and animal species. Common prairie inhabitants like badgers and bighorn sheep live next to recently reintroduced species such as the black-footed ferret and bison. Wind and water shaped the Badlands into the dramatic natural landscape of today. After his first visit to the area, architect Frank Lloyd Wright expressed his wonder in a simple, honest statement: "I was totally unprepared for that revelation called the Dakota Badlands." The Black Hills have been described as an "island of trees in a sea of grass" for the striking way they rise out of the plains. They are part of the North American Interior Range and host some of the tallest peaks east of the Rockies. Despite their history of mining and lumbering, the Black Hills today are primarily a recreational tourist attraction. The lands have been the focus of restoration and protection plans enacted over the last few decades, and these programs promise to preserve this valuable natural landscape for generations to come. As a central feature of South Dakota's economic and cultural personality, the Black Hills continue to dominate and define western South Dakota's natural beauty.

BADLANDS NATIONAL PARK

The 244,000 acres of Badlands National Park are the largest expanse of mixed-grass prairie under protection in the United States. It is not the grassland itself that makes this place unique; it is the towering rocks, deep canyons, and spires. These rocks contain layers from the recent Sharps Formation (28 to 30 million years old), which contains ash from ancient volcanic activity, to the Pierre Shale (69 to 75 million years old), the former bed of a Cretaceous sea. The Sharps and the Brule (30 to 34 million years ago) formations make up most of the dramatic topography here.

After deposition, about 500,000 years ago, erosion cut through these rock layers. What had been a flat landscape was carved by rainwater, exposing ancient layers of rock and soil and depositing sediment in streams, leading to the creation of the White, the Bad, and the Cheyenne rivers (all tributaries of the Missouri River). The process of erosion here is relatively quick. Scientists estimate the buttes here erode at a rate of about one inch per year and propose that the Badland formations will be completely gone in another 500,000 years. The Badlands Wall—a 60-mile long spine of buttes—was formed by wind, rain, and freeze-thaw activities.

But the Badlands contain more than unique vistas. They are home to the richest deposit of Oligocene fossils in the world. Remains of three-toed horses, the ancestors of modern deer, saber-toothed cats, turtles, and dinosaurs are found here. One of the most significant sites is the Pig Wallow Site, or Pig Dig. In 1993, visitors reported a spine protruding from the ground that scientists at first believed to be an ancient pig called Archaeotherium. However, excavation revealed it was the bones of Subhyracodon—an ancient, hornless rhinoceros. This dig was completed in 2008. Over 15,000 bones were excavated.

Badlands National Park contains 64,144 acres of wilderness and is surrounded by the Buffalo Gap National Grassland. Pronghorns, deer, bison, bighorn sheep, swift foxes, and endangered black-footed ferrets reside here. The latter has been reintroduced to the area and is one of two successful reintroductions of one of the world's rarest mammals.

The Lakota named this area Mako Sica, which means "bad land". French trappers who found the landscape difficult to travel concurred. The landscape was designated a national monument in 1939 and redesignated a national park in 1978. Management is concerned with visitor safety, controlling reduction of invasive plants, protecting fossil beds, and preserving fossils and other artifacts. Badlands National Park lies near the Black Hills National Forest, which contains Custer State Park, Mount Rushmore National Monument, Jewel Cave National Monument, and Wind Cave National Park. Badlands National Park contains part of the Pine Ridge Indian Reservation. Since 1976, the Oglala Lakota Nation and the National Park Service have comanaged this land, which contains many sites sacred to the tribe and comprises about half of the park's total size. This same area, the South Unit, contains unexploded munitions—remnants of its use as a World War II aerial bombing practice range. Badlands National Park is engaged in cleaning up these ordnances, which can potentially be detonated by cell phones.

Further Reading

Burnham, Philip. *Indian Country, God's Country: Native Americans and the National Parks.* Chicago: University of Chicago Press, 2000.

Raventon, Edward. *Island in the Plains: A Black Hills Natural History.* Boulder, CO: Johnson Books, 2003.

Shuler, Jay. *A Revelation Called the Badlands: Building a National Park, 1909–1939.* Interior, SD: Badlands Natural History Association, 1989.

BLACK HILLS NATIONAL FOREST

Native Americans called this area Paha Sapa, meaning hills that are black. The way these spruce and pine–covered hills rise above the flat prairie makes them look dark and dense. Located in western South Dakota and northeastern Wyoming, the Black Hills are 125 miles long and 65 miles wide. Human use dates to 10,000 years ago. More recently, Arapaho, Cheyenne, Kiowa, and Lakota visited these hills on spiritual quests and for peaceful wartime conferences. Euro-Americans explored here in the 1840s, but the land was little affected until 1874, when General George A. Custer, leading an army expedition, discovered gold. Mines, railroads, and towns were developed, followed by agriculture and range.

The Black Hills are also known as the Island in the Prairie for their seemingly isolated topography. The 1.2 million acres preserved as Black Hills National Forest are America's oldest mountains. They rose about 60 million years ago. Canyons, caves, and gulches mark this landscape along with grasslands, mountain meadows, lakes, and streams. Their highest point is Harney Peak (7,242 feet), also the highest peak east of the Rocky Mountains, where the Harney Peak Fire Tower, built in 1938 by the Civilian Conservation Corps, still sits.

Golden-mantled squirrels, chipmunks, pronghorns, mountain goats, and coyote make this area home, although mountain goats are not native to this region. In 1924, a Canadian park's donation of six goats to Custer State Park began their reintroduction. These six goats escaped their enclosures and gave birth to the current population of about 200 individuals. Mule deer, yellow-bellied marmots, red squirrels, white-breasted nuthatches, and turkey vultures also reside in the Black Hills National Forest. Three types of frogs are found here: striped chorus frog, western chorus frog, and northern leopard frog. Because their thin skin quickly absorbs contaminants, frogs are important indicator species for the health of the ecosystem. Northern leopard frog numbers are declining. Scientists attribute this to an increase in pesticide use, harvesting for bait, and loss of habitat.

Ponderosa pine forests represent a climax community in the Black Hills. Their open understory is swept with periodic fires, which the trees can resist. Removal of shade-tolerant species and debris makes it easier for new ponderosa pines to sprout. Fire, toppled trees, and bark beetle can disrupt this cycle and force the forest to begin a new cycle.

Black Hills National Forest. (Jeff Lorenz)

Aspens, grasses, and shrubs then take over the area. In 1893, multiple fires brought attention to the fragile forest and the need to manage it for timber. This led to the creation of the Black Hills Forest Reserve in 1897, which ensured protection from fire and irresponsible lumbering. One year later, the Black Hills Forest Reserve was the site of the first commercial timber sale on U.S. federal land. The reserve was renamed the Black Hills National Forest in 1907, two years after switching management to the newly established U.S. Forest Service. Today, forest staff burns slash piles to rid the forest of flammable dried needles, limbs, and treetops. Forest staff carefully monitors bloodroot, a flowering herb. Twenty-two locations contain bloodroot, usually in areas associated with beaver activity (dams and floodplains), wooded terraces, drainages, and north-facing slopes. There are few habitats in the Black Hills where it can thrive. In addition, invasive plants take over territory, making it difficult for the native species to spread.

Mount Rushmore National Memorial is in the Black Hills National Forest. This monument blasted 450,000 tons of rock from Mount Rushmore. Gutzon Borglum designed the sculpture, and carved the likenesses of Presidents George Washington, Thomas Jefferson, Theodore Roosevelt, and Abraham Lincoln between 1927 and 1941. Nearby is the 35,000-acre Norbeck Wildlife Preserve, established in 1920 to protect breeding grounds for wild game (elk, deer, bighorn sheep, mountain lions, and mountain goats) and birds (wild turkeys). The U.S. Forest Service manages 25,000 acres here; the rest is maintained by Custer State Park. At the heart of Norbeck Preserve is the Black Elk Wilderness. First designated in 1980, the wilderness now encompasses 13,605 acres.

Further Reading

Froiland, Sven G. *Natural History of the Black Hills & Badlands*. Sioux Falls, SD: Center for Western Studies, 1990.

Johnson, James R., and Gary E. Larson, *Grassland Plants of South Dakota and the Northern Great Plains*. Brookings: South Dakota State University, 1999.

O'Brien, Dan. *Buffalo for the Broken Heart: Restoring Life to a Black Hills Ranch*. New York: Random House, 2002.

BUFFALO GAP NATIONAL GRASSLAND

Across a vast expanse of apparent stillness and uniformity is a diverse community of plants and animals. Buffalo Gap National Grassland is the second largest national grassland in the United States. It is part of the Nebraska National Forest, managed by the U.S. Forest Service. The grassland contains 600,000 preserved acres spread across southwestern South Dakota, intermingled with private croplands and shelterbelts.

Buffalo Gap National Grassland is a mixed-grass prairie containing both tall-grass and short-grass communities, including western wheatgrass, blue grama, and needle-and-thread. In all, 43 species of grasses grow here as well as some 2,000 wildflowers. Grasslands emerge from climate and moisture somewhere between the humidity of forests and the aridity of deserts. They form a solid ground cover of grasses, which are one of the most productive ecosystems on the continent. The small surface area of their narrow leaves allows efficient photosynthesis. Their large underground root systems reach to deep layers of moister soil and helps grasses grow back after disturbances by grazers, mowing, or fire. In addition, the growing cells of grasses lie at the base of the plant instead of at the tip as in most plants. Thus, it can continue to grow if the plant is cut or grazed. In the last 200 years, more than half of the grasslands in the United States have been converted to agriculture.

Native woodlands of three types—deciduous, woody draws, and shrub patches—accompany grasslands and juniper breaks. Fires often jump over these areas, because the moist foliage is not as susceptible to fire as the drier grasses. Juniper breaks, which occur on north-facing slopes of river drainages, as on the Cheyenne River, have additional fire-proofing from their steep terrain. Woodlands are important habitat for wildlife that cannot live year-round on the harsh, windswept, and dry grasslands. Before dams and water control came to the Great Plains, woody areas were the only source of water. Year-round residents include amphibians and reptiles, porcupines, white-footed mice, and white-tailed deer. Coyote and red fox are frequent visitors. Conata Basin is home to a successful black-footed ferret reintroduction.

Avian life includes over 230 species. Native grassland residents are the western and horned meadowlarks and several birds of prey. Juniper breaks and woody draws, along with artificial ponds and impoundment (created by Ducks Unlimited) provide habitat for migrating shorebirds and waterfowl.

Further Reading

Manning, Richard. *Grassland: The History, Biology, Politics, and Promise of the American Prairie*. New York: Penguin Group, 1997.

Moul, Francis. *National Grasslands: A Guide to America's Undiscovered Treasures*. Lincoln: University of Nebraska Press, 2006.

O'Brien, Dan. *Buffalo for the Broken Heart: Restoring Life to a Black Hills Ranch*. New York: Random House, 2002.

JEWEL CAVE NATIONAL MONUMENT

Jewel Cave lies beneath just three square miles of surface area, but its length winds underground for 145 miles. It is the second longest cave in the world and has only one natural entrance. The largest room, Big Duh, is 570 feet long by 180 feet wide by 30 feet tall. Airflow from unexplored areas indicates many passages yet to be mapped.

Unlike most caves, which are carved by underground rivers, Jewel Cave was formed by groundwater. Here, acid-rich water slowly wore away the rock. The water worked its way underground some 40 million years ago, originating as rain. As it passed through carbon dioxide–rich soil (from decaying plant life), the rain became carbonic acid. It continued down through rock fractures, joining the water table. As the water rose, cracks in the limestone were submerged. When the water drained, it left behind mineral deposits. Cave formations, or speleothems, formed. In addition, the carbon from the water evaporated, and calcite hardened into stalactites, stalagmites, flowstone, draperies, and popcorn formations. Cave formations depend upon the movement of water.

Jewel Cave gets its name from the calcite crystal formations and gypsum strands. Some of the seeping water contained gypsum. When the water evaporated, fine needles, beards, flowers, and spiders of gypsum formed. Hydromagnesite speleothems were formed on the cave's walls when they were underwater. Magnesium concentrates precipitate as hydromagnesite and appear as chalky white deposits. Jewel Cave contains some hydromagnesite balloons, which occur when the deposits fill with air. Cave formations are still being formed, but Jewel Cave's crystals are no longer growing. They were formed when the cave was still filled with water, as calcite deposits on the cave walls known as spars.

Few signs of life are visible inside the cave. Springtails (insects) live near its entrances. In the deepest, darkest recesses, only microbes such as protozoa can survive. Bats utilize the cave, though they do not live there year-round. An estimated 1,000 bats hibernate inside the cave in winter. Local bat species include little brown myotis, long-legged myotis, western small-footed myotis, northern myotis, Black Hills fringed-tail myotis, Townsend's big-eared, and big brown bats. Hoary and silver-haired bats use Jewel Cave National Monument in summer before migrating further south. Myotis species make nursery colonies in the nearby ponderosa pine trees and rock crevices outside the cave in late spring. The monument contains one of the world's largest colonies of hibernating Townsend's big-eared bats.

Outside the cave, the monument's 1,275-acre ponderosa pine forest is home to elk, white-tailed and mule deer, eastern cottontail rabbits, red squirrels, and birds. Reptiles include bull snake, common garter snake, eastern yellow-bellied racer, milk snake, plains garter snake, plains hognose snake, prairie rattlesnake, redbelly snake, smooth green snake, and wandering garter snake. Various birds visit these forests as well. Great blue heron, turkey vulture, mallard, blue-winged teal, gadwall, bald eagle, sharp-shinned hawk, Cooper's hawk, red-tailed hawk, golden eagle, American kestrel, wild turkey, sandpiper, Wilson's phalarope, mourning dove, long-eared and northern saw-whet owls, white-throated swift, and rufous hummingbird are among them.

Jewel Cave was developed into a mildly successful tourist attraction in the first decade of the 20th century. Tours continued through a private group, the Jewel Cave Corporation, from 1928 through 1939. The National Park Service began caring for the cave in 1933, sharing rangers with Wind Cave. In the 1930s, the Civilian Conservation Corps built park structures and infrastructure. Until 1959, only two miles of cave had been discovered. By 1961, 15 miles were mapped by two climbing enthusiasts, Herb and Jan Conn. Much of the cave lies outside monument boundaries, beneath the Black Hills National Forest.

Further Reading

Conn, Herb, and Jan Conn. *Jewel Cave Adventure: Fifty Miles of Discovery in South Dakota*. Trenton, NJ: Cave Books, 1981.
Love, Judy L. *Jewel Cave National Monument*. Mount Pleasant, SC: Arcadia, 2008.

MISSOURI NATIONAL RECREATION RIVER

From its headwaters in the Rocky Mountains, the Missouri River flows 2,341 miles, meeting the Mississippi River at St. Louis, Missouri. It is America's longest river, just two and a half miles longer than the Mississippi River. The river drains about one-sixth of the United States and covers 529,350 square miles. Nearly 100 miles of undammed and unchanneled river are preserved as Missouri National Recreation River, a unit of the National Park System and part of the National Wild and Scenic Rivers System.

Missouri National Recreation River sits at the merger of glaciated and unglaciated areas of the Missouri Plateau. As with most northern high plains, the rock here was largely formed by ancient seas, including the Niobrara and Pierre Formations, which are some 80 million years old. Two plant communities line the riverbanks: mixed floodplain forest with willow and cottonwood and hardwood forests. On bluffs along the border with Nebraska, elm and oak woodland dominate. Sandbars contain early-stage growth such as grasses, sedges, and seedling willow and cottonwood. Further from the shore, forests mature, leaving cottonwood trees with an undergrowth of dogwood, sumac, wild grape, poison ivy, scouring rush, Kentucky bluegrass, and smooth brome. Hardwood forests along bluffs are communities of oak, mulberry, ash, walnut, and bur oak.

Small mammals such as mice, voles, shrews, weasels, mink, bats, rats, and ground squirrels are common along with coyote, common gray and red foxes, beavers, mule and white-tailed deer, opossums, porcupines, bobcats, gophers, mountain lions, striped skunks, cottontail and jackrabbits, river otters, woodchucks, raccoons, and badgers. Amphibians and reptiles include tiger salamanders, two species of toads, six species of frogs, snakes, and turtles. Former residents include grizzly bear, bison, and elk. Fish populations have changed due to dams that prevent migration, change habitat, and increase competition from other species. Natives include catfish, sauger, suckers, and paddlefish. Missouri National Recreation River staff manages endangered pallid sturgeon for recovery. Other sensitive species that use this habitat are interior least tern (endangered), bald eagle (threatened), and piping plover (threatened).

Before Euro-American settlement and development, the Missouri River was ecologically diverse. The natural flow of the river supported riparian areas, sandbars, islands, backwaters, sloughs, chutes, and braided channels. The river was used as a trading route by Omaha and Ponca natives, was traveled by the Lewis and Clark Expedition, and became the main waterway for trappers, traders, steamboats, and settlers. Flood control plans began in the early 20th century with two major dams, Fort Randall and Gavins Point, built in the 1940s. In its early days, the Missouri River carried a high content of sediments, earning it the nickname Big Muddy. Due to these dams, its waters now run clearer. The dams also changed the shape of the river and its shores, depleting sandbars, eroding banks, and creating a narrower channel. In addition, fewer nutrients reach fish, wildlife, and their habitat. Flood control, navigation, irrigation, hydropower, recreation, and water supply have further changed the flow and sediment in the river. Water quality and channel structure have also been affected. Within the park, engineering is not obvious, but flow and sediment regimes have been compromised. Dams and levees affect aquatic and terrestrial wildlife. Although the river will not be restored to a former state, a recovery program is underway by the U.S. Army Corps of Engineers and the U.S. Fish and Wildlife Service. The Missouri River is also affected by inflowing water from the James and the Vermillion rivers. These two rivers can contain high levels of fecal coliform bacteria that could affect recreation in the Missouri National Recreation River. Water is monitored for selenium, a natural heavy metal, ensuring that levels are within water quality regulations. Eight nonnative species of plants are under management control programs, including purple loosestrife, salt cedar, Russian olive, Canada thistle, and leafy spurge. Zebra mussels and Asian carp are nonnative fauna infesting waterways and driving out native species.

Missouri National Recreation River contains Spirit Mound, a symbolic hill associated with Native American legends contact with Euro-Americans. In 2002, a 160-acre plot was designated as Spirit Mound Historic Prairie. Restoration of this former ranchland will bring back prairie ecosystems.

Further Reading

Corps of Engineers, Omaha, NE. *Habitat Erosion Protection Analysis, Missouri National Recreation River, Nebraska and South Dakota*. Washington, DC: Storming Media, 2000.

Wilson, Jerry. *Waiting for Coyote's Call: An Eco-Memoir from the Missouri River Bluff*. Pierre: South Dakota State Historical Society, 2008.

Sand Lake National Wildlife Refuge

Sand Lake National Wildlife Refuge in northeastern South Dakota is one of the top birding sites in North America. It has been designated a globally important bird area and a wetland of international importance (by the Ramsar Convention on Wetlands). The environment here is prairie with deep potholes and lakes filled with blue waters, 11,000 acres of wetlands, 7,400 acres of grasslands, 200 acres of woodlands, and 2,580 acres of croplands. The James River flows gently through the refuge, which lies in the river's lowland valley at the center of the prairie-pothole region of the northern Great Plains. The river is a flight path for migratory birds that follow the natural marker and its resources for its 600-mile course.

Sand Lake National Wildlife Refuge hosts 266 species of birds, more than 100 of which nest and raise young on these grounds. Snow geese can number 250,000 during their fall migration and over one million in spring. Western grebes, white pelicans, and snow geese, along with thousands of waterfowl and migratory birds use this habitat. Sand Lake National Wildlife Refuge contains the largest Franklin gull rookery in the United States. Other nesters include white-faced ibis, Forster's terns, black terns, black-crowned night herons, and cattle egrets. Other avian sightings include grebes, common loons, double-crested cormorants, herons, egrets, American and least bitterns, tundra swans, sandhill cranes, plovers, snipes, gulls, terns, owls, belted kingfishers, woodpeckers, geese, ducks, a variety of hawks, osprey, prairie and peregrine falcons, merlins, American kestrels, golden and bald eagles, and northern harriers. The grasslands are habitat for greater prairie chicken, sharp-tailed grouse, ring-necked pheasant, and gray partridge. Forty species of mammals and many fish, reptiles, and amphibians use this landscape, including walleye and northern pike, white-tailed deer, and furbearers.

Farming and grazing depleted the natural prairie habitat beginning in the 1880s. Waterfowl all but disappeared from the landscape. Sand Lake and Mud Lake are the major open water sources here. While wetlands existed prior to development, two dams on the James River added acreage to this habitat. Sand Lake National Wildlife Refuge was established in 1935 as a breeding ground and refuge for migratory birds and wildlife. Recreation includes watching wildlife, education, photography, hunting, and fishing. The refuge is managed primarily for wildlife through water control; restoring native prairie through prescribed burns, grazing, and haying; controlling nonnative species; and cooperative agriculture. There is a 15-mile auto tour route with interpretive brochure. A short hiking trail, interpretive center, and picnic facilities are available.

Further Reading

Dolin, Eric Jay. *Smithsonian Book of National Wildlife Refuges*. Washington, DC: Smithsonian Institution Press, 2003.
Moul, Francis. *National Grasslands: A Guide to America's Undiscovered Treasures*. Lincoln: University of Nebraska Press, 2006.

WIND CAVE NATIONAL PARK

Beneath Wind Cave National Park's landscape of mixed-grass prairie and ponderosa pine forest lies a complex cave system. Wind Cave is currently mapped at 133 miles of passages, making it the third longest cave in the United States and the fourth longest in the world. The cave was formed in Madison limestone, the rock remains of a 350-million-year-old sea. When the limestone was forming, gypsum crystallized in the water and created odd shapes in the limestone. The gypsum was unstable and expanded

Wind Cave National Park. (Wayne Moran)

and shrunk as water entered and left. This fractured the limestone surrounding it. Some remains crystallized in cracks, and some was converted to calcite. This process released sulfuric acid into flowing fresh water as the ocean receded, which easily dissolved the soft limestone and formed cave passages. The first of these was formed 320 million years ago. This process also created significant boxwork formations and crystal fins. Slow waters that dissolved limestone in cracks around gypsum masses left the fillings standing on their own.

Seas came and went for 240 million years, leaving sediment and causing erosion. Then, 40 to 60 million years ago, tectonic activity in the event of the Black Hills Uplift further fractured the underground limestone, creating more cave passageways. Rather than gushing through, water seeped through cracks, causing the complex structure seen today.

Above the cave, eastern tall-grass and western short-grass meet in this mixed-grass prairie. In wet years, tall grasses dominate, while dry years leave more room for short grasses to grow. Wildflowers include creamy-white sego lily, purple coneflower, and golden-yellow sunflowers. This prairie is home to bison, elk, pronghorn, mule and white-tailed deer, turkey, coyote, badger, mountain lion, cottontails, and prairie dogs. The American Bison Society reintroduced bison to this landscape in 1911, making it one of the earliest reintroductions. Elk and pronghorn were added in 1914. Black bear are extirpated from the park; the last one seen in the Black Hills was in 1968. The grizzly bear was gone by 1894. The black-footed ferret was thought to be extinct in the 1960s, but a population was discovered in Wyoming in 1981, and they were reintroduced here from in 2007.

Two local brothers discovered Wind Cave in 1881, when they followed a whistling sound to an opening. It was made a national park in 1903, making it the seventh oldest national park and the first cave to be designated.

Further Reading

Costello, David. *The Prairie World*. New York: Thomas Y. Crowell, 1969.

Cushman, Ruth Carol, and Stephen R. Jones. *The Shortgrass Prairie*. Boulder, CO: Pruett, 1988.

Palmer, Art. *Wind Cave: An Ancient World Beneath the Hills*. Hot Springs, SD: Black Hills Parks and Forests Associations, 2001.

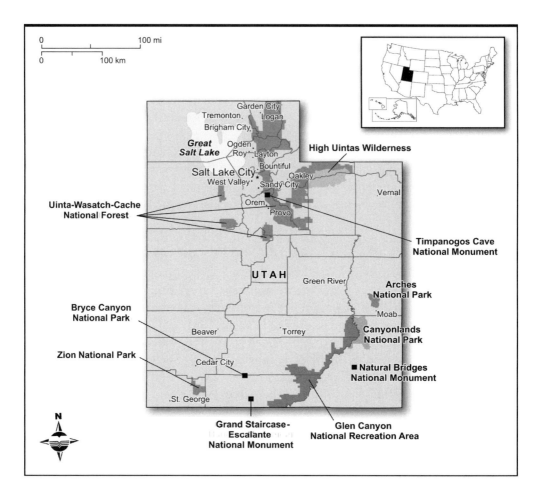

UTAH

Utah contains a diversity of climate types and ecosystems. Mountains, valleys, basins, and canyons stretch across a state largely dominated by desert conditions. Much of Utah sits on the Colorado Plateau, where erosion and buckling of sedimentary rock created the state's signature scenery. Natural arches, bridges, and hoodoos of bright red and orange decorate much of the southern landscape. In the northeast, the forested Wasatch and Uinta mountain ranges rise as contrast. Near the center of the state, the Great Salt Lake stretches for over 70 miles long and 30 miles wide. Though the water's salinity makes it unsuitable for most aquatic species, the lake's marshes and wetlands are critical habitat for avian life.

Utah draws many outdoor enthusiasts to the state's national parks and monuments, high-quality snow sport opportunities, and rich cultural heritage. These diverse characteristics result in a variety of environmental focuses across the state. Recreation and tourism are important issues that are vital to the health and welfare of the state's economy. Land, air, and water pollution; natural resource management; and the ability of the land to support agriculture and the livestock industry are major concerns. Many areas of Utah have enjoyed official environmental protection for many years (the state has eight national parks and many more federal and state natural recreation areas), but other areas have been drastically changed to suit the needs and uses of humankind. Watershed pollution is of particular concern, because the livestock industry and manufacturing activities have taken their toll. Even though mining was relatively limited compared to other mining states, these effects are still present.

Water quality of the Great Salt Lake is of public concern. As an entirely self-contained lake, there is no drainage outlet for this body of water. Heavy human habitation and use has resulted in an environmental issue that must be addressed. Significant amounts of mercury and selenium pollute the waters. Mercury harms wildlife dependent on the lake and can transform into the more dangerous methylmercury that enters the human food chain. The source of the mercury contamination is unknown, despite the fact that Great Salt Lake mercury levels have been studied for many years. Selenium is naturally occurring but is also a by-product of sewage discharge and industrial activity. are It can cause deformities and reproductive problems in bird species. The prospect of commercial oil shale development threatens the scenery and health of the state's red rock landscapes.

Arches National Park

Framing the desert landscape and snow-capped mountains, Delicate Arch symbolizes Arches National Park. With over 2,000 sandstone arches, this national park contains the largest concentration of arches in the world. Technically, an arch must have an opening of three feet, though this can be in any dimension. Landscape Arch's 306-foot opening makes it the park's longest arch. The movement of an underground salt bed known as the Paradox Formation formed these arches. The formation was deposited 300 million years ago by the evaporation of prehistoric seas. Salt deposits are thousands of feet thick. Sandstone formed on top of this layer, putting weight on the unstable salt and causing the rock to shift. Some rock was thrust up, some buckled downward. Seeping water and thawing created further cracks, and faults caused displacement. Together these processes created the unique formations seen in Arches National Park.

Part of the Colorado Plateau, the environment of Arches National Park is high desert, an arid landscape at 4,085 to 5,653 feet in elevation. Temperatures vary greatly, changing as much as 50 degrees in a single day. Summers are hot, winters are cold, and precipitation is light—only nine inches per year. Within park boundaries are riparian environments, ephemeral pools, dry arroyos, mixed grasslands, and bare rocks. Say's phoebes, black-throated sparrows, and western meadowlarks use the park's grassland habitat. Scrub jays, piñon jays, juniper titmice, and black-throated gray warblers live in the piñon-juniper forests. Turkey vultures and white-throated swifts are year-round residents, while winter hosts juncos and white-crowned sparrows. Migrant birds include great blue herons and Cooper's hawks. A total of 273 bird species have been recorded in the park, largely because of its rich riparian areas surrounding the Colorado River and Courthouse Wash. Songbirds include blue grosbeaks, yellow-breasted chats, spotted towhees, and canyon wrens. The peregrine falcon inhabits Arches National Park; it has been brought back from low numbers in the 1970s, when it was listed as an endangered species. The falcon suffered difficult reproduction and egg breakage due to spraying of the pesticide DDT in the region. Peregrines can be found along the Colorado River and its cliff walls, where they prey on small birds. Although they remain on Utah's endangered species list, they have been considered recovered by the federal list since 1999, when 1,650 nesting pairs were recorded in the United States. Only one nesting pair is known to use Arches National Park.

The bright yellow and turquoise hues of the collared lizard invigorate the red desert. Animals here are well adapted to the desert environment. Many are nocturnal, including kangaroo rats, wood rats (packrats), and other rodents. Foxes, bobcats, mountain lions, bats, and owls are active at night as well. At morning and dusk, mule deer, coyote, porcupines, desert cottontails, black-tailed jackrabbits, and songbirds are active. During the heat of midday, squirrels, chipmunks, lizards, snakes, hawks, and eagles are common. A unique subspecies, desert or Nelson's bighorn sheep, were once extinct in Arches National Park, but have now been reintroduced. They are better adapted to the desert than their mountain-dwelling relatives, the Rocky Mountain bighorns, with lighter coats, smaller bodies, and longer legs. Before Euro-American settlement, these sheep thrived, but diseases and competition from hunting and imported livestock depleted the population. In 1975, all of Utah contained only 1,000 individuals. In the 1980s, a single herd in Canyonlands National Park was used to garner sheep for Utah's Arches and Capitol Reef National Parks as well as Glen Canyon National Recreation Area. Utah now contains about 3,000 individual desert bighorn sheep, 600 within Arches National Park, gathering in two separate herds on the San Rafael Swell. The sheep need continued protection from development and tourist interruptions because of a high newborn mortality rate.

Ephemeral pools, or potholes, are sandstone basins ranging from one millimeter to several meters in depth that gather rain and sediment. These pools create their own unique ecosystems and organisms. Some insects, amphibians, and invertebrates use potholes to breed but live more permanently in larger bodies of water or on land. Mosquitoes, tadpoles, fairy shrimp, and spadefoot toads are such "drought escapers." Drought resistors such as snails and mites can survive short times when pools dry up by burrowing in the mud of the pool's floor. The protection of a shell or exoskeleton helps some animals retain water. Some organisms can survive losing 92 percent of their body water and can be rehydrated. Rotifers, tadpoles, and fairy shrimp eggs are such unique organisms.

Arches National Park's spectacular scenery was popularized by settlers around Great Salt Lake. They convinced leading railroad prospector Alexander Ringhoffer to publicize the region to the Rio Grande Western Railroad to gain support for a national park. Arches was designated Arches National Monument in 1929 and became a national park in 1971. During the 1950s, writer Edward Abbey worked as a park ranger here, recording impressions of the landscape in *Desert Solitaire* (1968).

In 2008, the Bureau of Land Management proposed oil and gas leasing in lands around Arches and Canyonlands National Parks, Dinosaur National Monument, and Desolation and Ninemile Canyons. They planned to bureau auction off 50,000 acres of adjacent land to oil and gas developers, which would have placed structures of the energy industry within sight of Arches, Dinosaur, and Canyonlands National Parks, spoiling unique vistas along with the integrity of these natural places. In February 2009, the Obama administration overturned this proposal and cancelled the auction, preserving 130,000 acres of natural scenery.

Further Reading

Abbey, Edward. *Desert Solitaire*. New York: Random House, 1985. (Originally published in 1968.)

BRYCE CANYON NATIONAL PARK

Without a doubt, it is geology that attracts the eye in Bryce Canyon National Park's 35,835 acres. Hoodoos dominate the landscape. The process of erosion forms these dramatic pillars. Park visitors have long enjoyed looking for shapes in the silhouettes of these colorful rocks of red, orange, and pink hues. Some formations have been given unusual names, such as the Poodle, the Sentinel, Sinking Ship, and Thor's Hammer.

About the same time dinosaurs were becoming extinct in the Cretaceous period (65 million years ago), southwestern Utah was covered with a mineral-rich freshwater lake. Iron, manganese, and calcium carbonate mixed to create the pink, red, yellow, and violet hues of the Claron Formation's limestone. Ten million years ago, uplift created Table Cliffs and Paunsaugunt plateaus, which were then slowly carved by rivers. Between the plateaus, a river of the same name carved the Paria Valley. Water passing through a gully at the edges of the Paunsaugunt plateau formed what geologists call fins. When snow and water freeze in the cracks of fins, the thaw breaks apart the rock. Cool nights and warm days create over 200 freeze-thaw cycles per year. When water expands as ice within the cracks of the rock, it breaks apart in a process called frost wedging. Meanwhile, acidic rain washes over the formations, dissolving the soft limestone. The park's lowest layer of gray and brown rock is part of the sedimentation of the Cretaceous Seaway, which extended from the Gulf of Mexico to the Arctic.

In addition to the hoodoos, Bryce Canyon National Park contains forests of piñon and junipers. At higher elevations, ponderosa pine, spruce, fir, and aspen host forest fauna. On exposed rock outcroppings, bristlecone pines thrive. Elevation in the park ranges between 6,000 and 9,100 feet. More than 400 plant species thrive here, including many summer wildflowers like the spiny orange paintbrush, the Nootka rose, and the sego lily. Bryce Canyon National Park is home to one threatened species, Utah prairie dogs, whose only habitat is in meadows of southwestern Utah. Although the park is stunning for its geology, many species use this habitat, including 310 species of birds; various small mammals such as squirrel and marmot; and larger mammals such as fox, mule deer, mountain lion, and black bear. Elk and pronghorn have been reintroduced nearby.

To the Paiutes, who lived in the area near the park when Euro-Americans arrived, the hoodoos were "legend people" whom the trickster-figure Coyote had paralyzed. Settlers came shortly after the 1870s exploration by Captain Clarence E. Dutton and John Wesley Powell. The park's namesake, Ebenezer Bryce, came with other Mormon settlers to Utah and, in 1875, settled in the Paria Valley to harvest timber. He remained until 1880. By the turn of the 20th century, tourists were coming to see the canyon near his land, and the first hotel was built on the rim. In 1929, 22,000 people visited the canyon. President Warren G. Harding declared the canyon a national monument in 1923, adding it to the Dixie (formerly Powell) National Forest. In 1924, it was designated Utah National Park and, in 1928, took on its current name. Bryce Canyon Natural History Association (a nonprofit organization established in 1961) and the park partnered to create the High Plateaus Institute. The educational facility and research organization opened its first season in 2008.

Visitors now number nearly two million per year. Bryce Canyon National Park has over 50 miles of hiking trails, many twisting among the hoodoos. Two backcountry trails—Riggs Spring Loop (9 miles) and Under-the-Rim Trail (23 miles)—require permits. Bryce Canyon Lodge is a national historic landmark designed by Gilbert Stanley Underwood. Since 1925, it has welcomed visitors and is the only remaining lodge from the old days of the Union Pacific Loop Tour, which ran between Bryce, Cedar Breaks, Zion, and Grand Canyon–North Rim. Horseback riding, skiing, snowshoeing, camping, and ranger programs are available in the park. Bicycles are limited to pavement. The park road runs 18 miles along the canyon rim, providing breathtaking vistas from a series of overlooks. From Rainbow and Yovimpa Points at the end of the road, a clear day rewards sightseers with views into New Mexico.

Further Reading
Fillmore, Robert. *The Geology of the Parks, Monuments, and Wildlands of Southern Utah.* Salt Lake City: University of Utah Press, 2000.
Williams, David B. *Naturalist's Guide to Canyon Country.* Guilford, CT: Falcon, 2000.

CANYONLANDS NATIONAL PARK

The Colorado River carves through this desert landscape of canyons, buttes, and mesas. Tributaries branch off to side canyons, cutting the landscape into sections known as the Island in the Sky, the Needles, and the Maze. This area of the Colorado Plateau in southeast Utah is a lightly disturbed remnant of the environment's undisturbed condition. The unique formations have more than visual impact. Erosion controls the distribution of rainwater and creates the chemical composition of soil. Canyonlands National Park is a high desert with temperatures that range as much as 50 degrees in a single day. Precipitation measures less than 10 inches in a year, and elevations range from 3,700 to 7,200 feet.

Claret cup cactus is among the 11 cacti species that thrive in the park. Bunchgrass and sod-forming grasses grow individually, in potholes, and in larger grasslands where soil has formed on the sandstone surface. Bunchgrasses, which grow in clumps, include Indian ricegrass and needle-and-thread. Sod-forming grasses are galleta and blue grama, which grow together and are important food sources for bighorn sheep and mule deer. Cheatgrass is a nonnative species that has established itself in the West and is often the first to sprout in disturbed areas after fire or grazing. Piñon and juniper comprise the forests of the Colorado Plateau. Utah juniper is a hearty tree, surviving inhospitable weather, drought, and poor soil conditions. Its secret is a root system that can be twice the size of the visible tree. Roots penetrate some 25 feet down and 100 feet laterally. They can self-prune when conditions are bad, cutting off nutrients from one branch to save the tree. Juniper provides shade in this open landscape, and its berries are food for jackrabbits, coyotes, and birds. Collard lizards are a common sight here, as are kangaroo rats.

Petrified wood and dinosaur tracks tell of life in the Jurassic period, 185 million years ago, when the landscape was comprised of sand dunes instead of desert, mountains, and canyons. The Navajo sandstone now here is the remnant of that landscape. It forms the canyons of Zion National Park and the petrified dunes at Arches National Park. The landscape itself is a relic of the past. Millions of years of geologic processes are visible in eroded sedimentary rock, which originally lay flat. Tectonic activity, former oceans, rivers, and mudflats shaped it. The red and white layers visible on Cedar Mesa sandstone reveal floods of iron-rich sediment.

The Colorado and the Green rivers that run through Canyonlands National Park have constantly shifting courses. As they carry and deposit sediment (sand, mud, and rocks), the current runs in serpentine channels, making it nearly impossible to determine river depth. Cataract Canyon is a spectacular display of wild river rapids 14 miles long. Boulders caught in the stream form rapids, but bedrock is 260 feet below the water's surface. Most rivers erode land, eventually cutting through to bedrock. Cataract Canyon, however, appears to be filling up. Millions of years of erosion created potholes, or ephemeral pools. These depressions in sandstone collect precipitation and sediment blown across the landscape and provide habitat for amphibians and insects specially adapted to surviving periods of drought or dehydration.

The Canyonlands Natural History Association supports the region's research and education. There are nearly eight million acres of preserved land in this region, combining lands of the National Park Service, the Bureau of Land Management (BLM), and the U.S. Forest Service. Cedar Mesa Primitive Area, managed by the BLM, contains numerous petroglyphs and pictographs. In December 2008, lands adjacent to Canyonlands and Arches National Park went up for auction. Conservation groups led by the Southern Utah Wilderness Alliance (SUWA) filed suit against the BLM land auction. In *Southern Utah Wilderness Alliance v. Allred*, SUWA claims that the BLM was rushing to complete land sales and leases for energy development before the change in presidential administration and ignored the environmental impacts of the planned actions. An environmentalist who won bids on all the adjacent lands, with no money or intention to buy, disrupted the auction. The sale of these lands would have affected Canyonlands as well as Arches National Park, Dinosaur National Monument, Nine Mile Canyon, and the Green River's Desolation Canyon. A group of 58 U.S. representatives asked President Obama to cancel these leases. The Obama administration overturned the auction in early 2009.

Further Reading

Baars, Donald L. *Canyonlands Country: Geology of Canyonlands and Arches National Parks*. Salt Lake City: University of Utah Press, 2001.

Baars, Donald L. *Colorado Plateau: A Geological History.* Albuquerque: University of New Mexico Press, 2000.

Webb, Robert H., Jayne Belnap, and John S. Weisheit. *Cataract Canyon: A Human and Environmental History of the Rivers in Canyonlands.* Salt Lake City: University of Utah Press, 2004.

GLEN CANYON NATIONAL RECREATION AREA

Glen Canyon National Recreation Area comprises 1.2 million acres of the Colorado Plateau around Lake Powell, including land in Utah and Arizona. Units of the National Park System, including Capitol Reef, Canyonlands, and Grand Canyon National Parks, and Grand Staircase–Escalante National Monument surround it. In contrast to those units, the Glen Canyon National Recreation Area, also managed by the National Park Service, places a higher emphasis on recreation than preservation of natural or wild conditions.

Lake Powell is an artificial lake created by the flooding of Glen Canyon in 1963 by a dam bearing its name. Plans to dam the Colorado River began in the 1940s. The U.S. Bureau of Reclamation mapped out a series of dams in the Colorado Plateau, many of which were protested by the environmental group, the Sierra Club. The Sierra Club succeeded in thwarting the bureau's plans for a dam at Echo Park, but the new location at Glen Canyon was hardly a better sacrifice. The original canyon was wild and scenic, with nearly 100 side canyons, wildlife, natural bridges and arches, pristine water, and archaeological sites. Water from Lake Powell feeds Los Angeles, Phoenix, and Las Vegas. The dam provides hydroelectric energy. Five marinas provide access to Lake Powell via houseboats, powerboats, jet skis, and kayaks. The national recreation area maintains four campgrounds and rents houseboats. Fishing for largemouth, smallmouth, and striped bass is allowed.

As the Colorado River runs through the Colorado Plateau, it exposes rock strata over 300 million years old. Glen Canyon contains Pennsylvanian, Permian, Moenkopi, and Chinle formations. Most of what is seen today above the lake is Navajo sandstone. The lake is only 13 percent of the total national recreation area. About 300 bird species have been recorded here, many unknown before the dam and lake. Animal life consists of kangaroo rats, rabbits, bats, rodents, jackrabbits, bighorn sheep, coyote, frogs, toads, and 28 reptiles—including four rattlesnake subspecies. Since the turn of the 20th century, the West has suffered a sustained drought. The water level in Lake Powell has dropped, revealing some of the lost, natural beauty of Glen Canyon. In 2006, over 100 square miles of land resurfaced for the first time since the dam was erected. Some of this land is being taken over by invasive species; tamarisk, tumbleweeds, and cheatgrass crowd out native willows and reeds. Some 11 percent of plants here are invasive and threaten the delicate ecosystem that includes federally endangered species such as Mexican spotted owls, Jones cycladenias, alcove primroses, southwestern willow flycatchers, northern leopard frogs, Colorado pike minnows, humpback chubs, and razorback suckers. Native fish of the Colorado River have had a difficult time surviving in the waters of Lake Powell. These fish, including three endangered species, can be found in the rivers of Glen Canyon National Recreation Area, but fish populations in the lake are nonnative and are stocked for sport fishing. In 1996, the nonprofit Glen Canyon Institute began studying and assessing the management of the area. It put together a Citizen's Environmental Assessment that recommended getting rid of the Glen Canyon Dam and, consequently, Lake Powell. The recreation area has not followed this recommendation. Friends of Lake Powell formed in reaction to Glen Canyon Institute, determined to preserve the lake, the dam, and the canyon.

Further Reading

Baars, Donald L. *Colorado Plateau: A Geological History.* Albuquerque: University of New Mexico Press, 2000.

Glick, David. "Glen Canyon Revealed." *National Geographic,* April 2006. http://ngm. nationalgeographic.com/2006/04/glen-canyon/glick-text.

Martin, Russell. *A Story That Stands Like a Dam: Glen Canyon and the Struggle for the Soul of the West.* New York: Henry Holt, 1989.

Reisner, Marc. *Cadillac Desert: The American West and Its Disappearing Water.* New York: Penguin Group, 2003.

GRAND STAIRCASE–ESCALANTE NATIONAL MONUMENT

R ock layers four billion years old colored vibrant pink, vermilion, gray, white, and brown form slot canyons, caves, alcoves, domes, pinnacles, monoliths, and sinkholes at Grand Staircase–Escalante National Monument. The monument preserves nearly two million acres of this stunning landscape. The monument contains three regions: the Grand Staircase, the Kaiparowits Plateau, and the Canyons of the Escalante. It is adjacent to Bryce Canyon National Park and Glen Canyon National Recreation Area. On its western border are the Paunsaugunt Plateau and Paria River. At the center of the monument is the Kaiparowits Plateau, a long ridge running east to west, also called Fifty-Mile Mountain. It ends at the Colorado River in Glen Canyon. In its eastern portion, the Kaiparowits Plateau is steep; its western edge descends in a shallow slope. It is the largest roadless pieces of land in the contiguous United States

Piñon-juniper forest and sagebrush dominate the upper part of Grand Staircase–Escalante National Monument. The upper canyon is filled with Gambel oak and pointed manzanita. Riparian areas feature Fremont cottonwood, horsetail, sedges, and scouring rushes, while the lower monument includes rabbitbrush, saltbush, sagebrush, cacti, yuccas, Indian paintbrush, penstemon, and sego lily. The monument's 59 species of mammals include mule deer, bighorn sheep, cougar, mountain lion, cottontail rabbit, coyote, and reintroduced elk, as well as 200 species of birds, including the rare peregrine falcon and bald eagle. Other wildlife includes 46 reptiles and amphibians and 6 fish species, including brown, cutthroat, and rainbow trout.

Recent paleontological excavations have found dinosaur fossils, most significantly, the Gryposaurus monumentensis. This 75-million-year-old dinosaur measured 30 feet long and 10 feet tall with 800 teeth in its jaw. Ruins and petroglyphs from the Fremont and ancestral Puebloan people can be found here. Euro-Americans traveled through during the 19th century, but none settled on this land. Some perceived President Clinton's designation of Grand Staircase–Escalante National Monument as a political move to win Arizona's vote in the 1996 election. Although the monument is in Utah, Clinton announced the designation at Grand Canyon National Park in Arizona. His preservation of Grand Staircase–Escalante National Monument thwarted local plans to open a coal mine on what is now preserved land. Detractors also questioned whether so much land could be set aside by a president as a monument. Environmentalists were also wary of this designation, because they had sought wilderness status. But the monument stands. Since its inception, Utah has set aside land in a School and Institutional Trust Lands program, which is managed to specifically add funds to public schools. The monument contained some of these lands, and Congress negotiated a trade for $13 million and mineral rights to other federal lands in Utah. This is the first monument to be administered by the Bureau of Land Management rather than National Park Service.

Roads within Grand Staircase–Escalante National Monument remain controversial. A 19th-century statute granted the state of Utah's right to build highways on public lands. Although the Federal Land Policy and Management Act repealed this in 1976, existing rights remain. Local county officials claim dirt roads on monument land, even erecting signage and bulldozing grades. The Bureau of Land Management seeks control of these same roads.

Further Reading

Chesher, Greer K., and Liz Hymans. *Heart of the Desert Wild: Grand Staircase Escalante National Monument.* Bryce, UT: Bryce Canyon Natural History Association, 2000.

Keiter, Robert B., Sarah B. George, and Joro Walker, eds. *Visions of the Grand Staircase-Escalante: Examining Utah's Newest National Monument.* Salt Lake City: Utah Museum of Natural History and Wallace Stegner Center, 1998.

Larmer, Paul, ed. *Give and Take: How the Clinton Administration's Public Lands Offensive Transformed the American West.* Seattle, WA: Mountaineers Books, 2004.

GREAT SALT LAKE

Covering some 1,700 square miles, Utah's Great Salt Lake is the largest lake in the Western Hemisphere and the fourth largest terminal lake in world. To the east are Salt Lake City and the Wasatch Mountains, to the west is the Bonneville Salt Flat, and to the south are the Oquirrh and Stansbury mountains. The Great Salt Lake can create its own weather. When cold air from the North and West sweeps across its warm water, moist clouds form, dumping rain or snow on nearby land and mountain ranges. During the Pleistocene epoch(32,000 to 14,000 years ago), a much larger lake was here—Lake Bonneville. This lake was 10 times the size of its remaining descendant, the Great Salt Lake. It spread over Utah, Idaho, and Nevada. In addition to the Great Salt Lake, it left behind Utah Lake, Sevier Lake, Rush Lake, and Little Salt Lake. Because of its shallowness, the Great Salt Lake has fluctuated between 950 to 3,000 square miles.

The Great Salt Lake's salinity is higher than sea water, varying from 5 to 27 percent. Average ocean salinity is 3.5 percent. Most of the Great Salt Lake's salt is left over from prehistoric Lake Bonneville. Rivers and streams that feed into the lake deposit new salts. It is fed by three rivers that originate in the Uinta Mountains in Utah's northeast—the Jordan, Weber, and Bear—and they deposit over one million tons of minerals in the lake annually. Evaporation is the lake's only outlet, which creates its high salinity as well as high density. Not much can live in such a salty environment. There are no fish. The lake is home to brine shrimp, brine flies, bacteria, and algae. Brine flies provide food for native and migrating birds. Brine shrimp—also known as "sea monkeys"—dominate the south arm of the lake, though they swim through northern sections as well. These shrimp and their eggs, known as cysts, are harvested for sale in the United States as fish food and are fed to harvested prawns in Asia. They are also used to test toxins, drugs, and chemicals.

Wetlands along the shores of the Great Salt Lake host native birds and migratory shorebirds and waterfowl, such as red-necked phalarope, American avocet, black-necked stilt, marbled godwit, snowy plover, western sandpiper, long-billed dowitcher, tundra swan, American white pelican, white-faced ibis, California gull, eared grebe, peregrine falcon, bald eagle, and several kinds of duck and geese. Particularly important is the migrating Wilson's phalarope. This area contains the largest staging population in the world. Specially protected areas are around Hat, Gunnison, and Cub islands, where American white pelicans nest. Bear River Bird Refuge, administered by the U.S. Fish and Wildlife Service, contains the lake's largest freshwater marshes. This refuge was created in 1928, when an epidemic of avian botulism left hundreds of thousands of birds dead. Settlers had rerouted water from the Bear River, and migrating birds found no place to rest. In the 1980s, high water levels flooded the fresh water with salt; only in 2000 did the refuge fully recover. Bear River Bird Refuge is part of a network of sites across the Americas intended to preserve migration stops to ensure bird survival beyond borders.

A railroad runs the width of Great Salt Lake in the southern portion, at the Promontory Peninsula. The lake is divided into three sections by the causeway of this railroad line, keeping the lake's waters from mixing. There are three 100-foot breaches. The

Great Salt Lake. (Reto Fetz)

northwest arm, known as Gunnison Bay, does not have tributaries flowing into it, so it is saltier than the northeast and southern arms. The northern arm appears an unusual reddish-purple due to a type of bacteria and a species of algae that emits beta-carotene. South of the causeway, blue-green and green algae dominate the biota and tint the water green.

Because of fluctuating water levels, the determination of islands and peninsulas in Great Salt Lake is uncertain. According to the U.S. Geological Survey, eight islands have historically never been submerged and are named islands. Though in low water, they have been known to connect to the mainland. Others say there are between 7 and 11 named island, in addition to rocks, shoals, and small islands. Antelope Island State Park offers views, hiking, biking, and beach access. But most of the lake is not fit for tourism because of pollution, a foul smell from decaying insects, and its constantly changing levels, which make it difficult to develop lakeside destinations.

Researchers from the U.S. Geological Survey and the U.S. Fish and Wildlife Service found extremely high levels of methylmercury in the lake water, some 25 nanograms per liter. They tested several species of ducks for mercury content and released warnings to hunters not to consume common goldeneye, northern shoveler, and cinnamon teal. In the 1980s, the high lake waters flooded the eastern shore, damaging residential neighborhoods and Interstate 80. The state of Utah responded with the West Desert pumping project at Hogup Ridge. This water control station regulated the level by making the lake larger to increase evaporation. It deposited water from the Great Salt Lake into a desert, creating the Newfoundland Evaporation Basin about 25 miles away. The pumps have not been in use since 1989 but are maintained in case levels rise dramatically again.

Minerals, salt, and oil have been extracted from the Great Salt Lake. The oil is not of good quality, but over 3,000 barrels have been captured from shoreline wells. Sodium chloride (salt), potassium sulfate (potash), and magnesium chloride are taken from solar evaporation ponds at the northeast end of the lake. Private companies pay the state for these products. The Great Salt Lake is owned by the state of Utah. Wildlife on the lake is managed through private duck clubs, state waterfowl management areas, and a federal bird refuge. These areas include Bear River Migratory Bird Refuge, Gillmor Sanctuary, Great Salt Lake Shorelands Preserve, Salt Creek Public Shooting Grounds, Harold Crane, Locomotive Springs, Ogden Bay, Timpie Springs, and Farmington Bay Management Areas.

Further Reading

Czerny, Peter G. *The Great Great Salt Lake*. Provo, UT: Brigham Young University Press, 1976.

Stum, Marlin. *Visions of Antelope Island and Great Salt Lake*. Logan: Utah State University Press, 1999.

HIGH UINTAS WILDERNESS

In northeastern Utah, between the Wyoming Basin to the north and the Uinta Basin to the south, lie the glacier-carved Uinta Mountains. The range runs east to west for some 60 miles, with secondary ridges created by glacial basins and canyons running north to south. The pre-Cambrian rock of these mountains is colored in places by exposed quartzite and shale, adding splashes of pink and gray. The High Uintas Wilderness protects several of the state's highest 13,000-foot peaks, including the highest, Kings Peak, measuring 13,528 feet above sea level.

This is the largest alpine area in the intermountain west and the source of the headwaters of Utah's largest waterways. Forests below the alpine tree line are thick with Engelmann spruce, subalpine fir, and lodgepole pine. Lakes, streams, rivers, wetlands, and meadows break these forests, providing crucial habitat for wildlife. Elk, mule deer, moose, mountain goats, bighorn sheep, coyote, cougar, black bears, river otters, and pine martens are common species. Seventy-five percent of all bird species in Utah are found here, including ptarmigan and a variety of raptors.

Designated a wilderness area in 1984, the High Uintas Wilderness is managed jointly by the Ashley and the Uinta-Wasatch-Cache National Forests. The former manages the majority of the wilderness area's 456,705 acres. There are many signs of human use in the wilderness, both past and present. Grazing rights that existed before wilderness designation have been allowed to continue. The Natural Resources Conservation Service tracks water and climate changes through two SNOTEL sensors in the wilderness area. Early 20th-century dams left their mark on the landscape and are currently being managed under the Central Utah Project Completion Act, although the dams themselves are protected historic structures. The wilderness area also contains Native American artifacts, Spanish tree markings, and pioneer cabins and salt houses.

Impacts from recreation are a top priority. Although only foot and horse travel are permitted, visitor use and misuse are evident. Native vegetation has changed, trees have been damaged, soil is compacted and eroded, water is contaminated, litter and human waste are found, and illegal structures have been built. These elements diminish the landscape's sense of solitude intended by the wilderness designation. The Forest Service enforces regulations, collects and removes trash, restores damaged sites, and maintains trails and signs. They focus on visitor education through the Leave No Trace curriculum, a national program meant to inform visitors of their impacts. Visitors are asked to acknowledge a code of seven principles of outdoor ethics: (1) plan ahead and prepare, (2) travel and camp on durable surfaces, (3) dispose of waste properly, (4) leave what you find, (5) minimize campfire impacts, (6) respect wildlife, and (7) be considerate of other visitors.

Further Reading

Fradkin, Philip L. *Sagebrush Country: Land and the American West.* Tucson: University of Arizona Press, 1989.

Howard, Lynna P. *Utah's Wilderness Areas: The Complete Guide.* Boulder, CO: Westcliffe, 2005.

NATURAL BRIDGES NATIONAL MONUMENT

Small and remote Natural Bridges National Monument is often considered the poor cousin of the Colorado Plateau's more spectacular rock formations. There are only three natural bridges here, but their seclusion is part of their charm. Formations are not arches standing out on open valleys, but bridges nestled within canyons. Arches are former cliffs created from top-down erosion, while natural bridges are formed by water running through rock. The national monument also contains striking, almost pure white sandstone canyons.

A five-mile path and an auto tour loop provide views of all three bridges: Kachina, Sipapu, and Owachomo—all named in the Hopi language. Owachomo is the oldest bridge here, but recent rock falls are decreasing its width, threatening to collapse the bridge. Its nine-foot thickness makes the arch seem elegant and delicate. Its height is 106 feet, its span is 180 feet, and its width is 27 feet. Kachina Bridge, on the other hand, is growing. Four thousand tons of sandstone separated and collapsed from the bridge, increasing its opening. Its current dimensions are 210 feet high, 44 feet wide, and

93 feet thick; its span is 204 feet. It is named after rock art—both painted and carved—on its base of figures that appear to be dancing. It is the most recently formed bridge in the monument. Sipapu, which is the Hopi term for an opening between this and the spiritual world, is 220 feet high, 31 feet wide, 53 feet thick, and has a 268-foot span,

Natural Bridges National Monument is in a high desert environment. It is slightly wetter than its neighbors, receiving an average of nine inches of rain per year. In wet years, wildflowers bloom in spring and sometimes in late summer if rains are plentiful. Cacti, yucca, and mosses are good drought resistors that use their leaves to reduce the effects of the harsh sun. Utah juniper has adapted to the lack of water; it can cut off nutrients from certain branches, ensuring the survival of the whole plant. Riparian areas are decorated with monkey flower, columbine, maidenhair fern, cottonwoods, and willows. This hot, dry environment favors small mammals, reptiles, and amphibians. Kangaroo rat, desert cottontails, and rats are common, though mostly nocturnal. Mule deer and mountain lion migrate between desert and mountain elevations. Ephemeral pools contain small, drought-resistant organisms. Natural Bridges National Monument also contains biological soil crust—a collection of cyanobacteria, lichens, green algae, microfungi, and mosses. This layer prevents erosion, balances nutrients, and holds in moisture. Also called cryptobiotic soil crust, it is actually a layer of living plant life common to high desert canyons. The cyanobacteria bind rock and soil when wet, making a stable surface. It also converts nitrogen into a form usable by other plants. This soil crust can also store water and nutrients for later use by plants.

The remoteness of Natural Bridges National Monument leaves the night sky incredibly dark. So dark, in fact, that it was designated the world's first international dark sky park by the International Dark-Sky Association. The sky is striking because of its distance from city lights and because of the lack of pollution. The National Park Service is beginning to value the night sky as a natural resource worth preserving as much as land, flora, and wildlife. The park has upgraded lights in the visitor center, parking areas, and campgrounds to minimize light pollution and enhance visitors' views of the Milky Way.

The bridges were featured in a 1904 issue of *National Geographic* magazine, bringing them to the attention of President Theodore Roosevelt, who established the monument in 1908. It was Utah's first tract of land added to the National Park Service. In 1908, Natural Bridges National Monument was chosen as a solar power demonstration site. In 1992, the National Park Service partnered with the U.S. Department of Energy and the Utah Department of Natural Resources to operate 50 kilowatts of power, providing the monument and community with clean energy.

Further Reading

Fillmore, Robert. *The Geology of the Parks, Monuments, and Wildlands of Southern Utah.* Salt Lake City: University of Utah Press, 2000.

Shaffer, Rick. *Parks after Dark: Beginner's Guide to Stargazing National Parks.* Tucson, AZ: Western National Parks Association, 2006.

TIMPANOGOS CAVE NATIONAL MONUMENT

From 9,500 feet, the highest elevation in Timpanogos Cave National Monument, are spectacular views of American Fork Canyon. The American Fork River flows through the monument's Wasatch Mountains, but protection of the 250 acres preserved here was inspired by what lies out of view—the underground cave reached only by a remote entrance at the top of a one-and-a-half-mile trail.

Beneath the mountains are the three caverns of Timpanogos Cave. They display colorful formations of green and yellow caused by nickel deposits in the crystal structure, calcite, and aragonite. Timpanogos is unique in its abundance of helictites, which spiral up to 10 inches in length. Chime Chamber contains hundreds of these formations. Timpanogos Cave and the surrounding area contain marine fossils from the ancient sea that covered Utah more than 340 million years ago. Horn corals, crinoids, and brachiopods are preserved as white deposits in the limestone.

Wildlife continues to use the landscape, which is comprised of four plant communities: riparian, coniferous, mountain brush, and subalpine. Montane chaparral and shrub forests grow on south-facing slopes with poor soil, supporting Gambel oak, bigtooth maple, curlleaf mountain mahogany, rubber rabbitbrush, and cliff rose. Coniferous forest contains mostly Douglas and white fir as well as forbs, grasses, and shrubs in the understory. Quaking aspen groves are also common here. Timpanogos Cave National Monument contains 55 mammal species, including mountain goats, bighorn sheep, mule deer, moose, mountain lions, black bears, ringtail cats, long-tail weasels, raccoons, squirrels, chipmunks, packrats, and bats. Townsend big-eared bats, known for their large pink ears, use local caves for winter hibernation (though not the main Timpanogos Cave). Recent frequent disturbances have, however, startled these bats and caused them to leave the cave for the harsh winter weather outside. Their population is declining quickly, and they are listed as a threatened species. Very little lives within the cave. The lack of light prevents the growth of organic matter for food. Research is being done on the cave's microbes by Crandall Lab at Brigham Young University.

The monument's two species of fish, brown and rainbow trout, inhabit the American Fork River. There are some 20 reptile species, but the four most common are Great Basin rattlesnake, gopher snake, rubber boa, and sage lizard. The area's 51 bird species include golden eagles, peregrine falcons, red-tailed hawks, American dippers, canyon wrens, orange-crowned warblers, western tanagers, Steller's jays, violet-green swallows, and broad-tailed hummingbirds.

The main threat to the cave is water quality. Monument staff carefully monitor the flow of water, watching nearby grazing activities, off-road vehicle routes, and visitor impacts such as camping, fires, and outhouses. Although there is no significant water contamination at this time, contamination would have irreversible effects upon the environment and formations within.

Further Reading

Martin, George V. *The Timpanogos Cave Story: The Romance of Its Exploration*. Salt Lake City, UT: Hawkes Publications, 1973.

Trimble, Stephen A. *Window into the Earth: Timpanogos Cave*. Tucson, AZ: Western National Parks Association, 1983.

Uinta-Wasatch-Cache National Forest

Created in 1897 as the Uinta Forest Reserve, the Uinta-Wasatch-Cache National Forest represents a 2007 merger of the Uinta and the Wasatch-Cache national forests. Together, they contain 1.3 million acres and nine wilderness areas: Deseret Peak, High Uintas, Lone Peak, Mount Naomi, Mount Nebo, Mount Timpanogos, Twin Peaks, Mount Olympus, and Wellsville Mountains Wildernesses.

The national forest contains a wide variety of ecosystems. The Desert Peak Wilderness is semiarid, populated with sagebrush and grass, giving way to the alpine environment. The High Uintas Wilderness contains the dramatic glacier-carved peaks and idyllic mountain lakes of the Uinta range, with its forests of aspen, Engelmann spruce, fir, and lodgepole pine broken by meadows and wetlands. Elk, mule deer, moose, mountain goats, black bears, bighorn sheep, coyote, river otters, pine martens, cougars, ptarmigans, and raptors find suitable habitat here. Mount Timpanogos Wilderness holds a diverse array of vegetation. In addition to aspens and various pines and firs, Gambel oak, maple, and chokecherry decorate this landscape. It is home to the Rocky Mountain goat and many waterfalls.

Deseret Peak (11,031 feet), Mount Timpanogos (11,753 feet), and Mount Nebo (11,928 feet) are the highest peaks in the forest. In nearby Big Creek Canyon live a herd of wild horses. Bonneville cutthroat trout are a sensitive species living in the Bear River watershed throughout Wyoming, Idaho, and Utah. They are currently reestablishing their population. The Wasatch shooting star, a delicate purple wildflower, is also a sensitive species in the state, growing only in Big Cottonwood Canyon. There are 69 caves in the forest, including the Timpanogos Cave National Monument, which was set aside in 1922. Its 250 acres include three limestone caves.

The Uinta-Wasatch-Cache National Forest is just outside the Salt Lake City metropolitan area, which is expanding at one of the highest rates in the West. Heavy use has prompted the U.S. Forest Service to expand conservation education and land restoration. NatureWatch, a program run jointly between the U.S. Forest Service and local private partners, aims to guide nature viewing by showing the public locations of wildlife and teaching safe and noninvasive viewing ethics. By partnering with local businesses, NatureWatch hopes to spur local economies as well.

In August 2008, a fire swept through the Corner Canyon area of the forest, burning 808 acres. The U.S. Forest Service has formulated a plan to lay down wood straw mulch and reseed 140 acres with the goal of reducing soil erosion from storms and spring snowmelt. Forest staff will install 50 gully relief trenches in Cherry Canyon and 1,500 feet of temporary wire and silt fencing to keep water from flooding residential areas.

Further Reading

Goodman, Doug, and Daniel C. McCool, eds. *Contested Landscape: The Politics of Wilderness in Utah and the West*. Salt Lake City: University of Utah Press, 1999.

Howard, Lynna Prue. *Utah's Wilderness Areas: The Complete Guide*. Boulder, CO: Westcliffe, 2005.

Huggard, Christopher J., and Arthur R. Gomez. *Forests under Fire: A Century of Ecosystem Mismanagement in the Southwest*. Tucson: University of Arizona Press, 2001.

ZION NATIONAL PARK

High in the hanging gardens of Zion National Park, the Zion snail makes its home. The unique geography of the 229-square-park makes this the crustacean snail's only refuge. Seventy-five species of mammals, 290 species of birds, 32 reptiles and amphibians, and 8 species of fish exist in Zion, whose very name means refuge.

Zion National Park's unique desert canyon environment creates a variety of ecosystems in unusually close proximity. The park ranges in elevation from 3,666 to 8,726 feet and has three main ecologic zones: rim, canyon, and river. Each contains plants and animals uniquely adapted to its conditions—from mountain sheep to desert tortoises. Some 800 native species of plants—including cacti, ferns, grasses, shrubs, trees, and wildflowers—give Zion the most diverse flora in all of Utah.

The most stunning thing about Zion National Park, however, is its rocks. At the southwestern edge of the Colorado Plateau, Zion is part of a formation called the Grand Staircase. Nearby Bryce Canyon forms the top of the staircase; Arizona's Grand Canyon comprises the bottom. When rain falls on the plateau, it shapes the soil and rocks, which gather into rivers. The Virgin River rushes through Zion to the Mojave Desert, meeting the Colorado River at Lake Mead.

The origins of Zion Canyon's geologic layers are as varied as they are colorful. They reflect millennia of environmental change. Ocean fossils are found in the bottom-most layer, known as the Moenkopi Formation. Directly above this lies evidence of a retreating sea and ancient forests. Findings of petrified wood suggest frequent flooding and pooling of water. Dinosaur footprints have been found in the layer of Kayenta mudstone just above the Moenkopi. Near the top layer of the canyon, Navajo sandstone has hardened into the shape of windswept sand dunes. These layers were later forced upward to create the Colorado Plateau, which sits about 11,000 feet above sea level. Rainwater eroded the rock, forming the dramatic canyons seen throughout the region today.

Zion National Park's landscape has been a refuge for humans for more than 12,000 years, when ancient hunter-gatherers first traversed the landscape. Fifteen hundred years ago, the Virgin Anasazi found the fertile Virgin River at the bottom of Zion canyon, a unique spot for the cultivation of crops, which could otherwise not be grown in desert conditions. The river; the wide, level, canyon floor; and the length of the growing season allowed them to thrive for nearly 800 years, until, archaeologists believe, they were driven away by drought and overuse. Since this time, the land has been home to Paiute and Mormon pioneers, who all struggled with similar environmental difficulties.

Explorer John Wesley Powell and artist Thomas Moran proclaimed the beauty of Zion during their 19th-century explorations. The land now within the national park was first preserved as Mukuntuweap National Monument in 1909 and was christened Zion National Park in 1919. The federal government's Civilian Conservation Corps built a road through the park to encourage visits by automobile tourists. At the time of its completion on July 4, 1930, the one-mile Zion–Mount Carmel tunnel, which cuts through the walls of the canyon, was the longest tunnel road in the United States. In 1937, the Kolob Canyons section was added to the park's domain.

By 2000, visitation had become so high that the park became the first in the lower 48 states to prohibit private vehicles from its scenic road. Four thousand to 5,000 cars a day were making the drive. Parking was impossible, and traffic detracted from the experience and endangered both wildlife and human lives. A shuttle service from Springdale was established, which now runs from May to October. In winter, visitors are welcome to drive themselves. At the end of the six-mile road, the Narrows is popular hike that introduces visitors to the back side of the canyon. While squeezing through the narrowing limestone of the canyon, visitors can appreciate the delicate side of the monumental park. Another hike, the 14-mile trek to Kolob Arch, rewards hikers with a view of one of the largest freestanding arches in the world.

The nonprofit Zion Natural History Association supports the National Park Service in protecting and studying Zion National Park's landscape, which is threatened. California condors were released in nearby Vermillion Cliffs, and sightings increased in the park throughout the 1990s. The North Creek section of the park is home to a population of 100 cougars, but the tourist sections are ecologically imbalanced, because the predators stay away from human disturbances. The result is overgrazing by the nonmigrating herd of mule deer. This means fewer wildflowers, less diversity of species, and erosion. Cougar conservation is controversial, because there have been attacks on livestock and pets in communities adjacent to the park. The park also battles with cottonwood trees, which are part of an older forest that is no longer regenerating. Visitors can participate in conservation work through field studies programs and lectures run by the Zion Canyon Field Institute.

Further Reading

Eves, Robert L. *Water, Rock & Time: The Geologic Story of Zion National Park*. Salt Lake City: University of Utah Press, 2005.

Fillmore, Robert. *The Geology of the Parks, Monuments, and Wildlands of Southern Utah*. Salt Lake City: University of Utah Press, 2000.

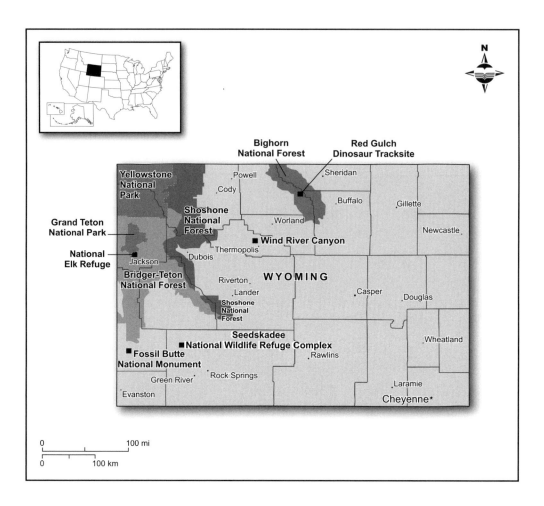

WYOMING

In Wyoming, the high plains run into the Rocky Mountains, which dramatically rise throughout its western portion. The Continental Divide cleaves the state in two, dividing the flow of water. Elevation ranges from 3,125 feet in the Belle Fourche River to 13,804 feet at the top of Gannett Peak. The mountains are broken by grassy flat basin, part of the intermontane basins. Though it was Wyoming's unusual geyser and geothermal features that sparked its first preserved natural area, the state is now part of grander ecosystem efforts at environmental conservation.

Hay, wheat, and barley thrive in the dry climate of Wyoming's eastern plains. The dryness also means that natural vegetation is sparse. The result is that ranging animals need more support acreage than in other areas of North America. Half of the land in Wyoming is owned by the federal government. The majority of federal land is designated as national parks, but a significant portion is used for mining. Mining is the largest economic force in the state. Natural gas, petroleum, and coal are the predominant commodity. The tourism industry in Wyoming is significant as well. Nearly six million people visit Wyoming every year, and half of those visitors spend time in one of the nation's most popular destinations, Yellowstone National Park. Grand Teton National Park, Shoshone National Forest, the eastern Great Plains, and Devil's Tower also draw many people to the state. The wonders of western Wyoming are wild and breathtakingly rugged.

As the home of the first national park in the world, the state has a long history of conservation action. Yellowstone was the testing ground for responsible human access to natural wonders. The early history of Yellowstone, despite its good intentions, was plagued by visitors who, out of either ignorance or carelessness, had a negative impact on many of the natural wonders in the park. Protection has strengthened Yellowstone's landscape and ecosystem. Today the park is one of the best examples of the struggle between human use and environmental preservation. The region is also among the first to recognize that national park boundaries mean nothing to wildlife and ecosystem health. The Greater Yellowstone Coalition, founded in 1983, encourages ecosystem management in the connected lands and waters of 20 million acres in two national parks, six national forests, three national wildlife refuges, as well as state and private lands. Because of efforts to protect the region, the Greater Yellowstone Ecosystem is among the world's largest preserved temperate ecosystems.

BIGHORN NATIONAL FOREST

North-central Wyoming is home to the one-million-acre Bighorn National Forest. This, Wyoming's most diverse landscape, ranges from desert and canyonlands to grasslands, meadows, and alpine peaks. Low-elevation mountain forests of ponderosa pine and Douglas fir give way to Englemann spruce and lodgepole pine and, finally, subalpine fir. Bighorn National Forest is noted for its large mountain meadows, rich with grasses and wildflowers.

The Bighorn River skirts the western edge of the National Forest. Native Americans named the waterway after the plentiful herds of bighorn sheep that grazed at the river's mouth. Lewis and Clark, in turn, named this mountain range after the river. This landscape was crossed by Jim Bridger, Lewis and Clark, Red Cloud, Plenty Coups, and Buffalo Bill. The forests of the Big Horn Mountains provided timber, beaver pelts, big game, and medicinal plants. Portions of the National Forest were first set aside in 1897 as the Bighorn National Reserve.

Cloud Peak Wilderness, which preserves 189,039 acres of the Big Horn Mountains, follows 27 miles of the range's spine, encompassing pine- and spruce-filled summits as well as meadows, wetlands, valleys, hundreds of lakes, and streams. The region had been preserved in 1932 as Cloud Peak Primitive Area; it earned its wilderness designation in 1984. Cloud Peak Wilderness contains the highest peak in the Bighorn National Forest, Cloud Peak, which rises 13,175 feet above sea level. Its eastern slope contains the last glacier in the range.

The biggest threat to Bighorn National Forest is white pine blister rust. In Tensleep Canyon, Shell Canyon, and Red Grade Road, the fungus has reached epidemic proportions. No fungicides have yet been developed to prevent the disease, which could kill up to 75 percent of limber pine populations on national forest, Bureau of Land Management, state, and tribal lands. Forest staff collects seeds of trees found to be resistant to the rust and uses the seeds to repopulate damaged forests. Trees with white pine blister rust are more susceptible to mountain pine beetle infestation. The national forest allows some beetle kill as a natural process of the changing forest ecosystem; dead trees provide shelter and nesting sites for small mammals and birds. The openings created by dead trees increase habitat diversity, allowing grasses, forbs, and shrubs to thrive. Forest staff manages the beetles, however, through harvesting areas at risk of beetle infestation. Forest staff also monitors mountain lakes for acid rain deposits.

Bighorn National Forest maintains 32 campgrounds and seven lodges, two visitor centers, two ski resorts, picnic areas, scenic byways, and 1,500 miles of trails. Timber is still taken from the forest, and land is reserved for cattle and sheep grazing.

BRIDGER-TETON NATIONAL FOREST

Part of the greater Yellowstone ecosystem, the 3.4-million-acre Bridger-Teton National Forest sits adjacent to Grand Teton National Park and the National Elk Refuge. The forest is larger than neighboring Grand Teton and Yellowstone national parks combined. A portion of what is now Bridger-Teton National Forest was first preserved as part of the first national forest, the Yellowstone Park Timber Land Preserve (or Yellowstone Forest Reserve, later renamed Wyoming National Forest in 1908), in 1891. Land was added, mostly by President Theodore Roosevelt, to include the Wind River and Wyoming ranges. In 1973, two national forests were combined. In addition to being next to two national parks, Bridger-Teton adjoins two other national forests: the Caribou-Targhee and Shoshone. It includes the southern portion of the Wind River Range and parts of the Salt River and the Wyoming ranges. Rivers include the Yellowstone, Snake, and Green; lakes number 1,500.

Named for legendary trapper and wilderness guide Jim Bridger, the national forest sits on three sides of Jackson Hole, a 40-mile-long valley. Over one million acres of three wilderness areas lie within the forest: Bridger Wilderness (428,169 acre), Gros Ventre Wilderness (287,000 acres), and Teton Wilderness (585,468 acres). The Bridger Wilderness, in the Wind River Range, contains a 100-mile stretch of the Continental Divide. This range contains 40 peaks over 13,000 feet in elevation, including Wyoming's tallest, Gannett Peak (13,804 feet). Bridger Wilderness contains seven of the largest glaciers in the contiguous United States. Teton Wilderness is a vast volcanic landscape between the two national parks where Two Ocean Creek, as its name suggests, divides, flowing east to the Atlantic and west to the Pacific drainages.

Riparian systems, shrublands, forests, alpine tundra, and wildflower parks are among the vegetation zones and habitats within Bridger-Teton National Forest. Four research natural areas are specifically intended for scientific investigations. Growing in the forest are sagebrush, willows, grasses, lupines, lodgepole pines, Engelmann spruces, whitebark pines, aspens, and Douglas firs. Wildflowers include arrowleaf balsamroot and Indian paintbrush. Coyote, elk, moose, mule deer, bighorn sheep, mountain lions, beavers, pikas, marmots, pronghorns, bison, and black and grizzly bears inhabit these habitats. The area hosts 335 bird species, including trumpeter swans, sandhill cranes, dippers, Clark's nutcracker, osprey, and bald and golden eagles. All told, the Bridger-Teton National Forest provides habitat for 74 mammal species, 25 fish species (including the rare Snake River cutthroat trout), and 6 species each of amphibians and reptiles. Threatened and endangered species include grizzlies, wolves, black-footed ferrets, and peregrine falcons. Kendall Warm Spring is home to a unique two-inch-long fish called Kendall Warm Springs dace. These fish turn colorfully purple (males) and green (females) during summer breeding. Another unique feature of Bridger-Teton National Forest is Periodic Spring—a cold-water geyser that flows at 18-minute intervals in late summer. It flows down a ledge and hillside to Swift Creek.

Management of the national forest ensures the health of this habitat for wildlife. The Lower Gros Ventre Habitat Enhancement Project of 2006 planned the prescribed burn of some 20,000 acres to create better grazing areas for big game in the Gros Ventre Corridor. These winter and transitional ranges contain regenerated aspen and provide for bighorn sheep, elk, mule deer, and moose. This is a joint venture of the Wyoming Game and Fish Department, Grand Teton National Park, and National Elk Refuge, with financial support from the Foundation for North American Wild Sheep, the Wyoming Governor's Big Game License Coalition, and the Rocky Mountain Elk Foundation.

In June 1925, a one-mile-long part of a mountain collapsed, damming the Gros Ventre River. Below the dam, a lake formed, known as Lower Slide Lake. In 1927, the dam collapsed and flooded the town of Kelly. The Gros Ventre Slide area includes an interpretive trail about this natural disaster. The 3,000 miles of road and trail includes the 72-mile Wyoming Range National Recreation Trail and 175 miles of the Continental Divide National Scenic Trail. Three alpine ski areas, including Jackson Hole Mountain Resort, and eight resorts lie with national forest boundaries. Bridger-Teton National Forest has issued 300 outfitter-guide permits, the most in the region. Jackson Hole Mountain Resort has taken significant steps to reduce its carbon emissions through alternative energy sources and promotes tree planting through its ski pass sales. Hunting, pack trips, climbing, river trips, fishing, mountain biking, and Nordic sports are all allowed.

A commercial compost project uses forest slash and horse manure (from outfitters) to improve reclaimed areas on the Togwotee Pass Highway. Oil wells have existed in the national forest since the 1940s, and today some 150,000 acres are leased. Less than half that land is in production. Only 14 wells are operating in the forest (as of 2006), and plans for an additional three are being discussed. In 2005, the U.S. Forest Service put in force a rule that all off-road vehicles must follow designated motorways. Bridger-Teton National Forest began developing a motorized trail system the next year.

Further Reading

Clark, Tim W. *The Natural World of Jackson Hole: An Ecological Primer.* Moose, WY: Grand Teton Natural History Association, 1999.

FOSSIL BUTTE NATIONAL MONUMENT

In the cold sagebrush desert of southwestern Wyoming, fossils at Fossil Butte National Monument reveal a contrasting ancient landscape. Fifty million years ago, this landscape was subtropical. Sycamore and palms grew tall, creating habitats for alligators, crocodiles, bats, turtles, stingray, snakes, insects, and small horses. The oldest known bat fossils have been found here. Fossil Butte National Monument's fossils are important for their detail, variety, and numbers. The monument contains only one percent of the total fossil deposits in the bed of the ancient Fossil Lake. The 50-mile-long by 20-mile-wide original Fossil Lake existed for about two million years and was the smallest of three local ancient lakes that comprise the Green River Formation. The monument contains

13 square miles of the 900-square-mile lake bed. The other two are Lake Gosiute and Lake Uinta, collectively referred to as the Green River Lake System, within Wyoming, Utah, and Colorado. The fossils of the Green River Formation are one of the world's best collections of Tertiary-period aquatic species.

Fossils are contained in two rock layers—the Wasatch and the Green River formations. The Wasatch ranges in tone from red to purple to yellow and gray and contains fossilized teeth and bone, mostly of Eocene-era mammals (primates and horses). They reveal life surrounding the lake, while the Green River Formation represents sediment from the lake bed itself. It lies over, under, and cuts through the middle of the more consistent Green River Formation, which is clearly seen in exposed slopes at Fossil Butte, Cundick Ridge, Ruby Point, and throughout Fossil Basin. Small, steep valleys cut through the high desert. Fossil Butte and Cundick Ridge and Wasatch Saddle create the eastern edge of Chicken Creek watershed, which drains more than half the monument land.

Three hundred elk winter here. A population of about 100 pronghorn spend the other three seasons. Wildlife includes three amphibians—the Utah tiger salamander, chorus frog, and northern leopard frog—along with 44 species of mammals, including mule deer, moose, jackrabbits, cottontail rabbits, pygmy rabbits, least chipmunks, and Richardson's ground squirrels. Only two reptile species, the wandering garter snake and the short-horned lizard, reside in Fossil Butte National Monument. Ninety-three species of birds live in forests, sagebrush, and grasslands here, including golden eagles, red-tailed hawks, northern harriers, black-billed magpies, common ravens, gray jays, green-tailed towhees, sage grouse, mountain bluebirds, western meadowlarks, Brewer's sparrows, and American robins. Aspen groves contain the most diverse bird life, including house wrens, tree swallows, black-capped chickadees, black-headed grosbeaks, orange-crowned warblers, yellow warblers, and red-naped sapsuckers. Birds preferring Douglas fir forests are the yellow-rumped warbler, common raven, chipping sparrow, Steller's jay, and red-breasted and white-breasted nuthatch. Mixed-conifer forests contain western tanagers, mountain bluebirds, Clark's nutcrackers, and Hammond's flycatchers. Birds dependent upon sagebrush habitat are the vesper sparrow, western meadowlark, and golden eagle.

The landscape of Fossil Butte National Monument is high desert sagebrush steppe. Snow accounts for most of the precipitation here, with only 9 to 12 total inches a year. A 2003 study documented 520 plant species. Scientists identified 14 types of vegetation zones: aquatic, aspen, barren, alkali sagebrush, basin big sagebrush, mountain shrub, saline, wet meadow, and willow. Three different sagebrush communities exist within the monument. Basin big sagebrush is found below 7,200 feet, with basin big sage, bluegrasses, and wheatgrasses growing in fertile soils. Above 7,200 feet, mountain big sagebrush grows its namesake species along with wheatgrasses, bluegrasses, and forbs. Deep clay soils of all elevations contain the alkali sagebrush type, with low sagebrush growing in soils of high salinity and alkalinity. Forested areas contain limber pine, Douglas fir, and aspen. Mountain shrub ecosystems contain mountain mahogany, Utah serviceberry, and mountain snowberry. Wet meadows contain Baltic rush, silver sagebrush, willows, and sedges.

Created in 1972, Fossil Butte National Monument was meant to preserve the fossils in the Wasatch and the Green River formations. However, its modern environment is just as valuable. It is one of the only remaining areas in southwestern Wyoming that is not used for livestock grazing. The fossil beds were first discovered in the mid-19th century. Many private quarries still operate nearby. The Green River Formation contains some 213 billion tons of oil shale—the largest deposits in the world. The Bureau of Land Management (BLM) has leased some land in the Green River Formation to oil companies, which are interested in extracting shale oil because of the rising prices of oil. The BLM claims that there are over 800 billion barrels of recoverable oil stored here—three times the amount of oil in Saudi Arabia. In 2006, much of the Piceance Creek Basin was leased to oil shale development, which has historically been too expensive to be profitable. Oil shale extraction is more disruptive of the land and produces more air pollution. Monument supporters are worried it could leak toxic arsenic and selenium, which would drain into the Colorado River Basin.

Further Reading

Knight, Dennis H. *Mountains and Plains: The Ecology of Wyoming Landscapes*. New Haven, CT: Yale University Press, 1994.

Krauss, Clifford. "The Cautious U.S. Boom in Oil Shale." *New York Times*, December 21, 2006. http://www.nytimes.com/2006/12/21/business/21shale.htm?_r=1.

GRAND TETON NATIONAL PARK

Grand Teton National Park preserves the dramatic peaks of the Teton Mountain Range, marked by 12 peaks above 12,000 feet elevation, rising 7,000 feet above the valley. Uplifted some two to three million years ago, they are the youngest mountain range in the Rockies but expose some of the continent's oldest rocks. Their signature jagged western slopes were formed as the ground lifted up on the western side, tilting the uplift back into the earth. On their eastern slope, they roll gently to the Teton Valley. The tallest peak is a series of three, known as Grand Teton, rising 13,770 feet above sea level. Surrounding it, are the "cathedral" peaks known as Nez Perce, Middle Teton, Mount Owen, and Teewinot Mountain.

Glaciers, some still visible today, carved the canyons and basins, which are now Lakes Leigh, Bradley, Jenny, and Taggart. The Snake River flows through the valley to the east through previous glacial moraines. Jackson Lake is a remnant of that Ice Age activity, as well. The valley is sagebrush, while mountains are marked with meadows and alpine lakes. There are four main habitat areas within Grand Teton National Park: alpine, coniferous forest, sagebrush flat, and wetland-riparian. More than 1,000 plant species exist here—100 different grass species alone, which grow in all four habitats. Sagebrush flats contain bigleaf and low sagebrush. Along the Snake River, narrowleaf cottonwood and willows dominate, marked with balsam poplar. Glacial moraines in the canyons and slopes support aspen and conifers such as lodgepole, whitebark, and limber pines as well as spruce-fir forest species of blue and Engelmann spruce and Douglas and subalpine fir. Alpine altitudes support lichens and the ground cover alpine forget-me-nots. Lichens, ferns, berry-bearing shrubs, and wildflowers also grow in the area.

Sixty-one species of mammals reside here. Elk, moose, bison, mule deer, pronghorns, beavers, badgers, pine martens, long-tailed weasels, wolverines, pikas, golden-mantled ground squirrels, muskrat, river otters, yellow-bellied marmots, mountain goats, bighorn sheep, mountain lions, coyote, wolves, and black and grizzly bears. Birds include a variety of species, from large raptors such as golden eagle and osprey to the smallest bird in North America, the calliope hummingbird. Other avian species include trumpeter swans, bald eagles, western tanagers, and sage grouse. The park also contains four reptile species—three snakes and one lizard, the latter only confirmed in 1992. Also found here are six amphibian species, including two whose populations are declining: the boreal toad and the leopard frog. Grand Teton National Park sits adjacent to the National Elk Refuge. Park staff manages the elk herd, which is now exceeding its sustainable count of 11,000 individuals. The park's reduction program allows hunters with permits to weed out the herd. While Grand Teton National Park contains an abundance of elk, its bighorn sheep herd is the smallest and most isolated herd in Wyoming. Scientists are currently monitoring the 100 to 125 animals to ensure their survival. The Teton Range herd of bighorn sheep have taken to wintering at higher elevations because of habitat loss at lower elevations. Researchers are worried that such a small herd may be susceptible to disease, avalanches, or severe winter weather. Trout fishing is popular here, but only one species is a native—the Snake River cutthroat trout. Lakes and rivers swim with mountain and Utah suckers, mountain whitefish, redside shiners, Paiute and mottled sculpins, and longnose and speckled dace—all natives. Introduced species include rainbow, eastbrook, lake, and brown trout; Utah chub; arctic graylings, and bluehead suckers.

Although it is a small national park, Grand Teton's 310,000 acres was not easily come by. When Yellowstone National Park was created in 1872, some of the land that is now Grand Teton National Park was designated the Teton Forest Reserve. Proposals for national park designation began in 1917, but Jackson Hole residents fought the bills. Yellowstone National Park Superintendent, Horace Albright, took billionaire philanthropist John D. Rockefeller, Jr., on a tour of the area in 1926. Impressed, Rockefeller started purchasing parcels of land around the forest reserve under the name Snake River Land Company. Between 1927 and 1940, he bought farms and ranches totaling 35,000 acres. The Park Service preserved the peaks and lakes of the Tetons in 1929 as Grand Teton National Park but did not include any of the Snake River Valley floor. Rockefeller tried to donate his lands but was met with opposition that was only culled when he threatened to sell his holdings back to development. President Franklin D. Roosevelt did not wish to pass up the opportunity to preserve this important landscape and sidestepped the national park designation process by issuing a presidential declaration naming 221,000 acres Jackson Hole National Monument. Locals and Congress fought to undo the president's work, but these efforts failed, and, in 1950, the national monument became part of the national park.

Grand Teton National Park is part of the 11-million-acre Greater Yellowstone Ecosystem. As of April 2008, the park runs entirely on green power. Threats to the park habitats include mountain pine beetle infestations of lodgepole and whitebark pine trees. Interactions between human visitors and wildlife are a major concern for the safety of both parties. In 2007, the park partnered with the Greater Yellowstone Coalition to create the Wildlife Brigade, a team of rangers and volunteers to educate the public and monitor human-wildlife interactions. They also ensure proper food storage and disposal in campgrounds and picnic areas throughout the park. One female black bear was euthanized last year due to reliance on human food. The first U.S. Wildlife Migration Corridor runs through Grand Teton National Park lands. Known as the Path of the Pronghorn, this 150-mile tract protects the seasonal migration route of pronghorn antelope. Their trip through the park, through Bridger-Teton National Forest, and ending in Wyoming's Upper Green River Valley is the longest migration of a land mammal in the contiguous United States. The route was mapped through studies done by the Wildlife Conservation Society. The National Park Service and the U.S. Forest Service have signed the agreement, but they are, as of late 2008, awaiting signatures from private landowners and the Bureau of Land Management.

Further Reading

"Ancient Pronghorn Path Becomes First U.S. Wildlife Migration Corridor." *Environmental News Service,* June 17, 2008. http://www.ens-newswire.com/ens/jun2008/2008-06-17-091.asp.

Craighead, Frank C. *Naturalist's Guide to Grand Teton and Yellowstone National Parks.* New York: Falcon, 2006.

Righter, Robert W. *Crucible for Conservation: The Struggle for Grand Teton National Park.* Moose, WY: Grand Teton Natural History Association, 1984.

National Elk Refuge

Ten thousand elk graze on the National Elk Refuge's 23,754 acres, the largest winter gathering of elk in the world. This herd also makes the longest migration of any elk herd in the lower 48 United States. The refuge is between Grand Teton National Park and the town of Jackson. An estimated 900,000 elk rely on the Greater Yellowstone Area. In summer, they roam the mountains, but in winter, they prefer lower elevations and meadows where food is still available. These elk are known as the Jackson Elk Herd. They were protected and then used to replenish and reintroduce elk to other areas.

The National Elk Refuge also provides habitat to more than 1,000 bison—the largest herd in the National Wildlife Refuge System. The refuge maintains habitat for birds, fish, and other game. Elk hunting is permitted in the fall. The Shoshone-Bannock tribes are permitted a ceremonial bison hunt each year. Rituals and traditional scouting and hunting techniques are used to hunt the permitted five bison, which are used for meat. This hunt is permitted by an agreement with the U.S. Fish and Wildlife Service in the

2005 Bison and Elk Management Plan and Environmental Impact Statement, which was finalized in 2007. A local tradition has Boy Scouts gather the shed elk antlers to sell at auction. They donate 80 percent of their profits to the refuge for care of the elk. In winter, visitors can take a guided sled ride in the refuge.

Further Reading

Bauer, Erwin A., and Peggy Bauer. *Elk: Behavior, Ecology, Conservation*. St. Paul, MN: Voyageur Press, 1996.

Smith, Bruce, Eric Cole, and David Dobkin. *Imperfect Pasture: A Century of Change at the National Elk Refuge in Jackson Hole, Wyoming*. Moose, WY: Grand Teton Natural History Association, 2004.

RED GULCH DINOSAUR TRACKSITE

Although this land was long under the administration of the U.S. Bureau of Land Management as the Red Gulch/Alkali National Back Country Byway, in 1997, it attained striking scientific importance. That year, a visitor reported the location of dinosaur tracks. Upon investigation, these tracks were found to cover some 40 acres with 125 separate trackways and more than 1,100 individual tracks.

The extent and number of tracks makes Red Gulch Dinosaur Tracksite unique, but it also is one of the few sites representing the middle Jurassic period. This new discovery transformed how scientists imagined the prehistoric landscape here. They had thought the entire Bighorn Basin was filled with an ancient sea called the Sundance Sea. To the west of the current state of Wyoming was a volcanic arch that stretched from Mexico to Canada. The east was bound by shallow water and coastline from central Wyoming to the Dakotas. The dinosaur tracksite suggests the ocean level dropped some 167 million years ago, leaving beaches and tidal flats. Ripple marks in the rock surface support this theory. Trace fossils of burrowing annelid worms have been found here as well as ancient pollen from the layer just above the tracksite, giving scientists an idea of the flora of the time, which seems to have consisted of cycads, fern spores, various conifers, and some one-celled organisms.

Dinosaur footprints left impressions in limy mud along the shoreline. These hardened and were covered by successive layers of mud and sand and were thus preserved. Erosion later exposed the fossils. The tracks reveal that this was an area populated by bipedal dinosaurs. Most appear to be theropods, three-toed meat-eating dinosaurs weighing between 15 and 400 pounds. Other tracks suggest ornithopods, or plant eaters. So little is known about the middle Jurassic period that scientists cannot identify specific species. In an area known as the Ballroom, 600 of the area's 1,000 tracks are concentrated. Scientist theorize that this could indicate a migration corridor or a narrow pathway. Others surmise the prints all show a south or southwesterly movement, into the water.

Further Reading

Foster, John. *Jurassic West: The Dinosaurs of the Morrison Formation and Their World.* Bloomington: Indiana University Press, 2007.

SEEDSKADEE NATIONAL WILDLIFE REFUGE COMPLEX

Seedskadee and Cokeville Meadows National Wildlife Refuges comprise this complex along Wyoming's Green River. The refuge's name comes from the region's first residents, the Shoshone. Seven hundred years ago, these people hunted bison, pronghorn, elk, mountain sheep, and sage grouse. *Sisk-a-dee-agie* means "river of the prairie chicken" in their language. Euro-American fur trappers interpreted this word as *seedskadee*.

In Seedskadee, 500 mammal species, 11 reptile and amphibian species, and 200 bird species find habitat. In the upland habitat, pronghorn, mule deer, and small mammals browse. Sage grouse and waterfowl depend on sagebrush communities, as do sage sparrows, sage thrashers, Brewer's sparrows, ferruginous hawks, and pygmy rabbits. Cottonwoods and willows grow along the riparian habitat of the Green River and are used by migrating songbirds like rufous hummingbirds, Wilson's warblers, yellow warblers, and northern orioles, as well as bald eagles, hawks, and great blue herons. Moose, mule deer, beaver, and porcupine find shelter for their young here. Wetlands nourish trumpeter swans, ruddy ducks, American avocets, long-billed dowitchers, sandpipers, white-faced ibis, redheads, cinnamon teals, pied-billed grebes, yellow-headed blackbirds, marsh wrens, sora rails, and muskrats.

The Green River region was used by fur trappers, passed over by emigrants, and grazed by cattle in winter. By 1886, range land was depleted. The combination of a drought, low prices for beef, and a harsh winter destroyed the cattle industry. This mismanagement of grazing land ended open-range practices. Ranchers erected fences across the western landscape to better manage land and cattle.

Seedskadee National Wildlife Refuge was established in 1965. When Flaming Gorge and Fontenelle Dams were built, wildlife gained habitat through the Colorado River Storage Project Act of 1956. Seventy-five miles west, Cokeville Meadows National Wildlife Refuge, created in 1992, sits along the Bear River. It includes 20 miles of the river, wetlands, and uplands. The refuge is still in the process of acquiring land. It currently contains about 8,000 protected acres, with approval to obtain a total 26,657 acres through additional purchases and conservation easements. Cokeville Meadows National Wildlife Refuge supports one of the state's most popular waterfowl nesting grounds. White-faced ibis and black tern nest here, and the area has been identified as ideal habitat for the reintroduction of trumpeter swans. In 2009, the refuge remained closed to public use, except for one viewing station along Route 30.

Seedskadee National Wildlife Refuge Complex staff manage for wildlife through hunting, prescribed burning, and seeding of native plants. They aim to bring invasive weeds like perennial pepperweed and Canada thistle under control with biological, mechanical, and chemical methods. Hunting, fishing, bird-watching, and boating on the Green River are popular recreational activities.

Further Reading

Butcher, Russell D. *America's National Wildlife Refuges, 2nd Edition: A Complete Guide.* Lanham, MD: Rowman and Littlefield, 2008.
Dolin, Eric Jay. *Smithsonian Book of National Wildlife Refuges.* Washington, DC: Smithsonian Institution Press, 2003.

SHOSHONE NATIONAL FOREST

What is now known as the Shoshone National Forest was the first land set aside as national forest. In 1891, the Yellowstone Timberland Reserve was created due in part to the travels and influence of soon-to-be President Theodore Roosevelt. In 1902, Roosevelt expanded the reserve and divided it into four units; the largest tract became the Shoshone National Forest in 1905 with the creation of the U.S. Forest Service. Shoshone National Forest contains the oldest remaining ranger station, the Wapiti Ranger Station, just west of the town of Cody. The national forest covers nearly two and a half million acres, with one a half million acres in the North Absaroka, Washakie, Fitzpatrick, and Popo Agie wildernesses. Yellowstone National Park lies to the west. This large expanse includes jagged peaks and alpine environments through all the montane vegetation zones to sagebrush flats. Up to 9,000 feet, lodgepole pine, Douglas fir, quaking aspen, and Rocky Mountain juniper grow, while subalpine fir, Engelmann spruce, whitebark pine, and limber pine spread upward. The forest contains parts of three mountain ranges: the Absaroka, the Wind River, and the Beartooth. The crest of the Continental Divide on its southern border divides the Shoshone National Forest from the Bridger-Teton National Forest. Shoshone National Forest is notable for its range of ecosystems and biodiversity.

Shoshone's sculpted peaks were created by the movement of glaciers, which also left behind hundreds of mountain lakes. Many predators reside here, including grizzly bears, mountain lions, wolves, and coyote. Grizzlies and wolves were reintroduced to the greater Yellowstone region in the 1990s. Shoshone National Forest has the distinction of being able to claim that all 50 of the known mammal species that existed here when Euro-Americans first entered the area still exist. Mammals include seven species of shrew, nine species of bat, pika, mountain cottontail, snowshoe hare, white-tailed jackrabbit, yellow pine, least, and Uinta chipmunks, four species of squirrels, mice, voles, weasels, skunks, northern pocket gophers, porcupine, swift and red foxes, beaver, raccoon, marten, coyote, gray wolves, black and grizzly bears, minks, wolverine, badger, river otter, mountain lion, Canada lynx, bobcat, elk, mule and white-tailed deer, moose, pronghorn, bison, mountain goat, and bighorn sheep. A few amphibians include the tiger salamander, boreal toad, and four frog species, as well as the American bullfrog. Reptiles are represented by three snakes—the rubber boa, intermountain wandering garter snake, and prairie rattlesnake—as well as the northern sagebrush lizard.

The U.S. Forest Service manages wildlife habitat, but populations are managed by state agencies. Prescribed burns are used to improve grazing lands and to encourage aspen communities. Aspens provide unique habitat for some wildlife. Forest staff will weed out unwanted conifers to maintain the aspen communities. Watersheds are restored by replanting damaged vegetation (due to early-20th-century roads and grazing). Streams and their banks benefit from these activities, as do the wildlife that use them. Shoshone National Forest staff pays particular attention to the needs of threatened and endangered species, four of which live within forest borders: the Canada lynx, grizzly bear, gray wolf, and bald eagle. Researchers estimate 125 grizzly bears occupy the Shoshone National Forest. Comprehensive management plans are in place for the Canada lynx and the grizzly bear; the latter has been helped by the Interagency Grizzly Bear Committee. Wolves from the Yellowstone reintroduction program have migrated to Shoshone.

Private, Bureau of Land Management, and the Wind River Indian Reservation (owned by Shoshone and Arapahoe) lands border Shoshone National Forest on its eastern edge. Montana's Custer National Forest forms the northern boundary. In the Popo Agie Wilderness are the famous climbing routes of the Cirque of the Towers. Shoshone National Forest contains 22 miles of the National wild and scenic river, the Clarks Fork of the Yellowstone River, as well as the Shoshone River's North and South Forks and the Wind River. Sixteen named and 140 unnamed glaciers lie within the national forest's Wind River Range, 44 in the Fitzpatrick Wilderness. The north slope of Gannett Peak contains the largest glacier in the U.S. Rockies but has lost one-quarter of its mass since 1980 due to global warming. Scientists predict that all the small glaciers will disappear by 2020.

The U.S. Forest Service has leased about 10 percent of Shoshone National Forest to industry. Forest staff allows for some logging for construction and wood pulp, mineral extraction, and grazing. The Wilderness Society has claimed some portions are falling to overgrazing by cattle in riparian zones and nonleased land. Also controversial are plans to build roads for logging and exploration of oil and gas interests. Another threat to the national forest are mountain pine beetle infestations in lodgepole pine and fir trees. Infestations of the insect kill trees, making forests more vulnerable to uncontrolled fires.

One of the most scenic drives in the United States—the Beartooth Highway—runs through the Shoshone National Forest, leading into the northeastern corner of Yellowstone National Park. Fly-fishing, white-water paddling, backpacking, climbing, pack trips, mountain biking, hunting, and hiking.

Further Reading

Clark, T. W., and M. R. Stromberg. *Mammals in Wyoming*. Lawrence: University of Kansas Museum of Natural History, 1987.

WIND RIVER CANYON

On the way to Yellowstone National Park is a 34-mile stretch of U.S. Route 20/ Wyoming Route 789 designated a Wyoming scenic byway. The road hugs the shores of the Wind River through the Wind River Canyon whose walls tower as high as 2,500 feet above the canyon floor, exposing black and pink shades of pre-Cambrian rock three billion years old. Wind River Canyon stretches between Wyoming's arid desert plains to the south and the northern confluence of the Wind and the Bighorn rivers, known as the Wedding of the Waters. A few miles north of the canyon, at the end of the scenic byway is Thermopolis, the world's largest mineral hot springs, in Hot Springs State Park.

The canyon has been a route for Native Americans and Western explorers. Mule deer, elk, marmots, and mink inhabit the canyon. Bighorn sheep were reintroduced in 1995. From 43 relocated individuals, the herd has grown to 100. Today, land within the canyon is owned by various parties—private individuals, the Wind River Indian Reservation, the state of Wyoming, the U.S. Bureau of Land Management, and the U.S. Bureau of Reclamation.

A recent proposed development in the canyon has some wondering about the impact of silt being deposited in the river. The portion of the Wind River that runs through the canyon is protected under the highest Wyoming state standards as a class 1 waterway.

Further Reading
Laurence Parent. *Scenic Driving Wyoming*. Guilford, CT: Falcon/Globe Pequot Press, 1997.

YELLOWSTONE NATIONAL PARK

The star attraction of Yellowstone National Park is, of course, its geysers. These unique geothermal features are what earned it the first national park designation in 1872. In all, the park contains some 10,000 thermal features. Most famous is Old Faithful, a predictable geyser that formed the centerpiece for the first lodge in the park. Yellowstone National Park's 2.2 million acres cross the borders of three states: Wyoming, Montana, and Idaho. Most park land is inside the Yellowstone Plateau, a gently rolling landscape surrounded on all but one side by mountains. These picturesque vistas sit atop an active volcano. In January 2009, earthquakes rattled the park, a reminder of this volatile landscape, which, scientists say, statistically should not erupt for a few hundred years.

Yellowstone National Park contains half of all the geothermal features on earth, more than 10,000 geysers, hot springs, mudpots, and fumaroles. Its 300 geysers are in seven main basins and account for two-thirds of the earth's total count as well as the world's tallest, Steamboat geyser. Yellowstone National Park is the only undisturbed geyser basin in the world. Those in Iceland and New Zealand have been drilled with wells.

Researchers come to Yellowstone National Park to learn about thermophilic bacteria and algae mats; their research is applied to energy production elsewhere.

One of the most fascinating landscape features of the park is the Grand Canyon of the Yellowstone—a deep gorge, dramatic in shape and color. For 20 miles between Upper and Tower Falls, the Yellowstone River has carved this canyon 800 to 1,200 feet deep. The Yellowstone River is the longest free-flowing river in the lower 48 states. It runs for 600 miles from Yount Peak, just south of Yellowstone National Park, to its confluence with the Missouri River in North Dakota.

Yellowstone National Park contains some 1,350 species of plants, 218 of which are nonnative to the area. Twenty-five years ago, the number of nonnative plants was 85. These include timothy and downy brome. Vulnerable areas include paved roads, back-country trails and campsites, rivers, and frontcountry developments. The park follows an integrated pest management program that educates the public, seeks early detection, and controls and eradicates species. Twenty species are highlighted as priorities, including musk thistle, leafy spurge, tall buttercup, spotted knapweed, yellow hawkweed, wooly mullein, Saint-John's-wort, and oxeye daisy. A native species, Yellowstone sand verbena, is an unusual plant that grows only on lakeshores within the park. It grows only up to four inches tall and spreads three feet wide, blooming with consistent white flowers in late summer. Sand verbena exists in warmer climates of deserts and tropical areas, so it is surprising to find it growing here, at 7,740 feet above sea level. The land's thermal activity might be responsible for this unique endemic species. Very little is known about this plant, including how it is pollinated. It is currently located only on the shores of Lake Yellowstone, with about 8,000 individual plants.

Sixty-seven mammal species live in Yellowstone National Park. The park contains the largest concentration of mammals in the contiguous United States, including black and grizzly bears, bighorn sheep, bison, bobcats, coyote, elk, lynx, moose, wolverines, mountain lions, and gray wolves. Amphibians include the boreal toad, chorus frog, spotted frog, and tiger salamander, but population numbers are not known and scientists believe more species will be discovered in the future. Park staff has been monitoring reptiles and amphibians since 1991, in cooperation with Idaho State University. Yellowstone National Park is not a major migration stop but does contain unique bird life. Species of particular concern are trumpeter swans, common loons, harlequin ducks, bald eagles, osprey, peregrine falcons, and endangered whooping cranes. Nonnative lake trout are taking over habitat of the native cutthroat trout in Yellowstone Lake.

Although most bison disappeared from their historic ranges during the 19th century due to overhunting and development, the land that is now Yellowstone National Park never completely lost its herd of wild bison. In 1902, a scant 50 individuals remained on this range. To ensure a future abundance of the animal, 21 bison were imported from a private herd and raised on a ranch in the Lamar Valley. In the 1920s, ranchers began interbreeding the two herds. In 1936, some ranched bison were placed in historic habitat. Today's herd numbers about 3,500. Wolves were reintroduced to their historic range here in 1995 and 1996, amid much controversy. They now number over 300 head in the greater Yellowstone area. In the 1970s, a biological study of the region's grizzly bear population revealed the bears' range covered some five million acres, only two million of which were within park boundaries. This realization, along with the growing field of ecosystem studies, led scientists and park managers to develop a conservation concept that extended beyond the park boundaries. They called it the Greater Yellowstone Ecosystem.

The Greater Yellowstone Area includes seven national forests, three national wildlife refuges, one Indian reservation, and one million acres of private land. The concept of ecosystem management has led to conflicts and controversy about the uses of this and all national parks. During the 1990s, private landowners adjacent to the park wanted to tap a geothermal feature and mine upriver. The government put a stop to both proposals by buying the land and the mining rights in exchange for other federal land.

Yellowstone National Park has long been on the front lines of the environmental movement. It was the nation's (and the world's) first national park, created in 1872. But with no precedent to follow, the park was poorly managed. Poachers were uncontrollable, leases were sold to private interests, and a laundry service operated near Mammoth placed clothes in hot pools. The U.S. Army intervened in 1886, bringing order to the wilderness (but also eradicating wolves). By 1916, a tourist infrastructure was being built, and the new National Park Service began to learn to manage landscapes and visitors. In 1933, supporters of the park established the Yellowstone Association. This organization has devoted itself to historic and scientific education within the park. It also sponsored organization of the Yellowstone Association Institute, founded in 1976.

Over four million people visit Yellowstone annually and are, ironically, one of the park's biggest threats, disturbing wildlife and bringing invasive plants. The most controversial visitor-use issue is the use and number of snowmobiles. In 2001, President Clinton established a ban on snowmobiles, but the ban was overturned during the next administration.

Wildfires significantly damaged Yellowstone National Park in 1988. Between mid-June and October, almost one and a half million acres were ablaze. Thirty-six percent of park land was lost when five fires crossed over from adjacent lands. Humans started at least one of the fires. A discarded cigarette ignited the North Fork Fire, which was responsible for the loss of 410,000 acres. Proposals have been before Congress since 1992, asking for protection of waters that flow into Yellowstone National Park. Geothermal development outside the park could have an effect on the temperature and flow of geysers and hot springs. The nonprofit Yellowstone Park Foundation supports research in the park and recently funded the Center for Wildlife Information Project, the Trumpeter Swan Recovery Project, and the Beaver Population Survey.

Further Reading

Craighead, Frank C., Jr. *For Everything There Is a Season: The Sequence of Natural Events in the Grand Teton-Yellowstone Area.* New York: Falcon, 2001.

Gruver, Mead. "Yellowstone Quakes Shake Loose Eruption Fears." *Discovery News Online,* January 12, 2009. http://dsc.discovery.com/news/2009/01/12/yellowstone-earth quakes-02.html.

Reinhart, Karen Wildung. *Yellowstone's Rebirth by Fire: Rising from the Ashes of the 1988 Wildfires.* Helena, MT: Farcountry Press, 2008.

Smith, Douglas W., and Gary Ferguson. *Decade of the Wolf: Returning the Wild to Yellowstone.* Guilford, CT: Lyons Press, 2006.

Glossary

All-Terrain Vehicle (ATV)   An off-road vehicle with low-pressure tires and a straddled seat that can handle a variety of terrain.

Alpine   The mountainous region above timberline.

Altitude   Elevation above sea level.

Anadromous Fish   Migrating fish, such as salmon, that swim from the sea to fresh water rivers to breed.

Aquifer   Underground porous rock that contains groundwater that is the source for wells and springs.

Arid   A lack of water, usually due to low precipitation, that prevents the growth of plant life and the existence of animal life.

Badlands   Barren land with eroded features such as ridges, peaks, and mesas.

Basalt   A dark, glassy, volcanic rock that is hard and dense.

Basin and Range   A landscape created by series of uplift and crustal falls that contains parallel mountain ranges interrupted by broad valleys, such as the Great Basin.

Batholith   Igneous rock that has melted and intruded surrounding strata at great depths.

Biodiversity (Biological Diversity, Diversity)   The number and variety of organisms and their environments. Can refer to ecosystems and genetic variation.

Biological (Cryptobiotic) Soil Crust   Living top layer of soil comprised of cyanobacteria, including lichen, green algae, microfungi, moss, and bacteria, usually found in deserts and arid landscapes.

BOX CANYON   A canyon or gorge with an opening on only one side.

BUTTE   A hill in a generally flat area that rises abruptly with sloping sides and a flat top.

CENTRAL FLYWAY   One of the migration routes followed by birds that stretches over the Great Plains; it narrows over Nebraska, resulting in a large concentration of species in that region.

CHRONIC WASTING DISEASE   A transmissible disease striking mule deer, white-tailed deer, elk, and moose, typified by chronic weight loss. It is progressive and always fatal.

CIRQUE   A steep depression at the top end of a mountain valley, usually containing water as a lake.

CLIMATE CHANGE   Any inconsistent, natural climatic events in geologic time, though often used interchangeably with the term *global warming*.

CLIMAX ECOSYSTEM (COMMUNITY)   The state of relative stability in an ecosystem in which organisms maintain a productive balance.

CONGLOMERATE   A rock made up of smaller pebbles cemented into one mass.

CONSERVATION   The management of natural resources for nature and humans, including responsible use, improvement, and protection of natural resources.

CONSERVATION EASEMENT   An agreement in which a landowner willingly restricts land use for the benefit of long-term conservation and environmental values.

CONTINENTAL DIVIDE   A location where water flows toward more than one drainage basin. Specifically in the United States, the Continental Divide of the Americas or Great Divide runs along the spine of the Rocky Mountains and separates waters flowing west to the Pacific Ocean and east to the Atlantic Ocean.

CRITICALLY ENDANGERED SPECIES   Any flora or fauna with declining numbers whose population is predicted to decrease by 80 percent within three generations. These species are at risk of becoming extinct.

CRYPTOBIOTIC SOIL CRUST   See biological soil crust.

CYANOBACTERIA   Former name of blue-green algae.

DESERT   A dry landscape receiving an average annual precipitation of less than 20 inches per year. A desert supports little or no vegetation on sandy, barren soil.

DIVERSITY   See biodiversity.

DUST BOWL   Any region that has become arid due to drought and dust storms. Historically, in the United States, the Dust Bowl was the period between 1930 and 1946 when the Great Plains experienced severe dust storms as a result of poor agricultural practices and drought.

ECOLOGY   The relationship of organisms to each other and their environment. The study of living things interacting in their environments.

ECOREGION   A larger unit of ecosystem; any area that shares climate, environment, and natural communities and has its own distinct biodiversity of flora, fauna, and ecosystems.

ECOSYSTEM   A local community of living organisms in their environment.

ENDANGERED SPECIES   An animal or plant in danger of extinction because of dwindling population, poor genetic diversity, or limited habitat caused by natural or human changes in the environment.

ENDANGERED SPECIES ACT OF 1973   Legal protection for flora and fauna threatened with extinction from human overdevelopment.

ENDEMIC   Native or limited to a particular region.

ENVIRONMENTAL PROTECTION AGENCY   An agency of the federal government that regulates chemicals and protects human health by ensuring the safety of air, water, and land.

EPHEMERAL POOL OR POND   A natural sandstone basin that collects rainwater seasonally and forms temporary ecosystems.

EROSION   The natural process of wearing away of land by wind or water. Erosion can be increased by human activities such as agriculture, development, or logging.

EXTINCTION   The disappearance of a species of flora or fauna due to failure to adapt to environmental changes, either natural or human-induced.

FOOTHILLS   The low-lying hills at the base of a mountain or range.

FOSSIL   The preserved impressions or remains of ancient animals and plants.

FOURTEENER   A mountain with elevation over 14,000 feet.

FUMAROLE   A hole in the earth's crust, usually in a volcanic area, emitting gases, smoke, and steam.

GEYSER   A natural hot spring that sporadically spouts water and steam.

GLACIER   A large mass of slow-moving ice created by compacted layers of snow.

GLOBAL WARMING   Natural warming periods in the geologic past or the current increase in temperatures thought to be expedited by human industry—that is, greenhouse gas emissions.

GNEISS   Composed of the same materials as granite, gneiss holds minerals in banded or foliated layers.

GORGE   A deep, narrow canyon with steep sides between mountains.

GRANITE   An igneous rock containing coarse, light minerals such as quartz and mica.

GRASSLAND   An expanse of land containing grass or grasslike vegetation and few trees, as in a meadow or prairie.

GREAT BASIN   A large, arid basin in the western United States, part of the basin and range province located between the Wasatch Mountains and the Sierra Nevada.

GREAT PLAINS   The prairie landscape west of the Mississippi River and east of the Rocky Mountains in the United States and Canada.

HABITAT   The environment that provides sustenance (food, water, shelter, and space) for a population of organisms.

HIGH PLAINS   The western part of the Great Plains, which rise in elevation in the states of Colorado, Kansas, Nebraska, Montana, New Mexico, Oklahoma, Texas, and Wyoming.

Hydroelectricity   The use of water to produce energy.

Ice Age   See Pleistocene epoch.

Igneous   Rock created by the hardening of molten substances, such as lava.

Indicator Species   An organism that readily conveys the effects of changing environmental conditions.

Integrated Pest Management   The control of pests (usually insects) with a combination of pesticides and other nonchemical methods.

Invasive Species   Opportunist nonnative flora or fauna that reproduce quickly, putting native species at risk.

Jurassic Period   The period between 200 and 150 million years ago, marked by dinosaurs and the appearance of primitive mammals and birds.

Krummholz   Stunted and twisted vegetation, usually trees, caused by exposure to severe winds at subalpine elevations.

Lek   The place where males of a species gather for mating displays.

Levee   An earthen or concrete embankment meant to prevent river flooding.

Limestone   A sedimentary rock.

Marsh   A low-lying wetland—with either fresh water or salt water and either tidal or nontidal—containing herbaceous vegetation and lacking peat deposits.

Mesa   A flat-topped hill with steep, clifflike sides.

Metamorphic   Rock created by extreme heat or pressure.

Migration Corridor   See wildlife corridor.

Miocene Epoch   23 million to 5.5 million years ago, characterized by the emergence of primitive apes, whales, and grazing animals.

Missouri Coteau   Also known as Missouri Plateau or Coteau du Missouri, a plateau that is part of the Great Plains stretching from the eastern Missouri River valley in central North Dakota to north-central South Dakota.

Montane   Highland regions below the subalpine zone characterized by cooler temperatures and higher rainfall than adjacent lowlands.

Moraine   The rocks, boulders, and stones deposited by a glacier.

Mountain   An elevation with relatively steep sides and substantial mass.

Mountain Range   A series of mountains that resemble each other in form, orientation, or origin.

Native   Having origins and existing in a particular place.

National Forest   Land owned by the federal government and managed by the U.S. Forest Service under the U.S. Department of Agriculture as multiuse areas that balance the needs of nature, wildlife, extractive industries (logging, mining), recreation, livestock grazing, and water distribution.

NATIONAL PARK   Land owned by the federal government and managed by the National Park Service under the Department of the Interior. Nature protection and sustainable recreation are prioritized; commercial use is prohibited.

OGALLALA AQUIFER, HIGH PLAINS AQUIFER   A large, shallow underground water table covering 174,000 square miles under the Great Plains used for agricultural irrigation and drinking water.

OLIGOCENE EPOCH   34 to 23 million years ago, marked by the spread of grasslands and a scarcity of mammals.

PATERNOSTER LAKES   A chain of glacially created lakes connected by a stream, climbing to a valley head and often ending in a cirque lake.

PATHOGENS   Microorganisms (bacteria, viruses, parasites) that spread disease.

PEAK   A mountain or its pointed summit.

PETRIFIED   A rocklike material created by the conversion of living material, such as wood, into mineral form.

PETROGLYPH   An ancient carved image on rock.

PHYSIOGRAPHIC PROVINCE   The subdivisions of a continent, defined by specific characteristics such as geography and environment.

PICTOGRAPH   An ancient image drawn or painted onto a rock surface.

PLAIN   A landscape that is relatively level and treeless.

PLATEAU   An elevated landscape with relatively level topography.

PLEISTOCENE EPOCH   Two and a half million to 120,000 years ago, characterized by glaciation and the emergence of the first humans.

PLIOCENE EPOCH   Five and a half million to three and a half million years ago, distinguished by the arrival of modern plants and animals.

POTHOLE   A natural hole worn into rock, usually filled with water.

PRAIRIE   A landscape characterized by flat or rolling grassland and few trees.

PRE-CAMBRIAN EON (SUPEREON)   4,567 to 542 million years ago, distinguished by the emergence of the first primitive forms of life.

PRESCRIBED BURN, CONTROLLED BURN   A fire set to manage or restore forest, agricultural land, or prairie.

PRESERVATION   The protection of nature from human activity.

PROTEROZOIC EON   2,500 to 542 million years ago, distinguished by the buildup of oxygen and the advance of primitive life forms.

RESERVOIR   A natural or manmade area used to store water.

RIPARIAN   Land and organisms surrounding flowing water in rivers and streams that are distinct from the outlying ecosystems.

ROCKY MOUNTAINS   The major mountain range of the western United States and Canada, forming the Continental Divide.

SANDSTONE   A sometimes-colorful sedimentary rock containing sandlike particles of quartz along with lime and silica.

SEDIMENTARY ROCK   A rock created from sediments deposited in water.

SENSITIVE SPECIES, SPECIES OF CONCERN   Any plant or animal with declining or vulnerable population that is likely to become endangered without conservation efforts.

SHALE   A sedimentary rock loosely bound with layers of fine, claylike particles.

SHELTERBELT   A wall of trees and shrubs planted to manage soil erosion and protect from wind and storms.

SPECIES   Living organisms that can interbreed with fertile offspring.

SPRINGS (HOT SPRINGS, MINERAL SPRINGS)   A place where groundwater seeps to the surface.

STRATA, STRATIGRAPHY   Layers of parallel rock, distinct in formation and composition, that reflect geological processes over time.

SUBALPINE   The mountain landscape just below timberline.

TALUS   A slope at the base of a mountain or cliff containing debris.

TARN   A small mountain lake in a cirque, or depression, created by a glacier.

TECTONIC   The movement of the earth's crust and the resulting structural formations.

TERTIARY PERIOD   65 million to 1.6 million years ago, distinguished by the appearance of modern plants, apes, and large mammals.

THREATENED SPECIES   Any plant or animal with declining population, likely to become endangered.

TRANSPIRATION   The process of water evaporating from the leaves of vegetation or animal pores.

TUNDRA   A high-latitude or high-altitude landscape distinguished by lack of trees, frozen subsoil, and low-lying vegetation such as lichens, mosses, grasses, stunted shrubs, and woody plants.

VEGETATION ZONE, LIFE ZONE   Categories used to distinguish ecological changes in elevation in relation to latitude.

WETLAND   A highly productive ecosystem characterized by saturated soil and the presence of shallow pools of water, including swamps, marshes, and bogs.

WILDERNESS AREA   Federally owned land protected under the U.S. National Wilderness Preservation System and managed primarily for nature protection. Motorized vehicles (including bicycles) and invasive activities such as logging, mining, grazing, and development are prohibited.

WILDLIFE CORRIDOR   A stretch of land protected from development and preserved for wildlife migration, which allows healthy breeding and increases effective population size.

BIBLIOGRAPHY

Abbey, Edward. *Desert Solitaire*. New York: Random House, 1985. (Originally published in 1968.)

"Ancient Pronghorn Path Becomes First U.S. Wildlife Migration Corridor." *Environmental News Service*, June 17, 2008. http://www.ens-newswire.com/ens/jun2008/2008-06-17-091.asp.

Argo-Morris, Lesley. "Ecological History of the City of Rocks." http://www.nps.gov/ciro/naturescience/naturalfeaturesandecosystems.htm.

Armstrong, David Michael. *Rocky Mountain Mammals: A Handbook of Mammals of Rocky Mountain National Park and Vicinity*. Boulder: University Press of Colorado, 2007.

Arno, Stephen F. *Mimicking Nature's Fire: Restoring Fire-Prone Forests in the West*. Washington, DC: Island Press, 2005.

Ashworth, William. *Ogallala Blue: Water and Life on the High Plains*. Woodstock, VT: Countryman Press, 2007.

Baars, Donald L. *The American Alps: The San Juan Mountains of Southwest Colorado*. Albuquerque: University of New Mexico Press, 1992.

Baars, Donald L. *Canyonlands Country: Geology of Canyonlands and Arches National Parks*. Salt Lake City: University of Utah Press, 2001.

Baars, Donald L. *Colorado Plateau: A Geological History*. Albuquerque: University of New Mexico Press, 2000.

Baden, John, and Don Snow, eds. *The Next West: Public Lands, Community, and Economy in the American West*. Washington, DC: Island Press, 1997.

Bailey, R. *Ecoregions of the United States*. Washington, DC: U.S. Department of Agriculture, U.S. Forest Service, 1980.

Baird, L., and Dennis Baird. *In Nez Perce Country: Accounts of the Bitterroots and the Clearwater after Lewis and Clark*. Moscow: University of Idaho Press, 2003.

Baker, John. *The Peregrine*. Moscow: University of Idaho Press, 1996.

Bamforth, Douglas B. *Ecology and Human Organization on the Great Plains*. New York: Plenum, 1988.

Barkley, Ted, ed. *Flora of the Great Plains*. Lawrence: University Press of Kansas, 1986.

Baron, Jill, ed. *Rocky Mountain Futures: An Ecological Perspective*. Forward by Paul R. Ehrlich. Washington, DC: Island Press, 2002.

Bauer, Erwin A., and Peggy Bauer. *Elk: Behavior, Ecology, Conservation*. St. Paul, MN: Voyageur Press, 1996.

Beemer, Rod. *The Deadliest Woman in the West: Mother Nature on the Prairies and Plains, 1800–1900*. Caldwell, ID: Caxton Press, 2006.

Benedict, Audrey DeLella. *The Naturalist's Guide to the Southern Rockies: Colorado, Southern Wyoming, and Northern New Mexico*. Golden, CO: Fulcrum, 2008.

Bezener, Andy, and Linda Kershaw. *Rocky Mountain Nature Guide*. Auburn, WA: Lone Pine, 1999.

Biel, Alice Wondrak. *Do (Not) Feed the Bears: The Fitful History of Wildlife and Tourists in Yellowstone*. Lawrence: University Press of Kansas, 2006.

Blouet, Brian W., and Frederick C. Luebke. *The Great Plains: Environment and Culture*. Lincoln: University of Nebraska Press, 1979.

Botkin, Daniel B. *Beyond the Stony Mountains: Nature in the American West from Lewis and Clark to Today*. New York: Oxford University Press, 2004.

Boucher, B. J. *Walking in Wildness: A Guide to the Weminuche Wilderness*. Durango, CO: Durango Herald Small Press, 1999.

Buchhotz, C. W. *Rocky Mountain National Park: A History*. Boulder: University Press of Colorado, 1987.

Burnham, Philip. *Indian Country, God's Country: Native Americans and the National Parks*. Chicago: University of Chicago Press, 2000.

Butcher, Russell D. *America's National Wildlife Refuges, 2nd Edition: A Complete Guide*. Lanham, MD: Rowman and Littlefield, 2008.

Byers, John A. *American Pronghorn: Social Adaptations and the Ghosts of Predators Past*. Chicago: University of Chicago Press, 1998.

Callenbach, Ernest. *Bring Back the Buffalo!: A Sustainable Future for America's Great Plains*. Berkeley: University of California Press, 2007.

Callicott, J. Baird, and Michael P. Nelson. *The Great New Wilderness Debate*. Athens: University of Georgia Press, 1998.

Cannings, Richard. *The Rockies: A Natural History*. Vancouver, Canada: Greystone Books, 2005.

Carrey, John, and Cort Conley. *River of No Return*. Cambridge, ID: Backeddy Books, 2003.

Cheek, Roland. *Montana's Bob Marshall Wilderness*. Chattanooga, TN: Skyline, 1999.

Chesher, Greer K., and Liz Hymans. *Heart of the Desert Wild: Grand Staircase Escalante National Monument*. Bryce, UT: Bryce Canyon Natural History Association, 2000.

Chronic, H. *Time, Rocks, and the Rockies: A Geologic Guide to Roads and Trails of Rocky Mountain National Park*. Missoula, MT: Mountain Press, 1984.

Chronic Wasting Disease Management on the Charles M. Russell National Wildlife Refuge Complex, Montana: Environmental Assessment, June 13, 2007.

Clark, Tim W. *The Natural World of Jackson Hole: An Ecological Primer*. Moose, WY: Grand Teton Natural History Association, 1999.

Clark, T. W., and M. R. Stromberg. *Mammals in Wyoming*. Lawrence: University of Kansas Museum of Natural History, 1987.

Clifford, Frank. *The Backbone of the World: A Portrait of a Vanishing Way of Life along the Continental Divide*. New York: Broadway Books, 2002.

Cohen, Shaul E. *Planting Nature: Trees and the Manipulation of Environmental Stewardship in America*. Berkeley: University of California Press, 2004.

Coleman, Jon T. *Vicious: Wolves and Men in America*. New Haven, CT: Yale University Press, 2006.

Corbridge, James N., and William A. Weber. *A Rocky Mountain Lichen Primer*. Boulder: University Press of Colorado, 1998.

Corps of Engineers, Omaha, NE. *Habitat Erosion Protection Analysis, Missouri National Recreation River, Nebraska and South Dakota*. Washington, DC: Storming Media, 2000.

Cosco, Jon M. *Echo Park: Struggle for Preservation*. Boulder, CO: Johnson Books, 1995.

Costello, David. *The Prairie World*. New York: Thomas Y. Crowell, 1969.

Craighead, Frank C., Jr. *For Everything There Is a Season: The Sequence of Natural Events in the Grand Teton–Yellowstone Area*. New York: Falcon Press, 2001.

Craighead, Frank C., Jr. *Naturalist's Guide to Grand Teton and Yellowstone National Parks*. New York: Falcon Press, 2006.

Cronon, Willian. *Nature's Metropolis: Chicago and the Great West*. New York: W. W. Norton, 1992.

Cunfer, Geoff. *On the Great Plains: Agriculture and Environment*. Bryan: Texas A&M University Press, 2005.

Cushman, Ruth Carol, and Stephen R. Jones. *The Shortgrass Prairie*. Boulder, CO: Pruett, 1988.

Czerny, Peter G. *The Great Great Salt Lake*. Provo, UT: Brigham Young University Press, 1976.

Day, Arthur Grove. *Coronado's Quest: The Discovery of the Southwestern States*. Westport, CT: Greenwood, 1982.

Disilvestro, Roger. "Is This a Bad Deal for Taxpayers?" *National Wildlife*, October/November 1997.

Dolin, Eric Jay. *Smithsonian Book of National Wildlife Refuges*. Washington, DC: Smithsonian Institution Press, 2003.

Droz, Dwight R. *City of Rocks*. Poulsbo, WA: Scandia Patch Press, 2006.

Ducey, James E. *Birds of the Untamed West: The History of Birdlife in Nebraska, 1750 to 1875*. Omaha, NE: Making History Press, 2000.

Dunlap, Thomas. *Saving America's Wildlife: Ecology and the American Mind, 1850–1990*. Princeton, NJ: Princeton University Press, 1991.

Elias, Scott A. *The Ice-Age History of National Parks in the Rocky Mountains*. Washington, DC: Smithsonian Institution Press, 1996.

Evans, Howard Ensign. *A Naturalist's Years in the Rocky Mountains*. Boulder, CO: Johnson Books, 2001.

Eves, Robert L. *Water, Rock & Time: The Geologic Story of Zion National Park*. Salt Lake City: University of Utah Press, 2005.

Ferguson, Gary. *The Great Divide: A Biography of the Rocky Mountains*. New York: W. W. Norton, 2004.

Ferguson, Gary. *Hawk's Rest: A Season in the Remote Heart of Yellowstone*. Washington, DC: National Geographic, 2003.

Fiege, Mark. *Irrigated Eden: The Making of an Agricultural Landscape in the American West*. Seattle: University of Washington Press, 2000.

Fielder, John, and Mark Pearson. *Complete Guide to Colorado's Wilderness Areas*. Boulder, CO: Westcliffe, 1994.

Fillmore, Robert. *The Geology of the Parks, Monuments, and Wildlands of Southern Utah*. Salt Lake City: University of Utah Press, 2000.

Flannery, Tim. *The Eternal Frontier: An Ecological History of North America and Its Peoples*. New York: Atlantic Monthly Press, 2001.

Fleharty, Eugene D. *Wild Animals and Settlers on the Great Plains*. Norman: University of Oklahoma Press, 1995.

Flores, Dan L. *The Natural West: Environmental History in the Great Plains and Rocky Mountains*. Norman: University of Oklahoma Press, 2003.

Foy, Paul. "Uproar over Federal Drilling Leases Next to Parks." *MSN Travel*. http://travel.msn.com/Guides/greenarticle.aspx?cp-documentid=732551>1=45002.

Frank, James, and Dan Klinglesmith. *Portrait of Pikes Peak Country*. Alberta, Canada: Altitude, 2000.

Franke, Mary Ann. *To Save the Wild Bison: Life on the Edge in Yellowstone*. Norman: University of Oklahoma Press, 2005.

Frazier, Ian. *Great Plains*. New York: Picador, 2001.

Freed, Elaine. *Preserving the Great Plains & Rocky Mountains*. Albuquerque: University of New Mexico Press, 1992.

Freinkel, Susan. *American Chestnut: The Life, Death, and Rebirth of a Perfect Tree*. Berkeley: University of California Press, 2007.

Froiland, Sven G. *Natural History of the Black Hills & Badlands*. Sioux Falls, SD: Center for Western Studies, 1990.

Galatowitsch, Susan M., and Arnold G. Van der Valk. *Restoring Prairie Wetlands: An Ecological Approach*. Hoboken, NJ: John Wiley, 1994.

Geist, Valerius. *Antelope Country: Pronghorns: The Last Americans*. Iola, WI: Krause, 2001.

Gellhorn, Joyce. *Song of the Alpine: The Rocky Mountain Tundra through the Seasons*. Boulder, CO: Johnson Books, 2002.

Gensbol, Benny, and Walther Thiede. *Collins Birds of Prey*. New York: HarperCollins, 2008.

Glick, David. "Glen Canyon Revealed." *National Geographic*, April 2006. http://ngm. nationalgeographic.com/2006/04/glen-canyon/glick-text.

Good, J.M.M., and Kenneth L. Pierce. *Interpreting the Landscape: Recent and Ongoing Geology of Grand Teton and Yellowstone National Parks*. Moose, WY: Grand Teton Natural History Association, 1997.

Goodman, Doug, and Daniel C. McCool, eds. *Contested Landscape: The Politics of Wilderness in Utah and the West*. Salt Lake City: University of Utah Press, 1999.

Graetz, Rick P. *Bob Marshall Country*. Helena, MT: Farcountry Press, 1985.

Grassy, John. *Audubon Guide to the National Wildlife Refuges: Rocky Mountains: Idaho, Colorado, Montana, Utah, Wyoming*. New York: St. Martin's Griffin, 2000.

Groom, Martha J., Gary K. Meffe, and C. Ronald Carroll. *Principles of Conservation Biology*, 3rd ed. Sunderland, MA: Sinauer Associates, 2005.

Gruver, Mead. "Yellowstone Quakes Shake Loose Eruption Fears." *Discovery News Online*, January 12, 2009. http://dsc.discovery.com/news/2009/01/12/yellowstone-earth quakes-02.html.

Guthrie, Carol W. *Glacier National Park: The First 100 Years*. Helena, MT: Farcountry Press, 2008.

Hagerman Fossil Council, Inc. *Equus Evolves: The Story of the Hagerman Horse*. Boise, ID: Black Canyon Communications, 2005.

Haines, Aubrey L. *The Yellowstone Story: A History of Our First National Park*. Boulder: University Press of Colorado, 1996.

Hansen, Wallace, Carolyn Dodson, and T. J. Priehs, eds. *Black Canyon of the Gunnison: In Depth*. Tucson, AZ: Western National Parks Association, 1993.

Hargreaves, Mary W. M. *Dry Farming in the Northern Great Plains: Years of Readjustment, 1920–1990*. Lawrence: University Press of Kansas, 1993.

Harrington, H. D. *How To Identify Grasses: And Grasslike Plants*. Athens, OH: Swallow Press, 1977.

Harvey, Alan E., James W. Byler, Geral I. McDonald, Leon F. Neuenschwander, and Jonalea R. Tonn. *Death of an Ecosystem: Perspectives on Western White Pine Ecosystems of North America at the End of the Twentieth Century*. General Technical, Report RMRS-GTR-208. Fort Collins, CO: U.S. Forest Service, Rocky Mountain Research Station, April 2008.

Harvey, Mark W. T. *A Symbol of Wilderness: Echo Park and the American Conservation Movement*. Seattle: University of Washington Press, 2000.

Heat-Moon, William Least. *PrairyErth, a Deep Map*. New York: Houghton Mifflin, 1999.

Henderson, Norman. *Rediscovering the Great Plains: Journeys by Dog, Canoe, and Horse*. Baltimore: Johns Hopkins University Press, 2001.

Hess, Karl. *Rocky Times in Rocky Mountain National Park: An Unnatural History*. Boulder: University Press of Colorado, 1993.

Higgins, Janis Lindsey. *Snowmass Village: Wild at Heart, A Natural History Guide Dedicated to Snowmass, Aspen, and the Maroon Bells Wilderness*. Snowmass, CO: Town of Snowmass Village, 2004.

Hilty, Jodi, William Z. Lidicker, Jr., and Adina Merenlender. *Corridor Ecology: The Science and Practice of Linking Landscapes for Biodiversity*. Washington, DC: Island Press, 2006.

Hirt, Paul W. *A Conspiracy of Optimism: Management of the National Forests since World War Two*. Lincoln: University of Nebraska Press, 1996.

Hood, William. *Searching for a Perfect State of Colorado: My Enlightening Experience Crossing the Weminuche Wilderness Area*. Boulder, CO: Bauu Institute, 2008.

Hoogland, John, ed. *Conservation of the Black-Tailed Prairie Dog: Saving North America's Western Grasslands*. Washington, DC: Island Press, 2005.

Howard, Lynna Prue. *Utah's Wilderness Areas: The Complete Guide*. Boulder, CO: Westcliffe, 2005.

Howe, Jim, Edward T. McMahon, and Luther Propst. *Balancing Nature and Commerce in Gateway Communities*. Washington, DC: Island Press, 1997.

Huggard, Christopher J., and Arthur R. Gomez. *Forests under Fire: A Century of Ecosystem Mismanagement in the Southwest*. Tucson: University of Arizona Press, 2001.

Isenberg, Andrew. *Destruction of the Bison: An Environmental History, 1750–1920*. Cambridge, UK: Cambridge University Press, 2000.

Jacobs, Randy. *Guide to the Colorado Mountains*, 10th ed. Robert M. Ormes, ed. Golden, CO: Colorado Mountain Club Press, 2000.

Jacoby, Karl. *Crimes against Nature: Squatters, Poachers, Thieves, and the Hidden History of American Conservation*. Berkeley: University of California Press, 2003.

Jenkinson, Clay S. *Theodore Roosevelt in the Dakota Badlands*. Dickinson, ND: Dickinson State University Press, 2006.

Jennings, Bob, Roger Burrows, and Ted T. Cable. *Birds of the Great Plains*. Auburn, WA: Lone Pine, 2005.

Johnson, James R., and Gary E. Larson, *Grassland Plants of South Dakota and the Northern Great Plains*. Brookings: South Dakota State University, 1999.

Johnson, S. R. *Conservation of Great Plains Ecosystems: Current Science, Future Options*. Norwell, MA: Kluwer Academic Publishers, 1995.

Johnsqard, Paul A. *Birds of the Rocky Mountains*. Lincoln: University of Nebraska Press, 2002.

Johnsqard, Paul A. *Great Wildlife of the Great Plains*. Lawrence: University Press of Kansas, 2003.

Johnsqard, Paul A. *Lewis and Clark on the Great Plains: A Natural History*. Lincoln: University of Nebraska Press, 2003.

Johnsqard, Paul A. *The Nature of Nebraska: Ecology and Biodiversity*. Lincoln: University of Nebraska Press, 2005.

Johnsqard, Paul A. *The Niobrara: A River Running through Time*. Lincoln: University of Nebraska Press, 2007.

Johnsqard, Paul A. *Prairie Birds: Fragile Splendor in the Great Plains*. Lawrence: University Press of Kansas, 2001.

Johnsqard, Paul A. *Prairie Dog Empire: A Saga of the Shortgrass Prairie*. Lincoln: University of Nebraska Press, 2005.

Jones, Stephen R. *The Last Prairie: A Sandhills Journey*. Lincoln: University of Nebraska Press, 2006.

Kavanagh, James. *The Nature of Colorado: An Introduction to Familiar Plants, Animals and Outstanding Natural Attractions*. Phoenix, AZ: Waterford Press, 2009.

Keiter, Robert B., and Mark S. Boyce. *The Greater Yellowstone Ecosystem, Redefining America's Wilderness Heritage*. New Haven, CT: Yale University Press, 1991.

Keiter, Robert B., Sarah B. George, and Joro Walker, eds. *Visions of the Grand Staircase–Escalante: Examining Utah's Newest National Monument*. Salt Lake City: Utah Museum of Natural History and Wallace Stegner Center, 1998.

Kershaw, Linda J., Jim Pojar, and Andy MacKinnon. *Plants of the Rocky Mountains*. Auburn, WA: Lone Pine, 1998.

Klinkenborg, Verlyn. "Splendor of the Grass." *National Geographic*, April 2007. http://ngm.nationalgeographic.com/2007/04/tallgrass-prairie/klinkenborg-text.html.

Knight, Dennis H. *Mountains and Plains: The Ecology of Wyoming Landscapes*. New Haven, CT: Yale University Press, 1994.

Krauss, Clifford. "The Cautious U.S. Boom in Oil Shale." *New York Times*, December 21, 2006. http://www.nytimes.com/2006/12/21/business/21shale.htm?_r=1.

Kurtz, Carl. *A Practical Guide to Prairie Reconstruction*. Iowa City: University of Iowa Press, 2001.

Ladd, Doug, and Frank Oberle. *Tallgrass Prairie Wildflowers: A Field Guide to Common Wildflowers and Plants of the Prairie Midwest*. New York: Falcon Press, 2005.

Lapinski, Mike. *Wilderness Predators of the Rockies: The Bond between Predator and Prey*. New York: Falcon Press, 2006.

Larmer, Paul, ed. *Give and Take: How the Clinton Administration's Public Lands Offensive Transformed the American West*. Seattle, WA: Mountaineers Books, 2004.

Levy, Dana. *American Wilderness: The National Parks*. New York: Rizzoli, 2009.

Lewis, Michael. *American Wilderness: A New History*. New York: Oxford University Press, 2007.

Lillie, Robert J. *Parks and Plates: The Geology of Our National Parks, Monuments, and Seashores*. New York: W. W. Norton, 2005.

Long, Kim. *Prairie Dogs: A Wildlife Handbook*. Boulder, CO: Johnson Books, 2002.

Longo, Peter Joseph. *Water on the Great Plains: Issues and Policies*. David W. Yoskowitz, ed. Lubbock: Texas Tech University Press, 2002.

Lopez, Barry. *Of Wolves and Men*. New York: Scribner, 1979.

Lott, Dale F. *American Bison: A Natural History*. Berkeley: University of California Press, 2003.

Lovejoy, Thomas E., and Jonathan Elphick. *Atlas of Bird Migration: Tracing the Great Journeys of the World's Birds*. Buffalo, NY: Firefly Books, 2007.

Madson, John, and Dycie Madson. *Where the Sky Began: Land of the Tallgrass Prairie*. Iowa City: University of Iowa Press, 2004.

Maher, Neil M. *Nature's New Deal: The Civilian Conservation Corps and the Roots of the American Environmental Movement*. New York: Oxford University Press, 2007.

Manning, Richard. *Grassland: The History, Biology, Politics, and Promise of the American Prairie*. New York: Penguin Group, 1997.

Martin, Russell. *A Story That Stands Like a Dam: Glen Canyon and the Struggle for the Soul of the West*. New York: Henry Holt, 1989.

Mathews, Daniel. *Rocky Mountain Natural History: Grand Teton to Jasper*. Portland, OR: Raven Editions, 2003.

Mattern, Joanne. *The Bighorn Sheep*. Mankato, MN: Coughlan, 1999.

Matthews, Anne. *Where the Buffalo Roam: Restoring America's Great Plains*. Chicago: University of Chicago Press, 2002.

McLean, J. S., F. A. Switzer, and J. R. Jowsey. *Wildflowers of the Northern Great Plains*, 3rd ed. Fenton R. Vance, ed. Minneapolis: University of Minnesota Press, 1999.

McPhee, John. *Rising from the Plains*. New York: Farrar, Straus and Giroux, 1987.

McPhee, John. *Basin and Range*. New York: Farrar, Straus and Giroux, 1981

Mech, L. David, and Luigi Boitani, eds. *Wolves: Behavior, Ecology, and Conservation.* Chicago: University of Chicago Press, 2007.

Merchant, Carolyn. *The Columbia Guide to American Environmental History.* New York: Columbia University Press, 2005.

Meyer, Herbert W. W. *Fossils of Florissant*. Washington DC: Smithsonian Institution Press, 2003.

Miller, Char, ed. *American Forests: Nature, Culture, and Politics.* Lawrence: University Press of Kansas, 1997.

Mohlenbrock, Robert. *This Land: A Guide to Western National Forests.* Berkeley: University of California Press, 2006.

Montgomery, David R. *Dirt: The Erosion of Civilizations.* Berkeley: University of California Press, 2008.

Moul, Francis. *The National Grasslands: A Guide to America's Undiscovered Treasures.* Lincoln: University of Nebraska Press, 2006.

Mutel, Cornelia F., and Stephen Packard, eds. *The Tallgrass Restoration Handbook: For Prairies, Savannas, and Woodlands.* Washington, DC: Island Press, 2005.

Nash, Roderick. *Wilderness and the American Mind.* New Haven, CT: Yale University Press, 2001.

National Audubon Society. *National Audubon Society Regional Guide to the Rocky Mountain States.* New York: Knopf, 1999.

National Geographic Society. *National Geographic Park Profiles: America's Hidden Treasures.* Washington, DC: National Geographic, 2009.

———— *National Geographic Guide to the National Parks of the United States, 5th Edition.* Washington, DC: National Geographic, 1997.

National Park Service. *Agate Fossil Beds National Monument, Nebraska.* Washington, DC: U.S. Department of the Interior, 1989.

National Park Service. *A Field Guide to the Wildlife and Habitats of the Grant-Kohrs Ranch.*

Neil, J. M. *To the White Clouds: Idaho's Conservation Saga, 1900–1970.* Pullman: Washington State University, 2005.

Newton, Ian. *The Migration Ecology of Birds.* Burlington, MA: Academic Press, 2007.

Nicholas, Liza, Elaine M. Bapis, and Thomas J. Harvey, eds. *Imagining the Big Open: Nature, Identity, and Play in the New West.* Salt Lake City: University of Utah Press, 2003.

Nolt, David. "Revamping the Charles M. Russell Wildlife Refuge Conservation Plan." *New West, Bozeman*, February 22, 2008. http://www.newwest.net/city/article/charles_m_russell_national_wildlife_refuge_conservation_plan_to_be_revamped/C396/L396.

O'Brien, Dan. *Buffalo for the Broken Heart: Restoring Life to a Black Hills Ranch*. New York: Random House, 2002.

Oelschlaeger, Max. *The Idea of Wilderness: From Prehistory to the Age of Ecology*. New Haven, CT: Yale University Press, 1993.

Oko, Dan. "The Debate That Roared: A Plan To Reintroduce the Grizzly in Idaho Causes Considerable Growling." *Outside*, March 1998.

Palmer, Bill. *Audubon Guide to the National Wildlife Refuges: South Central: Arkansas, Kansas, Louisiana, Missouri, Oklahoma*. New York: St. Martin's Griffin, 2000.

Pattie, Don. *Mammals of the Rocky Mountains*. Auburn, WA: Lone Pine, 2000.

Paulson, Deborah D., and William L. Baker. *The Nature of Southwestern Colorado: Recognizing Human Legacies and Restoring Natural Places*. Boulder: University Press of Colorado, 2006.

Pearson, Mark. *The Complete Guide to Colorado's Wilderness Areas*. Englewood, CO: Westcliffe, 2005.

Petrides, George A. *Trees of the Rocky Mountains & Intermountain West*. Illustrated by Olivia Petrides. Mechanicsburg, PA: Stackpole Books, 2005.

Phillips, Dave. "The Lost World/Comanche National Grassland." *Colorado Springs Gazette*, May 16, 2003.

Phillips, H. Wayne. *Central Rocky Mountain Wildflowers: Including Yellowstone and Grand Teton National Parks*. New York: Falcon Press, 1999.

Picton, Harold. *Buffalo Natural History & Conservation*. St. Paul, MN: Voyageur Press, 2005.

Postel, Sandra. *Rivers for Life: Managing Water for People and Nature*. Washington, DC: Island Press, 2003.

Powell, James Lawrence. *Dead Pool: Lake Powell, Global Warming, and the Future of Water in the West*. Berkeley: University of California Press, 2009.

Powers, Tom, and John Grassy. *Audubon Guide to the National Wildlife Refuges: Northern Midwest: Illinois, Indiana, Iowa, Michigan, Minnesota, Nebraska, North Dakota, Ohio, South Dakota, Wisconsin*. New York: St. Martin's Griffin, 2000.

Pritchard, James A. *Preserving Yellowstone's Natural Conditions: Science and the Perception of Nature*. Lincoln: University of Nebraska Press, 1999.

Punke, Michael. *Last Stand: George Bird Grinnell, the Battle to Save the Buffalo, and the Birth of the New West*. New York: Collins, 2007.

Pyne, Stephen J. *Fire in America: A Cultural History of Wildland and Rural Fire*. Seattle: University of Washington Press, 1997.

Raventon, Edward. *Buffalo Country: A Northern Plains Narrative*. Boulder, CO: Johnson Books, 2003.

Raventon, Edward. *Island in the Plains: A Black Hills Natural History*. Boulder, CO: Johnson Books, 2003.

Reinhart, Karen Wildung. *Yellowstone's Rebirth by Fire: Rising from the Ashes of the 1988 Wildfires.* Helena, MT: Farcountry Press, 2008.

Reisner, Marc. *Cadillac Desert: The American West and Its Disappearing Water.* New York: Penguin Group, 2003.

Righter, Robert W. *Crucible for Conservation: The Struggle for Grand Teton National Park.* Moose, WY: Grand Teton Natural History Association, 1984.

Rinella, Steven. *American Buffalo: In Search of a Lost Icon.* New York: Spiegel & Grau, 2008.

Robinson, Michael J. *Predatory Bureaucracy: The Extermination of Wolves and the Transformation of the West.* Boulder: University Press of Colorado, 2005.

Rockwell, David. *Glacier: A Natural History Guide.* Helena, MT: Falcon Press, 2007.

Roosevelt, Theodore. *Big Game Hunting in the Rockies and on the Great Plains, Comprising "Hunting Trips of a Ranchman" and "The Wilderness Hunter."* London: G. P. Putnam's Sons, 1899.

Rothman, Hal K. *Blazing Heritage: A History of Wildland Fire in the National Parks.* New York: Oxford University Press, 2007.

Runte, Alfred. *National Parks: The American Experience.* Lincoln: University of Nebraska Press, 1997.

Sample, Michael. *Glacier on My Mind.* Guilford, CT: Globe Pequot Press, 1997.

Savage, Candace. *Prairie: A Natural History.* Vancouver, Canada: Greystone Books, 2006.

Scheese, Don, and Wayne Franklin. *Mountains of Memory: A Fire Lookout's Life in the River of No Return Wilderness.* Iowa City: University of Iowa Press, 2001.

Schrepfer, Susan R. *Nature's Altars: Mountains, Gender, and American Environmentalism.* Lawrence: University Press of Kansas, 2005.

Schullery, Paul. *America's National Parks: The Spectacular Forces That Shaped Our Treasured Lands.* New York: DK Adult, 2001.

Schullery, Paul, and Lee Whittlesey. *Myth and History in the Creation of Yellowstone National Park.* Lincoln: University of Nebraska Press, 2003.

Schullery, Paul, and Lee Whittlesey. *Searching for Yellowstone: Ecology and Wonder in the Last Wilderness.* Missoula: Montana Historical Society Press, 2004.

Schultz, Elizabeth, and Kelly Kindscher. *The Nature of Kansas Lands.* Lawrence: University Press of Kansas, 2008.

Scott, Doug. *The Enduring Wilderness: Protecting Our Natural Heritage through the Wilderness Act.* Golden, CO: Fulcrum, 2004.

Sellars, Richard West. *Preserving Nature in the National Parks: A History.* New Haven, CT: Yale University Press, 1999.

Severson, K. E., and C. H. Sieg. *The Nature of Eastern North Dakota: Pre-1880 Historical Ecology.* Fargo: North Dakota State University, 2006.

Shaffer, Rick. *Parks after Dark: Beginner's Guide to Stargazing National Parks*. Tucson, AZ: Western National Parks Association, 2006.

Sharpe, Roger S., W. Ross Silcock, and Joel G. Jorgensen. *Birds of Nebraska: Their Distribution and Temporal Occurrence*. Lincoln: University of Nebraska Press, 2001.

Shuler, Jay. *A Revelation Called the Badlands: Building a National Park, 1909–1939*. Interior, SD: Badlands Natural History Association, 1989.

Sibley, David Allen. *Sibley Guide to Birds*.

Sibley, David Allen. *Sibley Field Guide to Birds of Western North America*. New York: Knopf, 2003.

Sierra Club. *The Sierra Club Guide to the National Parks of the Rocky Mountains and the Great Plains*. New York: Random House, 1995.

Smith, Bruce, Eric Cole, and David Dobkin. *Imperfect Pasture: A Century of Change at the National Elk Refuge in Jackson Hole, Wyoming*. Moose, WY: Grand Teton Natural History Association, 2004.

Smith, Douglas W., and Gary Ferguson. *Decade of the Wolf: Returning the Wild to Yellowstone*. Guilford, CT: Lyons Press, 2006.

Smith, Robert S., and Lee J. Siegel. *Windows into the Earth: The Geologic Story of Yellowstone and Grand Teton National Parks*. New York: Oxford University Press, 2000.

Southern Rockies Ecosystem Project. *The State of the Southern Rockies Ecoregion: A Report by the Southern Rockies Ecosystem Project*. Golden, CO: Colorado Mountain Club Press, 2004.

Spence, Mark David. *Dispossessing the Wilderness: Indian Removal and the Making of the National Parks*. New York: Oxford University Press, 2000.

Stahl, Greg. "20 Years since Borah Earthquake." *Idaho Mountain Express*, October 22–28, 2003. http://www.mtexpress.com/2003/03-10-22/03-10-22borah.htm.

Stegner, Page. *Adios Amigos: Tales of Sustenance and Purification in the American West*. Berkeley, CA: Counterpoint Press, 2008.

Stegner, Wallace. *Wolf Willow: A History, a Story, and a Memory of the Last Plains Frontier*. New York: Viking Compass Books, 1966.

Steinberg, Ted. *Down to Earth: Nature's Role in American History*. New York: Oxford University Press, 2008.

Stiller, David. *Wounding the West: Montana, Mining, and the Environment*. Lincoln: University of Nebraska Press, 2000.

Stohlgren, T.J. "Rocky Mountains." In *Status and Trends of the Nation's Biological Resources*, edited by M.J. Mac. Washington, DC: U.S. Department of the Interior, U.S. Geological Survey, 1998.

Stum, Marlin. *Visions of Antelope Island and Great Salt Lake*. Logan: Utah State University Press, 1999.

Sullivan, Noelle, and Nicholas Peterson Vrooman. *M-e Ecci Aashi Awadi: The Knife River Indian Villages*. Medora, ND: Theodore Roosevelt Nature & History Association, 1995.

Tekiela, Stan. *Birds of the Dakotas Field Guide*. Cambridge, MN: Adventure Publications, 2003.

Tekiela, Stan. *Birds of Montana Field Guide*. Cambridge, MN: Adventure Publications, 2003.

Trimble, Stephen. *Bargaining for Eden: The Fight for the Last Open Spaces in America*. Berkeley: University of California Press, 2008.

Trimble, Stephen. *Great Sand Dunes: The Shape of the Wind*. [City]: Western National Parks Association, 2001.

Turner, Jack. *Travels in the Greater Yellowstone*. New York: Thomas Dunne Books, 2008.

Tweit, Susan J., and Glen Oakley. *The San Luis Valley: Sand Dunes and Sandhill Cranes*. Tucson: University of Arizona Press, 2005.

Van Bruggen, Theodore. *Wildflowers, Grasses, and Other Plants of the Northern Plains*. Interior, SD: Badlands Natural History Association, 1992.

Van Driesche, Jason, and Roy Van Driesche. *Nature Out of Place: Biological Invasions in the Global Age*. Washington, DC: Island Press, 2004.

Waldt, Ralph. *Crown of the Continent: The Last Great Wilderness of the Rocky Mountains*. Helena, MT: Riverbend, 2004.

Wassink, Jan L. *Petersons Field Guide: The North American Prairie—Watchable Birds of the Black Hills, Badlands and Northern Great Plains*. Lyn Purl, ed. Missoula, MT: Mountain Press, 2006.

Weaver, J. E. *Prairie Plants and Their Environment: A Fifty Year Study in the Midwest*. Lincoln: University of Nebraska Press, 1991.

Webb, Robert H., Jayne Belnap, and John S. Weisheit. *Cataract Canyon: A Human and Environmental History of the Rivers in Canyonlands*. Salt Lake City: University of Utah Press, 2004.

Webb, Walter Prescott. *The Great Plains*. Lincoln: University of Nebraska Press, 1981.

Wheeler, Ray. *Wilderness at the Edge: A Citizen Proposal To Protect Utah's Canyons and Deserts*. Salt Lake City: Utah Wilderness Coalition, 1990.

White, Courtney. *Revolution on the Range: The Rise of a New Ranch in the American West*. Washington, DC: Island Press, 2008.

Williams, David B. *Naturalist's Guide to Canyon Country*. Guilford, CT: Falcon, 2000.

Williams, Roger L. *A Region of Astonishing Beauty: The Botanical Exploration of the Rocky Mountains*. Lanham, MA: Roberts Rinehart, 2003.

Williams, Terry Tempest. *Finding Beauty in a Broken World*. New York: Knopf, 2008.

Wilshire, Howard G., Jane E. Nelson, and Richard W. Hazlett. *The American West at Risk: Science, Myths, and Politics of Land Abuse and Recovery*. New York: Oxford University Press, 2008.

Wilson, Jerry. *Waiting for Coyote's Call: An Eco-Memoir from the Missouri River Bluff.* Pierre: South Dakota State Historical Society, 2008.

Wishart, David J., ed. *Encyclopedia of the Great Plains.* Lincoln: University of Nebraska Press, 2004.

Worcester, Don. *Texas Longhorn: Relic of the Past, Asset for the Future.* College Station: Texas A&M University Press, 1994.

Worster, Donald. *Dust Bowl: The Southern Plains in the 1930s.* New York: Oxford University Press, 2004.

Worster, Donald. *Nature's Economy: A History of Ecological Ideas.* New York: Cambridge University Press, 1994.

Worster, Donald. *Rivers of Empire: Water, Aridity, and the Growth of the American West.* New York: Oxford University Press, 1992.

Worster, Donald. *The Wealth of Nature: Environmental History and the Ecological Imagination.* New York: Oxford University Press, 1994.

Wright, R. Gerald, and Stephen C. Bunting. *The Landscapes of Craters of the Moon National Monument: An Evaluation of Environmental Changes.* Moscow: University of Idaho Press, 1994.

Zaslowsky, Dyan, and T. H. Watkins. *These American Lands: Parks, Wilderness, and the Public Lands.* Washington, DC: Island Press, 1994.

Zontek, Ken. *Buffalo Nation: American Indian Efforts to Restore the Bison.* Lincoln, NE: Bison Books, 2007.

Zwinger, Ann H. *Wind in the Rock: The Canyonlands of Southeastern Utah.* Tucson: University of Arizona Press, 1986.

INDEX

About the Author

Kelly Enright holds her PhD in American history from Rutgers University. Her interests are environmental and cultural history, anthropology, animal studies, and museum studies. She has worked as a researcher and consultant for the Wildlife Conservation Society and the American Museum of Natural History. She is the author of *Rhinoceros* and has two forthcoming publications, one on imaginary animals and another on the image of the Jungle in American culture.

St. Louis Community College
at Meramec
LIBRARY